PUBLICATIONS OF THE DEPARTMENT OF ROMANCE LANGUAGES
UNIVERSITY OF NORTH CAROLINA

General Editor: ALDO SCAGLIONE

Editorial Board: JUAN BAUTISTA AVALLE-ARCE, PABLO GIL CASADO, FRED M. CLARK, GEORGE BERNARD DANIEL, JANET W. DÍAZ, ALVA V. EBERSOLE, AUGUSTIN MAISSEN, EDWARD D. MONTGOMERY, FREDERICK W. VOGLER

NORTH CAROLINA STUDIES IN THE ROMANCE LANGUAGES AND LITERATURES

ESSAYS; TEXTS, TEXTUAL STUDIES AND TRANSLATIONS; SYMPOSIA

Founder: URBAN TIGNER HOLMES

Editor: JUAN BAUTISTA AVALLE-ARCE
Associate Editor: FREDERICK W. VOGLER

Other publications of the Department:
Estudios de Hispanófila, Hispanófila, Romance Notes

Distributed by:

INTERNATIONAL SCHOLARLY BOOK SERVICE, INC.
P. O. BOX 4347
Portland, Oregon 97208
U. S. A.

NORTH CAROLINA STUDIES IN THE
ROMANCE LANGUAGES AND LITERATURES
Number 139

NARRATIVE TECHNIQUE IN THE
LAIS OF MARIE DE FRANCE:
THEMES AND VARIATIONS

NARRATIVE TECHNIQUE
IN THE
LAIS OF MARIE DE FRANCE:
THEMES AND VARIATIONS
VOL. I

BY

JUDITH RICE ROTHSCHILD

CHAPEL HILL

NORTH CAROLINA STUDIES IN THE
ROMANCE LANGUAGES AND LITERATURES
U.N.C. DEPARTMENT OF ROMANCE LANGUAGES
1974

Library of Congress Cataloging in Publication Data

Rothschild, Judith Rice.

Narrative technique in the Lais of Marie de France.

(North Carolina studies in the Romance languages and literatures, no. 139)

Vol. 1 was originally presented as the author's thesis, The Johns Hopkins University.

Bibliography: p. 251

1. Marie de France, 12th cent. Lais. 2. Marie de France, 12th cent.—Technique. I. Title. II. Series.

PQ1494.L7R6 841'.1 74-12482
ISBN 978-0-8078-9139-1

DEPÓSITO LEGAL: V. 4.338 - 1974

ARTES GRÁFICAS SOLER, S. A. - JÁVEA, 28 - VALENCIA (8) - 1974

For
Anna Granville Hatcher

TABLE OF CONTENTS

	Page
PREFACE	11
INTRODUCTION	13
CHAPTERS	
I. *Equitan*	21
II. *Le Fresne*	48
III. *Bisclavret*	92
IV. *Les Deus Amanz*	139
V. *Yonec*	168
VI. *Milun*	211
BIBLIOGRAPHY	251

PREFACE

This first volume of a projected two-volume study of narrative technique in the *Lais* of Marie de France was originally submitted, less minor revisions, as a Ph. D. dissertation to The Johns Hopkins University. The investigation of Marie's narrative technique, which originated in a graduate seminar conducted by Professor Anna Granville Hatcher, focused upon all the known *Lais* of the 12th century poetess. In the dissertation, the results of my research are given in the form of detailed *explications de texte* for six poems, with comparative and contrastive reference to the entire collection. The remaining six poems are being treated in a similar manner.

I should like to take this occasion to thank Professor Hatcher, for the benefits of her scholarship and experience, and for her encouragement, for which I am inexpressibly grateful. For the always courteous assistance of the staffs of the Libraries of the University of Michigan, and of The Johns Hopkins University, especially that of Miss Martha Hubbard, Miss Adelaide Eisenhardt and Mrs. Ione Hoover, I wish to express my warm appreciation.

For the assistance which helped to bring this volume to publication, I am indebted to the Clark Charitable Trust of Boston for its generous grant, to the Publication Fund of Brandeis University, and to the Graduate School of Arts and Sciences, Boston University.

J. R. R.

Newton Centre, Mass.

INTRODUCTION

Since the first modern publication, at the beginning of the 19th century,[1] of the *Lais* of Marie de France, much has been written about this work, its author, the time when she lived,[2] and even about the identities of the individuals to whom she dedicated her *Lais* (and also her *Fables*).

Some scholars have attempted to establish the identity of the poetess as, variously, Marie de Compiègne,[3] Marie de Champagne,[4] Marie the daughter of Count Galeran of Meulan, and of his wife, Agnes.[5] Others would attribute to her an ecclesiastical identity: Mary, the abbess of Reading,[6] or the natural daughter of Geoffrey of Anjou (and thus the sister of Henry II),

---

[1] B. de Roquefort, *Poésies de Marie de France*, 2 vols. (Paris, 1819-25). Marie's works were first published during the Renaissance by Claude Fauchet, in his *Recueil de l'origine de la langue et poésie françoise* (Paris, 1581).

[2] E. A. Francis, "Marie de France et son temps," *Romania*, LXXII (1951), 78-99.

[3] Of this identification proposed by E. Mall, "Noch Einmal: Marie de Compiègne und das "Evangile aux femmes," *ZRPh*, I (1877), 337-56, a recent editor of the *Lais* declares that it "has been effectively disposed of" (cf. Alfred Ewert, ed. Marie de France: *Lais* (Oxford, 1947; reprinted 1958), p. ix). All references to the *Lais* in the present study are to Ewert's edition.

[4] E. Winkler, *Französische Dichter des Mittelalters: II. Marie de France* (Vienna, 1918).

[5] This identification suggested by U. T. Holmes, in his *History of Old French Literature* (New York, 1937), p. 189, is supported by later evidence presented by P. N. Flum, "Additional Thoughts on Marie de France," *Romance Notes*, III, i (1961), 53-6.

[6] Ezio Levi, "Maria di Francia e le abbazie d'Inghilterra," *Arch. Rom.*, V (1921), 472-93, especially 484-88.

who became the abbess of Shaftesbury.[7] As for the identification of the dedicatee of the *Lais*, a most convincing argument is made for the 'Young King.'[8] Among identifications suggested for the 'Count William' to whom she dedicated her *Fables* is that of William Marshall.[9]

Some studies have attempted to ascertain the chronology of Marie's *Lais*;[10] the sources of Marie's lays;[11] Marie's relationship to the Roman d'Énéas,[12] to the Breton lays,[13] to the Tristan legend,[14] and to other works.[15]

---

[7] J. C. Fox, "Marie de France," *Engl. Hist. Rev.*, XXV (1910), 303 ff., and XXVI (1911), 317 ff. Of all the identifications proposed, Ewert (*op. cit.*, p. ix) states that this is "the most plausible."

[8] Ezio Levi, "Il Re Giovane e Maria di Francia," *Arch. Rom.*, V (1921), 448-71. Levi thus differs from the identification of the 'noble king' as Henry II proposed by Warnke, Paris, Gröber, Suchier, Zingarelli, Crescini, Foulet, Winkler and Bertoni (whom Levi cites, p. 458).

[9] For an identification differing from that suggested by Ezio Levi of the *cunte Willalme*, cf. Sidney Painter, "To Whom were dedicated the Fables of Marie de France?", *MLN*, XLVIII (1933), 367-9.

[10] Maurice Delbouille, "Le nom et le personnage d'Equitan," *Le Moyen-Age*, LXIX (1963), 315-23; Ernest Hoepffner, *Les 'Lais' de Marie de France* (Paris, 1935); Hoepffner's article, "The Breton Lais," in *Arthurian Literature in the Middle Ages*, ed. R. S. Loomis (Oxford, 1959); Hoepffner's article, "Pour la Chronologie des Lais de Marie de France. I. — Le Lai de Lanval," *Romania*, LIX (1933), 351-70.

[11] For example, Tom Peete Cross, "Celtic Elements in the Lays of Lanval and Graelent," *Mod. Phil.*, XII (April 1915), no. 10, 1-60; "The Celtic Origin of the Lay of Yonec," *Revue Celtique*, XXXI (1910), 413-71. Also O. M. Johnston, "Sources of the Lay of the *Two Lovers*," *MLN*, XXI (1906), 34-9.

[12] J. J. Salverda de Grave, "Marie de France et Énéas," *Neophil.*, X, 56; Ernest Hoepffner, "Marie de France et l'*Énéas*,'" *Studi Medievali*, V (1932), 272-308.

[13] Lucien Foulet, "Marie de France et les lais bretons," *ZRPh*, XXIX (1905), 19-56 and 293-322; Ezio Levi, "I lai brettoni et la leggenda di Tristano" (reprinted from *Studj romanzi*, XIV) (Perugia, 1918).

[14] Lucien Foulet, "Marie de France et la Légende de Tristan," *ZRPh*, XXXII (1908), 161-83 and 257-89; Ernest Hoepffner, "Thomas d'Angleterre et Marie de France," *Studi Medievali*, VII (1934), 8-23. Indeed, Stefan Hofer ("Der Tristanroman und der Lai du Chievrefueil der Marie de France," *ZRPh*, LXIX (1953), 129-31, sees in Marie's lays a "Mosaik aus Tristanschen Motiven." But, apart from the over-obvious instance of *Chievrefueil*, he gives no examples.

[15] Lucien Foulet, "Thomas and Marie in their relation to the Conteors," *MLN*, XXIII (1908), 205-8; M. Wilmotte, "Marie de France et Chrétien de Troyes," *Romania*, LII (1927), 353-5.

Other studies, less positivistic, have been devoted to "love and adventure" in the Lais;[16] or to a consideration of the "problem" or "problems" within each individual poem;[17] or to a discussion of the folklore elements in the lays.[18] A recent study has investigated the fundamental distinction between the *aventure*, the *lai*, and the *conte*.[19] Yet it is notable that very few studies maintain that there is a unity in the ensemble of the *Lais*.[20] There is still even less mention of Marie's narrative technique.[21]

The purpose of the present investigation was to discover, by a close reading (and many re-readings) and comparison of the *Lais* (which has never before been offered), Marie's narrative technique. I wished also, if possible, to discover an artistic unity for the ensemble.

About Marie's narrative art there can be formulated several generalizations (which are as true for the group of twelve *Lais* as for the large sampling offered here.). First, there is never a simple, uncomplicated plot of "boy meets girl, they fall in love and live happily ever after." Secondly, with the one exception of *Chevrefoil* (and that this must be an exception is obvious), Marie never begins her tale *medias in res:* each story unfolds in linear progression. Within the sequence of events recounted in an individual story there may be, however, temporal shifts, either backwards or forward: these occur for several reasons. Thirdly, Marie

---

[16] Camilla Conigliani, "L'Amore e l'avventura nei "Lais" di Maria di Francia," *Arch. Rom.*, II (1918), 281-95.

[17] Leo Spitzer, "Marie de France, Dichterin von Problem-Märchen," *ZRPh*, L (1930), 29-67.

[18] Mary H. Ferguson, "Folklore in the *Lais* of Marie de France," *RR*, LVII (1966), (February), no. I, 3-24.

[19] Martín de Riquer, "La 'aventure', el 'lai' y el 'conte' en María de Francia," *Fil. Rom.*, II (Fasc. I, num. 5), Gennaio-Marzo 1955, 1-19.

[20] Cf. however, Spitzer, *op. cit.*, S. Foster Damon, "Marie de France: Psychologist of Courtly Love," *PMLA*, 44 (1929), 968-96. In both these articles there is also discussion of the symbolic value of the lays.

[21] As to Marie's narrative art, one can find a few meager statements, e. g., Ewert, *op. cit.*, p. xi: "The titles of the lais are for her an important consideration." Cf. also E. Hoepffner's remark that Marie "... aime tant à indiquer la valeur d'un objet." ("Marie de France et les Lais anonymes," *Studi Medievali* (Nuova Serie), 4 (1931), 4.)

takes great pains to locate exactly the setting for her tales;[22] her sense of "place" or topography is highly acute. Fourthly, a very characteristic device of Marie's artistry is "the story within the story that becomes a story to be told within the framework of the story." Moreover, the use of one-line summary is frequent; such a summary tends to occur, after an expanded narration of one phase of a journey, in order to recount rapidly the return-trip, or to summarize the duration or a situation with which the reader is already familiar.

Very important, but very difficult to summarize, is Marie's use of sensuous details in the presentation of physical objects, or places. At times she will offer a picture inviting to visualization rich and dense with descriptive details; more often, the details are vaguely, poetically, suggestive. And occasionally, in presenting a physical background, the details we might have expected are entirely lacking, with the positive effect of conveying a sense of mystery, of nowhereness. Always we feel that Marie has "chosen," and the significance of her choice can always, eventually, be found. — In her description of persons, she will sometimes present a woman's figure before our eyes (and the women she so distinguishes form an interesting and diverse company). But no such treatment is accorded to the men who move through her stories.

Equally important, and equally difficult to indicate in summary form, is Marie's presentation of character. It is true that she seldom lets a character develop in the sense of changing, of acquiring new possibilities different from those inherent. Yet there is "development through revelation." Generally, Marie's technique is to attribute to the characters conventional traits (traits which countless other persons could share with them, and perhaps, mainly, her stock epithets refer to an individual's reputation). Then, gradually (or sometimes suddenly) as the story unfolds, these amorphous entities take on shape, with qualities, with contours of their own that make them unforgettable, for

---

[22] Cf. Hoepffner, "Marie de France et les Lais anonymes," p. 19: "Il est de règle chez Marie de France de situer l'aventure qu'elle raconte de la manière la plus précise. Sur ses douze lais, seul le lai de *Bisclavret* se contente d'une vague indication: 'en Bretagne.'"

Marie allows them to reveal qualities whose existence we did not even have a chance to suspect.

In her *Lais* Marie uses certain basic narrative motifs or themes; these may be either primary or secondary elements of the individual plot structure. Throughout the lays these themes are repeated, often multiply, each time with a different variation. Upon these variations S. Foster Damon[23] attempts to build a system of classification of the *Lais,* according to analogues or parallels (which he confines to pairs of poems or groups of four) in the treatment of certain themes (i.e., selfishness and its opposite; the father-son relationship). After a discussion of the parallelism which he sees in the lays (which I, too, have found, but sometimes between more than the two of the four lay-combination), Damon then comments upon Marie's narrative method:

> ... It is perfectly obvious how Marie's mind has been working, whether or not she was conscious of it. Her workmanship, however, is usually so cool and deliberate that to imagine her completely ignorant of all this parallelism is going a bit too far. This same parallelism moreover, disproves Schofield's contention that Marie did virtually nothing to the materials of which she built her stories. "For originality in conception or combination, we look in vain in her work," he wrote. "The great success she achieved, was apparently due to her graceful, flowing style, her good taste, and possibly to her unusual opportunities." [24] And elsewhere: "She does not seem to have done more than recount what she has read or heard." [25]

Professor Schofield came to this conclusion, I think, because in his search for analogues he noted the similarities but not the differences. Now when a writer uses well-known themes, his art lies in subtilizing the original or in varying from it. The variation is in itself an emphasis. So we judge the Greek dramatists; so we must judge Marie.

---

[23] Damon, *op. cit.*
[24] W. H. Schofield, "The Lays of Graelent and Lanval," *PMLA*, XV (1900), 163, quoted by Damon, *op. cit.*, p. 972.
[25] Schofield, *ibid.*, p. 175, quoted by Damon, *ibid.*

Damon was not the only critic to note the repetitions in Marie's lays, and to comment upon them; so did Ernest Hoepffner [26] a few years later, as follows:

> On le sait, et on l'a déjà dit, [27] Marie aime à se répéter elle-même. D'invention un peu courte, elle ne craint pas de reprendre d'un lai à l'autre non seulement les mêmes expressions, mais quelquefois les mêmes thèmes. Ainsi, dans *Yonec* aussi bien que dans *Guigemar*, elle montre la femme innocente, enfermée par le mari jaloux, et exprimant sa juste indignation. *Milun* et *Fresne* racontent l'histoire d'un enfant exposé par ses parents qu'il finit par retrouver. [28] Mais les répétitions textuelles ne portent que sur des vers isolés ou sur de courts passages; et dans les épisodes que Marie reprend elle n'accumule jamais, comme ici [dans *Guingamor*] des répétitions aussi nombreuses et des ressemblances aussi frappantes. Au contraire, quand Marie est obligée par son récit de reprendre un thème déjà traité, on constatera qu'elle évite avec soin de se répéter de trop près. [29]

In connection with these two scholars' views on Marie's repetitions and her narrative technique, it may be pertinent to cite Bédier's evaluation [italics mine] of Marie: [30]

> ... Marie de France nous dit qu'elle a composé ses lais pour être lus, et lus en collection. C'est bien une femme qui devait, l'une des premières, écrire ces légendes. Marie l'a fait avec charme, *sans grand talent*. Il faut le dire, *sa valeur poétique est médiocre*, et sa maîtresse forme est, auprès d'une certaine grâce sobre, *la sécheresse d'imagination*. Sent-elle toujours l'intérêt des récits qu'elle

---

[26] "Marie de France et les Lais anonymes," *Studi Medievali* (Nuova Serie), IV (1931), 1-31.

[27] At this point Hoepffner cites Joseph Bédier (*Romania*, XXXIV (1905), 279-80), but the pagination given by Hoepffner is not correct; it should read pp. 479-80.

[28] Hoepffner is not exactly correct in this remark. Of the two lays in question, it is only in *Le Fresne* that a child is *exposé*, and by only one parent (the other does not even know of the child's birth). In *Milun* the parents do not "expose" the child; they entrust it to the care of the mother's sister.

[29] Hoepffner, *op. cit.*, pp. 16-17.

[30] "Les Lais de Marie de France," *RDM*, CVII (1891), 835-63.

répète? On en pourrait douter; car *elle prend de toutes mains, sans choix:* l'un de ses contes, *Équitan,* est un vilain fait-divers, *qui serait répugnant, s'il était moins sot. Elle raconte les scènes les plus violentes ou les plus tendres, du même ton placide, sans en paraître touchée:* c'est d'ailleurs une garantie que ses poèmes doivent être infiniment proches des originaux, de ces contes oraux qu'elle a reçus des jongleurs bretons; *elle est trop peu artiste, trop peu imaginative pour y avoir beaucoup ajouté.* Elle aligne avec calme ses petits octosyllabes, dont les rimes plates semblent n'avoir d'autre valeur que celle d'un procédé mnémotechnique. Aucune splendeur dans le style, aucune passion dans le récit, rien que la grâce d'une émotion très faible, à fleur de peau. Mais aussi, *nul bavardage, nulle rhétorique:* une langue agile et fine, dont la gracilité même n'est pas sans charme. *Elle s'arrête sur le seuil de l'art....* [31]

What a wholesale condemnation of Marie's artistry! Surely this unjustified series of charges results from the most serious misunderstanding, even misreading, of the *Lais,* and in the course of the present study every one of Bédier's judgments will be refuted. Marie's repetitions or parallels, far from being indicative of a poverty of imagination, are revelatory of her subtlety and invention. And as for the unity of the totality of the *Lais,* it lies in the multiplicity of the many thematic threads which she has so carefully and skilfully woven together.

---

[31] *Op. cit.,* pp. 857-8.

EQUITAN

The lay of *Equitan* discloses a tripartite external structure, introduced by a Prologue of twelve verses, and ending in a short Epilogue of only four lines. The three divisions of the narrative are presented in descending order of length: the first portion (172 lines) is more than double the length of the second part (78 verses), the final section (48 lines) slightly longer than one half the number of lines in the middle portion. In the first part, we learn of King Equitan, his seneschal and the seneschal's wife, and how the King finally wins the love of the lady; in the second, Equitan and the lady conspire to kill the husband so that the King can marry her; the third section relates how the well-devised plan goes astray, resulting in the deaths of both the King and the lady.

In the Prologue Marie speaks of the Breton tradition of the lay, and tells the name of the protagonist: (1-12)

    Mut unt esté noble barun
    Cil de Bretaine, li Bretun.
    Jadis suleient par prüesce,
  4 Par curteisie e par noblesce
    Des aventures que oïeent,
    Ki a plusur gent aveneient,
    Fere les lais pur remembrance,
  8 Que [hum] nes meïst en ubliance.
    Un en firent, ceo oi cunter,
    Ki ne fet mie a ublïer, [1]

---

[1] Is there ont a moralistic intent in this line (*Ki ne fet mie a ublïer*) which accords with and serves as a counterpart to Marie's moralizing at the close of the lay?

D'Equitan que mut fu curteis, [2]
12   Sire de Nauns, jostis' e reis. [3]

After having stressed in eight lines the courtesy and nobility of the Bretons and their love of composing lays (this is the only lay which opens this way), Marie now mentions this Equitan, one of the noble Bretons; he will be the protagonist of our story, but it is not as such that he is first presented to us: he is simply one of the noble Bretons, about whom lays are composed. Thus he emerges from the background of massive nobility.

As for the Prologue, it would seem that Marie's intent is to give a very noble tone (given the use of the terms 'courtesy,' 'nobility' and 'worthiness') to what will be a very ignoble story. And surely Marie's characterization of King Equitan as "curteis" is highly significant.

Equitan has a loyal seneschal: (13-28)

> Equitan fu mut de grant pris
> E mut amez en sun païs;
> Deduit amout e drüerie:
> 16   Pur ceo maintint chevalerie.
> Cil met[ent] lur vie en [nu]n cure
> Que d'amur n'unt sen e mesure;
> Tels est la mesure de amer
> 20   Que nul n'i deit reisun garder.
> Equitan ot un seneschal,
> Bon chevaler, pruz e leal; [4]
> Tute sa tere li gardoit
> 24   E meinteneit e justisoit.
> Ja, se pur ostïer ne fust,
> Pur nul busuin ki li creüst
> Li reis ne laissast sun chacier,
> 28   Sun deduire, sun riveier.

---

[2] For the puzzling names of Equitan and Nauns, cf. Maurice Delbouille, "Le nom et le personnage d'Equitan," *le Moyen-Age,* LXIX (1963), 315-23.

[3] Note the necessity of remembrance (or of non-forgetfulness) mentioned three times (in just four lines!) in the Prologue. Furthermore, twice the negated verb *ublïer* is used: first, of the lays as a group *Que [hum] nes meïst en ubliance* (8), then of a particular lay *Ki ne fet mie a ublïer* (10).

This particular Prologue departs from Marie's usual technique of promising to tell us a certain story.

[4] The first instance of the recurring motif of loyalty.

In the next section, we are introduced to a new character, as well as being informed about Equitan himself. This passage can be divided into four parts of four lines each, with the first and last given over to details concerning the King.

In the first four lines of this passage (13-16), and especially in the third and fourth verses, we have the first characterization of Equitan. This is the first time in Marie's *Lais* that we have a man who goes after women; all the other lovers love only one lady. What a contrast this characterization of Equitan affords us, after the introduction in which *curteisie* and nobility were so strongly emphasized.

In the second group of four lines (17-20), we find Marie's indictment of people such as Equitan, an indictment of sensuality itself. Equitan is already judged, even before his story has been unfolded. And there is no other lay like this.

In the third group of four lines (21-4), the seneschal is presented, whose good qualities are emphatically if briefly mentioned. The seneschal takes over the duties of the King when the latter is enjoying himself.

The reader should remember that Equitan was called a judge: ("jostis'" 12). It is rather odd that this information should be given us, gratuitously, as it were. Is there (perhaps) an implication that Equitan himself will (somehow) be judged in the course of the narrative; first, by the reader or listener, because of Equitan's actions; secondly, by his people when the King does not wish to marry; and finally, by his people once again, and by the loyal seneschal, after the King's death? And does not this apparently irrelevant mention of justice anticipate the final justice done to Equitan, and to the lady as well? In that connection, the statement that the seneschal also administered justice (24) will acquire a further and ironical significance at the end of the narrative! [5]

In the four concluding lines (25-8), we learn that Equitan is never prevented by anything whatever (unless to wage war) from enjoying himself. He is the complete sensualist.

The seneschal has a wife unequalled in beauty: (29-37)

---

[5] This is the first of several instances of what we may call the reversal of roles, with the seneschal assuming the king's duties.

> Femme espuse ot li seneschals,
> Dunt puis vient el païs granz mal[s].
> La dame ert bele durement
> 32 E de mut bon affeitement,
> Gent cors out e bele faiture;
> En li former uvrat nature: [6]
> Les oilz out veirs e bel le vis,
> 36 Bele buche, neis ben asis.
> El rëaume n'aveit sa per.

After the description of the sensual Equitan, and the noble, good seneschal, now we are told that the seneschal has a beautiful wife. Contrasting with the brief mention of the seneschal and his moral qualities is the lengthy portrait of the wife,[7] in which her physical qualities are emphasized.

In the line immediately preceding the description praising the lady's beauty and charm, not only is the lady (like Equitan before) judged by Marie; the final outcome of the story ("Dunt puis vient el païs granz mal[s]": 30) is disclosed. There is a sort of causal relationship between *granz mal[s]* (in 30) and the lady's beauty.

The King makes the acquaintance of the lady: (38-42)

> Li reis l'oï sovent loër.
> Soventefez la salua,
> 40 De ses aveirs li enveia;
> Sanz veüe la coveita,
> E cum ainz pot a li parla.

In this very short passage, we find the medieval *topos* of falling in love through hearsay. It is obvious that Equitan intends to add another woman to his collection.

Equitan finds her most beautiful: (43-53)

> Priveement esbanïer [8]
> 44 En la cuntree ala chacier.
> La u li seneschal maneit,

---

[6] Notice the Ovidian element, the reference to the goddess Natura.

[7] Because of its length, the physical description of a woman offered here is in striking opposition to Marie's usual procedure.

[8] Is there not a double meaning intended in the phrase *Priveement esbanïer?*

> El chastel u la dame esteit,
> [Se] herberjat li reis la nuit,
> 48   Quant repeirout de sun deduit.
> Asez poeit a li parler,
> Sun curage e sun bien mustrer.
> Mut la trova curteise e sage,
> 52   Bele de cors e de visage,
> De bel semblant e enveisie;

In a series of three lines (45-7), each of which is given over to one of the three principal characters, we have the presentation of the future *ménage à trois*.

There is clearly deep significance that the ruse invented by the King involves his taking the role of hunter (*chacier*, 44). For we shall soon see that it is the hunt and the pursuit of the seneschal's wife that the King intends — and of which the lady is still unaware.

Equitan's conversation with the lady, anticipated in the previous section ("E cum ainz pot a li parla": 42), is elaborated here. Indeed, lines 49-50 ("Asez poeit a li parler, / Sun curage e sun bien mustrer") prepare the way for the King's later declaration of love.

In this lay, the reader does not really feel a definite given moment when the action begins. We learn that Equitan can see the lady (51) and talk to her (49) — but precisely *where* they are and *when* these events take place we do not know.[9] (Yet we do know he has sent gifts to the seneschal's wife, and that he is covetous of her.) The gradual *entrée en matière* harmonizes with the Prologue where King Equitan is not individualized, but rather is presented as just a member of a group.

The King is wounded by one of Cupid's arrows: (54-62)

> Amurs l'ad mis a sa maisnie.
> Une s[e]ete ad vers lui traite,
> 56   Que mut grant plaie li ad faite,
> El quor li ad lancie e mise;
> N'i ad mestier sens ne cointise;
> Pur la dame l'ad si suspris,

---

[9] Indeed, the absence of visualizable scenes is a characteristic feature of this lay.

60 Tut en est murnes e pensis.
   Or l'i estut del tut entendre,
   Ne se purrat nïent defendre:

In this passage we find another Ovidian allusion, the cliché of the Arrow of Love.[10] Equitan is the only protagonist in Marie's lays of whom it is specifically said that he is wounded by Love's arrow. The use of the cliché is in agreement with the insistent mention of *curteisie,* in a superficial, even cheap sense.

In Marie's auctorial comment in the final couplet, we learn that Equitan is doomed ("Or l'i estut del tut entendre, / Ne se purrat nïent defendre"). All his obedience to the lady is anticipated here, for he will be her helpless victim. His destiny will be a fate which Equitan will have to undergo completely.

In the night Equitan laments: (63-88)

   La nuit ne dort ne [ne] respose,
64 Mes sei meïsmes blasme e chose.
   'Allas,' fet il, 'queil destinee
   M'amenat en ceste cuntree?[11]
   Pur ceste dame que ai veüe
68 M'est un' anguisse al quor ferue
   Que tut le cors me fet trembler.
   Jeo quit que mei l'estuet amer;
   E si jo l'aim, jeo ferai mal:
72 Ceo est la femme al seneschal.
   Garder li dei amur e fei,
   Si cum jeo voil k'il face a mei.
   Si par nul engin le saveit,
76 Bien sai que mut l'en pesereit.

---

[10] Love-symbolism is not excessively used in Marie's lays; *Equitan* is the second of four lays (cf. *Guigemar, Lanval, Eliduc*) where it is found.

[11] In the opening couplet of his lament (65-6), Equitan reveals his surprise that his amorous adventure has boomeranged. According to Jeanne Wathelet-Willem ("Equitan dans l'œuvre de Marie de France," *le Moyen-Age,* LXIX (1963), 325-45), this would mean that Marie has failed to offer a convincing character study: "Mais pour Equitan, cette attitude de victime correspond mal à ses entreprises de conquête, le personnage manque d'unité" (336)! But, obviously, Equitan is being presented to us as no longer "uni", but torn; he has discovered a new aspect of himself: he the conqueror of women finds himself conquered by a woman. As for his opening question, of course he knows that his visit to the seneschal's wife was the result of his own scheming; but he now suspects that Fate had a hand in it.

> Mes nepurquant pis iert asez
> Que pur li seië afolez.
> Si bele dame tant mar fust,
> 80 S'ele n'amast u dru eüst!
> Que devendreit sa curteisie,
> S'ele n'amast de drüerie?
> Suz ciel n'ad humme, s'ele amast, [12]
> 84 Ki durement n'en amendast.
> Li seneschal, si l'ot cunter, [13]
> Ne l'en deit mie trop peser;
> Sul ne la peot il nient tenir:
> 88 Certes jeo voil od li partir.'

In accordance with the blurred effect already noted is the total lack of any stage-setting for Equitan's soliloquy (63ff.). He must be in his bed-room (cf. 90: *Enprés se jut* ...). During the first part of his monologue, is he standing at a window, or pacing the floor as he argues with himself? We hear his voice eerily coming out of nowhere.

This lament is remakable for the conflict between Equitan's various sentiments. At its beginning, he does show some sense of moral values, and feels compassion for the seneschal; at its close, the seneschal no longer counts.

In the first eight lines (63-70), Equitan talks about his destiny. (As we will see more and more, he creates his own destiny.) In the next six verses (71-6), we see him struggling with the moral problem involved ('Et si jo l'aim, jeo ferai mal'), apparently with deep earnestness. His compassion for the seneschal is genuine, and shows understanding of his vassal's position. [14] Yet this is the last time we shall ever see Equitan in this mood!

---

[12] Note the emphasis given to the lady's love in 80, 82, and 83, echoing the King's assertion in 70 *(Jeo quit que mei l'estuet amer)*. And how ironic is it that Equitan speaks of the ennobling effects of love (83-4): for he will degenerate, and so will the lady.

[13] The recurring motif of knowledge (e.g., knowledge acquired through hearsay).

[14] In retrospect, lines 75-6 ('Si par nul engin le saveit, / Bien sai que mut l'en pesereit') are grimly humorous. What Equitan here anticipates is not his own end: what he foresees, with deep compassion, is the seneschal's grief. But when the end comes, we do not see a grieving seneschal, whom we must pity, but a brutal executioner!

In the next eight lines (77-84), Equitan tries to work himself out of his problem. In 77-8 ('Mes nepurquant pis iert asez / Que pur li seië afolez'), the adversative *mes* clearly indicates a reversal in his argument: it is better the seneschal suffer than the King! In the last four verses (81-4), he mentions the need for the woman, for the maintenance of her *curteisie*, of *drüerie*. The ennobling effects of love (83-4) have become one of the *topoi* of courtly love, but we will see a quite different effect upon the lady and King Equitan.

In 85-88, the moral problem is no longer posed for the King: his compassion for his vassal has entirely disappeared. Equitan now proceeds to make his own laws concerning the lady ('Sul ne la peot il nient tenir: / Certes jeo voil od li partir'). The *certes* in the passage's final line indicates that the King has convinced himself completely.

The King continues to lament: (89-100)

```
     Quant ceo ot dit, si suspira;
     Enprés se jut e si pensa.
     Aprés parlat e dist: 'De quei
 92  Sui en estrif e en effrei?
     Uncor ne sai ne n'ai seü
     S'ele fereit de mei sun dru;
     Mes jeo savrai hastivement.
 96  S'ele sentist ceo ke jeo sent,
     Jeo perdrei[e] ceste dolur.
     E Deus! tant ad de ci que al jur!
     Jeo ne puis ja repos aveir:
100  Mut ad ke jeo cuchai eirseir.'
```

In the very first verse of this section, we learn that Equitan sighs. Is Marie making fun of him — that he is acting like a courtly lover who sighs? Or is his a sensuous sigh? (He may have been visualizing what it would be to share the seneschal's wife with the seneschal.)

Although Equitan rationalizes his distress at the beginning of this passage, at its close he reveals, twice (in 98 and 100), his nervous impatience to talk with the lady: when will the night end?

At dawn, the king goes out to hunt, only to return: (101-6)

> Li reis veilla tant que jur fu;
> A grant peinë ad atendu. [15]
> Il est levez, si vet chacier;
> 104 Mes tost se mist el repeirer
> E dit que mut est deshaitiez.
> Es chambres vet, si s'est cuchiez. [16]

The King's impatience for daybreak is echoed in the opening couplet of this short passage. At dawn, he starts to carry out his stratagem, but finds his forces unequal to the task. In this passage the rapidity of action (summed up in only four verses) contrasts markedly with the slow preceding scene of the King's lament.

The seneschal grieves over the King's indisposition: (107-10)

> Dolent en est li senescaus:
> 108 Il ne seit pas queils est li maus
> De quei li reis sent les friçuns;
> Sa femme en est dreit' acheisuns.

The King's unhappiness (*deshaitiez*, 105) is now reflected in the feeling of the loyal vassal (*dolent*, 107), who cannot understand what causes his lord to shiver so. The seneschal is so worthy and compassionate; his concern for the King reminds us of the King's brief moment of compassion for his vassal (cf. 71-6). In the final line of this passage, Marie's auctorial aside serves to point up the grim irony of the seneschal's ignorance, and his concern.

Equitan sends for the vassal's wife: (111-16)

> Pur sei deduire e cunforter [17]
> 112 La fist venir a li parler.

---

[15] A continuation, from the preceding section, of the motif of grief and pain.

[16] Is this the same chamber as the one in which Equitan and the seneschal are later bled, and in which the King, with his mistress, will die?

[17] Once more, the motif (*sei deduire*) of Equitan's love of pleasure mentioned on three previous occasions (17; 28; 48). Note also that the verb *sei deduire* is used here in the scene preceding the King's talk with the lady in which he finally convinces her of the rightness of their love.

And the accompanying verb *cunforter* anticipates the 'comfort' (cf. 115) which the lady will give to the King by becoming his mistress.

>   Sun curage li descovri,
>   Saver li fet qu'il meort pur li;
>   Del tut li peot faire confort
> 116 E bien li peot doner [l]a mort.

In the opening couplet we learn of Equitan's pretext ("Pur sei deduire e cunforter") given to the husband so that the King may speak privately with the lady. And speak he does! The reader can not fail to be struck by the extraordinary amount of conversation there is in this lay; from 113-176, there will be nothing but talk.

Whereas the evening before Equitan had merely made polite conversation with the lady, at this moment [18] he lays bare his most intimate feelings, twice mentioning his certain death unless she would comfort him.

The lady objects to his request: (117-48)

>   'Sire,' la dame li ad dit,
>   'De ceo m'estuet aveir respit:
>   A ceste primere feiee
> 120 Ne sui jeo mie cunseillee.
>   Vus estes rei de grant noblesce;
>   Ne sui mie de teu richesce
>   Que [a] mei [vus] deiez arester
> 124 De drüerie ne de amer.
>   S'avïez fait vostre talent,
>   Jeo sai de veir, ne dut nïent,
>   Tost me avrïez entrelaissie[e],
> 128 Jeo sereie mut empeiree.
>   Së [is]si fust que vus amasse
>   E vostre requeste otreiasse,
>   Ne sereit pas üel partie
> 132 Entre nus deus la drüerie.
>   Pur ceo që estes rei puissaunz
>   E mi sire est de vus tenaunz,
>   Quidereiez, a mun espeir,
> 136 Le danger de l'amur aveir.
>   Amur n'est pruz se n'est egals.
>   Meuz vaut un povre[s] hum lëals,

---

[18] Although we know that the King is in bed (cf. 106), we must wonder about the lady: is she seated or standing (cf. 112-13: "La fist venir a li parler. / Sun curage li descovri")?

> Si en sei ad sen e valur,
> 140 [E] greinur joie est de s'amur
> Quë il n'est de prince u de rei,
> Quant il n'ad lëauté en sei.
> S'aukuns aime plus ha[u]tement
> 144 Que [a] sa richesce nen apent,
> Cil se dut[e] de tute rien.
> Li riches hum requid[e] bien
> Que nus ne li toille s'amie
> 148 Qu'il volt amer par seignurie.'

In the lady's objection [19] we are struck by her lack of moral protest, of shocked reaction. Not once does she insist upon her love and fidelity to her husband, who has been presented as such a good and loyal man! Yet even more arresting is the legal and pedantic tone of her words. She offers a series of moralizations which she has at her instant command (in terms of which she visualizes the situation of the King as her lover), enouncing them so unhesitatingly and so rapidly that we are stunned! There will be another long speech of hers (the third and last) in which her preparedness and foresight will be equally in evidence.

The first four lines of this speech (117-20) shock us; for where we might have expected some remark about her husband, there is none. The lady has no moral values whatever; she is utterly and consistently bad, in contrast to the King, who will degenerate. In her the King, who had expected to add another woman to his series of amorous conquests, has more than met his match.

The lady does not say 'no' to the King's request for her love: she merely asks him for time to think! Yet the rest of her speech tells him exactly what she thinks. In this, lies the humor of her speech.

In the following four lines (121-4, and note the lady's emphasis upon his nobility, 'Vus estes rei de grant noblesce'), the lady takes for granted something we have never seen taken for granted

---

[19] On three occasions the lady's words to the King are reproduced in direct address; each time they are prefaced by the title 'Sire.' Of the three speeches, the one above is the longest.

It is also to be pointed out that preceding every speech of the lady to Equitan, his words to her are reported briefly in indirect discourse, serving, as it were, to prompt her lengthy utterances.

before: as the prerequisite for love, she sets up the equality of social rank.

Then (in the next four verses, 125-8) the lady makes a pronouncement having nothing whatever to do with social status: she predicts, accusingly, that he will abandon her as soon as he has had his pleasure. Her words are an expression of what any vulgar woman would think.

She proceeds to talk about the inequality in love (the following eight lines, 129-36), reminding him of the difference in their status. Referring to the relationship between her husband and the King (which recalls Equitan's sentiments expressed in his lament) she expresses the fear that he would carry over his *seigneurie* into their love-relationship. Indeed, she foresees that he would always be the master. Then, turning aside from their particular situation, she proceeds to generalize about the calamitous consequences of "inequality in love": twelve lines (137-148) are devoted to her arguments,[20] which end with another reference to the inevitability of *seigneurie* being exercised by the one of higher rank. The lady's prediction, as we shall see, will never materialize; to the contrary, the King will become her servant in every respect. In this situation, too, we will have a case of reversal of roles.

The King reproves her for her uncourtly attitude: (149-75)

<pre>
      Equitan li respunt aprés:
      'Dame, merci! Nel dites mes!
      Cil ne sunt mie fin curteis,
152   Ainz est bargaine de burgeis,
      Que pur aveir ne pur grant fieu
      Mettent lur peine en malveis liu.
      Suz ciel n'ad dame, s'ele est sage,
156   Curteise e franche de curage,
      Pur quei d'amer se tienge chiere,
      Que el ne seit mie novelere,
      S'el n'eüst fors sul sun mantel,
160   Que uns riches princes de chastel
      Ne se deüst pur li pener
</pre>

---

[20] In the lady's conclusion, note the term *richesce* (in 144) five lines from the end of her speech which repeats the *richesce* (in 122) used five lines from its beginning.

E lëalment e bien amer.
Cil ki de amur sunt nov[e]lier
164 E ki se aturnent de trichier,
Il sunt gabé e deceü;
De plusurs l'avum nus veü.
N'est pas merveille se cil pert
168 Ki par s'ovreine le desert.
Ma chiere dame, a vus m'otrei!
Ne me tenez mie pur rei,
Mes pur vostre hum e vostre ami!
172 Seürement vus jur e di
Que jeo ferai vostre pleisir
Ne me laissez pur vus murir! [21]
Vus seiez dame e jeo servant,
176 Vus orguilluse e jeo preiant!'

In his reply, Equitan shows himself to be a most persuasive speaker. He has probably spoken such words many times before — and never meant them — but this time he means them completely.

Yet the first thirteen lines of Equitan's speech (149-62) are puzzling in two respects. Why does Marie allow him to speak so wisely, even nobly, if we are meant to believe that his character has begun to degenerate? (We are reminded of Guigemar (cf. 512-516, *Guigemar*) who also speaks with dignity and authority on the same subject; yet up to the time of that speech, he had been presented as the personification of innocence.) Moreover, why does Marie let the King speak such good sense in the name of *curteisie*, which he so falsely represents? The mention of *curteisie* is ironic, for up to the time Equitan met the lady, *curteisie* was equated with sensousness! (And we will see this "courtly" lover sink even lower in the moral scale.) Perhaps it is to demonstrate some more how Equitan creates his own destiny that Marie allows him to speak in such a way.

Just as the lady had moralized to him, now the King moralizes (in the following six verses, 163-8) to her, preaching about those who are fickle. (In doing so, he unknowingly uses terms that

---

[21] Here the King reiterates what he had already told her (cf. 114, "Saver li fet qu'il meort pur li," and 116, "E bien li peot doner [l]a mort").

describe his own downfall,[22] while pretending to distinguish himself from the others.) It is interesting that Equitan should lash out at fickleness, since up to the time of meeting the lady, he was the embodiment of inconstancy; after meeting her, he will no longer be *novelier,* for she will not let him go. His love for her will be a sickness, which will lead to his death (and to hers).

In the impassioned words (169-71) with which he pledges himself to her, we may note the term 'vostre hum' reminiscent of the expression of fealty between lord and vassal. Here it is the King himself who insists on the reversal of rôles, as he promises to serve her as her vassal.

His final plea (172-6) is triply effective. Although the words may sound fixed and common-place, expressions that any suppliant lover would utter, they nevertheless reflect deep feeling, and (hopeful) joy. Yet in reality these words of Equitan have a sinister ring, for as he pledges his service ('Seürement vus jur e di / Que jeo ferai vostre pleisir') he renounces his own will, giving himself entirely to love and to its consequences. We may point again to the pathological nature of his love for the lady; to the reader who knows that the King will be the complete victim of this evil love, these are ominous words. In the closing couplet we find another reference to the reversal of roles ('Vus seiez dame e jeo servant, / Vus orguilluse e jeo preiant!').

The lady grants him her love: (177-84)

>   Tant ad li reis parlé od li [23]
>   E tant li ad crië merci
>   Que de s'amur l'aseüra,
> 180   E el sun cors li otria.
>   Par lur anels s'entresaisirent,
>   Lur fiaunce[s] s'entreplevirent.
>   Bien les tiendrent, mut s'entr'amerent;
> 184   Puis en mururent e finerent.

---

[22] In verse 165 ("Il sunt gabé e deceü"), the word 'deceü' can signify 'deceived' as well as 'disappointed,' both of which are applicable here.

[23] The verb *parler* will acquire another level of meaning after this scene. Occurring four times (42; 49; 112; 177) before the lady grants her favors to the King, it has no sexual implications; whereas after she has acceded to Equitan's request, in its four subsequent instances (118; 200; 205; 279) the verb may well have an erotic connotation.

We now learn (in the first four lines of this passage) the favorable results of the discussion between the lady and the King, as Equitan gains his wish.[24] In the next two lines (181-2) we are shown the ceremony in which the lovers pledge their faith. In the final couplet, Marie interrupts the progression of the narrative, moving to the future. She prophetically announces the end of Equitan's and the lady's story in unmistakable terms, the first line so tender, the last, so heavy and final: "Bien les tiendrent, mut s'entr'amerent; / Puis en mururent e finerent." (Note the double predication of their end *(mururent, finerent)*,[25] giving an unmistakable note of finality to both this particular passage and to the lovers' story.)

Equitan plans a way to be alone with the lady when he wishes: (185-96)

> Lung tens durrat lur drüerie,
> Que ne fu pas de gent oïe.
> As termes de lur assembler,
> 188 Quant ensemble durent parler,
> Li reis feseit dire a sa gent
> Que seignez iert priveement.
> Les us des chambres furent clos;
> 192 Ne troveissez humme si os,
> Si li rei pur lui n'enveiast,
> Ja une feiz dedenz entrast.
> Li seneschal la curt teneit,
> 196 Les plaiz e les clamurs oieit.[26]

In this narrative passage summarizing Equitan's rendez-vous with the lady, we are given two details: the ruse for their meetings, and the arrangements for the chamber-doors. Both details,

---

[24] Does *E el sun cors li otria* refer to the physical act of the lady's giving herself, or merely to her promises, to her words ("mun cors vus otrei"), as the preceding line had referred to the King's words? The last seems the more likely: Marie would be deliberately refraining from announcing the moment of their first act of love-making.

[25] This use of repetition will be found once again toward the close of the lay.

[26] Equitan's second ruse, like his first, is equally successful.
The reader may well wonder whether the seneschal is not very perceptive. Or is he so loyal, and/or so busy seeing to the duties of the kingdom, that he has no suspicions?

apparently irrelevant here, will become important in the third section of our poem.

Here we note the third presentation of the seneschal, for whom our sympathies have been gradually engaged: he is always so good, so kind, so loyal, and always so much in the background. Just as the seneschal had acted as *jostisier* when the King gave himself up to frivolous pleasures, we see him again replacing the King when the King is making love to his own wife!

As in the lay of *Guigemar*, the majority of action within a major narrative division will take place in a bedroom. In this second part of our poem, there will be a change of scene to the King's residence. Yet the vagueness of setting continues: where is *la curt* (105)?

The lady hears that the King's people resent his refusal to marry: (197-204)

>   Li reis l'ama mut lungement,
>   Que d'autre femme n'ot talent:
>   Il ne voleit nule espuser,
> 200   Ja n'en rovast oïr parler.
>   La gent le tindrent mut a mal,
>   Tant que la femme al seneschal
>   L'oï suvent; mut li pesa, [27]
> 204   E de lui perdre se duta.

The phrase *la femme al seneschal* in 202 (noted before when Equitan debated the propriety of his love, 72) is a reminder of the seneschal who is holding court for the King who is betraying him!

This brief passage represents the turning-point in the story. In the first line (197) we learn about the King's love for the lady; this is the second successive instance when a reference to their lasting love (cf. 185) has begun a passage. In the next verse, we are told of the King's total lack of interest in other women; as for the possibility of marriage, he never wanted to hear that mentioned (the following couplet, 199-200).

---

[27] The motif of hearsay and reporting, extremely important in Marie's lays.

"EQUITAN" 37

In 201-4 we learn first, of the resentment of the King's people which gradually increased until the lady hears of it, then of her grief, and of her fear of losing her lover.

In the King's presence, the lady weeps: (205-211)

>   Quant ele pout a lui parler
>   E el li duit joie mener,
>   Baisier, estreindre e acoler
> 208 E ensemblë od lui jüer,
>   Forment plura e grant deol fist.
>   Li reis demanda e enquist
>   Que [ceo] deveit e que ceo fu.

Although there is more conversation (beginning at 205, and continuing to the end of 260), there is still no individualized staged scene (and there will be none, until almost the very end of the story). We will hear the lovers' speak, but *where* they are we do not know.

This brief section (205-211), describing the first moments of the lovers' next meeting, offers a most effective contrast of joy and grief: we are reminded of the happiness they usually had together, the happiness Equitan was expecting them to have, to be told instead of the lady's tears and overwhelming sorrow. Four lines of potential joy, followed by one line of the sadness that was reality: the heavy line "Forment plura e grant deol fist" (209).

The lady discloses her fears: (212-20)

> 212 La dame li ad respundu:
>   'Sire, jo plur pur nostre amur,
>   Que mei revert a grant dolur: [28]
>   Femme prendrez, fille a un rei,
> 216 [E] si vus partirez de mei;
>   Sovent l'oi dire e bien le sai.
>   E jeo, lasse! que devendrai?
>   Pur vus m'estuet aver la mort; [29]
> 220 Car jeo ne sai autre cunfort.'

---

[28] The opening couplet of the lady's words may be considered as an anticipation of the end of the lovers' story. Observe, too the use of the verb *revert* (214) which will reappear twice again toward the close of the lay (cf. 299-300; and 233-5).

[29] Note the dramatic irony of these words, for (in one sense) they will come true.

This brief passage is problematic: why does the lady not mention the situation which motivates her lament to the King? For now she only talks about her grief; it is as if she were remembering her words to him the first time (their difference in rank, and his certain desertion of her). The most important thing for the lady is that she is right: we are struck by her sententious tone as she asserts he will leave her to marry someone of his own rank.

Her closing words are reminiscent of Equitan's first words to her: just as he claimed to be dying for love of her (cf. 114), and needed her comfort, now she will have to die for love of him, since she knows no other comfort.

Equitan assures her that her fears are in vain: (221-8)

<blockquote>
Li reis li dit par grant amur:
'Bele amie, n'eiez poür!
Certes, ja femme ne prendrai
224 Ne pur autre [ne] vus larrai.
Sacez de veir e si creez:
Si vostre sire fust finez, [30]
Reïne e dame vus fereie;
228 Ja pur [nul] humme nel lerreie.'
</blockquote>

The King lovingly consoles her, assuring her that he will never marry another woman (for he well knows her obsession with social status): that he would take her for wife and queen, if only she did not have a husband.

The lady offers a suggestion of her own: (229-36)

<blockquote>
La dame l'en ad mercië
E dit que mut li sot bon gre,
E si de ceo l'aseürast
232 Que pur autre ne la lessast,
Hastivement purchacereit
A sun seignur que mort sereit;
Legier sereit a purchacier,
236 Pur ceo k'il li vousist aidier. [31]
</blockquote>

---

[30] Note that the verb *finez* (here referring to the husband) is repeated from line 184 (where it pertained to the lovers: "Puis en mururent e *finerent*").

[31] The lady in *Equitan* is the first of two wives (the other is in *Bisclavret*) who use a lover to destroy their husbands.

After the lady asks once more for the King's assurance of his fidelity, she seizes upon the phrase intended by Equitan only hypothetically (" 'Si vostre sire fust finez, / Reïne e dame vus fereie' "), and suggests a plan which will make of them both criminals.

Equitan promises his assistance to her in any undertaking: (237-40)

> Il li respunt que si ferat:
> Ja cele rien en li dirrat
> Quë il ne face a sun poeir,
> 240 Turt a folie u a saveir.

This entire brief passage echoes the King's words to the lady during their first interview (" 'Seürement vus jur e di / Que jeo ferai vostre pleisir' ": 172-3). Once again we are given an instance of the major theme of the lay, that of reversal: reversal not only of role (here, the King to serve, the lady to command), but as we will later see, reversal of situation.

The phrase *Turt a folie u a saveir* in the final couplet summarizing Equitan's total obedience to the lady's desires seems so fixed and set; yet it is not formulaic in Marie's lays. It is found only once more, and in a similar situation: it is used in *Lanval* (125-6) when the protagonist of that name promises his unswerving obedience to the fairy's commands.

The lady reveals the details of her murderous plan: (241-60)

> 'Sire,' fet ele, 'si vus plest,
> Venez chacer en la forest,
> En la cuntree u jeo sujur;
> 244 Dedenz le chastel mun seignur
> Sujurnez; si serez seignez,
> E al terz jur si vus baignez.
> Mis sire od vus se seignera [32]
> 248 E avuec vus se baignera;
> Dites li bien, nel lessez mie,
> Quë il vus tienge cumpainie!
> E jeo ferai les bains temprer

---

[32] The bleeding of King Equitan and his seneschal reminds us of a situation in the *Tristan* story, with the difference that the lady in *Equitan*, unlike Iseut, is not to be bled.

252 E les deus cuves aporter,
     Sun bain si chaut e si buillant,
     Suz ciel n'en ad humme vivant [33]
     Ne fust escaudez e malmis,
256 Einz que dedenz [se] fust asis.
     Quant mort serat e escaudez,
     Vos hummes e les soens mandez;
     Si lur mustrez cumfaitement
260 Est mort al bain sudeinement.'

The lady's second long speech in which she discloses each carefully formulated step of her plan reminds us of her first speech to the King, with its series of crude and vulgar formulas. Because the lady so quickly appropriates the King's suggestion, we wonder if this is a parallel to her quick-wittedness which was demonstrated in that first speech. Or has she been planning the murder for some time (and we know of the love-affair's long duration), waiting for the opportune moment to reveal her plot?

In the first detail of her plot ("'Sire, ... 'si vus plest, / Venez chacer en la forest, / En la cuntree u jeo sujur' "") it is clever that Marie has the lady unknowingly repeat the situation which led to the love-affair. The second detail (the King's bleeding) is simply a continuation of what has been going on before (yet then it was Equitan's pretext to be alone with the lady). [34] The third detail (the tub of boiling water) is completely new; upon it the murder of the seneschal will depend.

As for the King's part in the lady's plan (249-50), Equitan need only be sure to keep her husband company. We will soon learn how well the King carries out this instruction!

Most remarkable are the lady's detailed arrangements for the bath intended for her husband. As she tells of her part in the plan, we are struck by the verb *temprer* ("'E jeo ferai les bains temprer' "). Surely this verb is employed deliberately for its ironic overtones; the lady will heat the water to just the right degree of temperature! Indeed, she twice insists upon the extreme

---

[33] From 254 to the end of the lady's speech, notice the recurring opposition between life and death.

[34] And we will see how Equitan will act when he next is bled.

heat of the water intended for her husband ("'... si chaut e si buillant'": 253), [35] so hot that anyone would be scalded (255).

Moreover, the lady is absolutely certain of the effect of the scalding water on her husband, taking his death for granted ("Quant mort serat e escaudez'": 257), speaking of it in a dependent clause in which the fact more important to the lover is presented first. [36] Furthermore, we learn that not only has the lady very carefully planned the execution of her husband's death, but its announcement as well!

The King assents to her plan: (261-2)

> Li reis li ad tut graanté
> Qu'il en ferat sa volenté.

With his promise of absolute obedience to the lady's wishes, the second portion of the narrative ends.

The seneschal accepts the King's invitation to bathe with him: (263-70)

```
        Ne demurat mie treis meis [37]
264  Que el païs vet chacier li reis.
        Seiner se fet cuntre sun mal,
        Ensemble od lui sun senescal.
        Al terz jur dist k'il baignereit;
268  Li senescal mut le voleit.
        'Vus baignerez,' dist il, 'od mei.'
        Li senescal dit: 'Jo l'otrei.'
```

This third narrative section, just as did the second, opens with a summary of the passing of time indicating that the action is once more to move forward.

Now Equitan goes again to the country to hunt. We may remember the two reasons for hunting: to capture an animal to tame it, as a diversion, or to kill. And we know already what will be the King's intent, and who will be his quarry.

---

[35] The correspondence between the lady's warmth in her emotions toward her lover and the warmth of the hot water intended for her husband can not be fortuitous.

[36] Line 257 is a particularly effective use of the rhetorical figure of hysteron proteron.

[37] Given the fervor of his love, the reference to three months probably does not mean that the King waited that long before he saw the lady again.

It is meaningful that the first (and only) time that we hear the seneschal speak is to say 'I agree' (270). For here, the vassal who has been fulfilling the duties of his King, now grants something to his lord. The feudal verb *otreier* in the seneschal's assent must be a deliberate reminder of the other time when it was used: when the secenschal's wife granted her favors to the King ("E el sun cors li otria": 180).

The lady carries out completely her part of the plan: (271-6)

>   La dame fet les bains temprer
> 272 E les deus cuves aporter;
>   Devant le lit tut a devise
>   Ad chescune de[s] cuves mise.
>   L'ewe buillant feit aporter,
> 276 U li senescal dut entrer.

The opening couplet of this passage recalls the lady's words (spoken precisely twenty lines earlier), as she now fulfills her task to the letter. Yet would it not be highly improbable that the seneschal would sit down in the tub without first testing the water-temperature?

For the second time, notice the verb *temprer*, first mentioned for its ironic quality. But it is also a verb pertaining to the activity of a good housewife. Perhaps it is true that the lady was an accomplished housewife, and that her husband had learned to trust her preparations for the bath. If so, she could then expect him to jump into the tub without first testing the water.

This brief section offers, for the first time in the lay, a scene that invites to some degree of visualization: the two tubs that are placed "tut a devise" by the bed. Never before had a bed been mentioned. We have been told twice before that the King has lain down (and each time it was in conjuction with his love): after his first soliloquy (*Enprés se jut...* : 91), and then, in feigned illness (*... si s'est cuchiez*: 106). And we know that the King and the seneschal's wife went to bed together. How ingenious of Marie to specify the bed (connected both with the blood-letting and with their love-making) only when the lady is unwittingly preparing for their death. In the scene that follows, the bed will figure even more prominently.

Equitan's role fails to be fulfilled: (277-84)

> Li produm esteit sus levez: [38]
> Pur deduire fu fors alez. [39]
> La dame vient parler al rei, [40]
> 280 E il la mist dejuste sei;
> Sur le lit al seignur cucherent [41]
> E deduistrent e enveiserent.
> Ileoc unt ensemble geü,
> 284 Pur la cuve que devant fu.

This short passage is triply puzzling. First of all, why did the seneschal get up from bed? He and the King have been bled; they are soon to bathe. We learn that he wanted to amuse himself, and therefore, went out (*Pur deduire fu fors alez*: 278). This may well be the first and only occasion when the seneschal has ever been able to relax — he has been so busy, taking over the King's duties! Moreover, his departure from the bed-chamber is as if he has escaped already from his wife's plot.

As for Equitan, he had only one thing to do in the plot — to keep the husband company. Why did he fail to do so? Why did he not also go out with the seneschal?

Thirdly, why does Equitan, knowing that the husband is at large, run the risk of being discovered together with the wife?

---

[38] We may wonder whether the seneschal's designation as *li produm* is in any way ironic, or simply indicative of Marie's sympathetic attitude toward that character who has always been presented as so worthy and so decent?

And note the couplet just above (275-6): with the rescriptive clause ... *U li seneschal dut entrer* reflecting the confidence of the lovers, it is almost as if Marie were warning the reader that the husband will escape.

[39] The use of *deduire* is very significant; it reminds us of the King who spends his time in pleasureable activities (and we remember that the verb *deduire* is so important to the King's characterization, cf. 28). Furthermore, the verb serves to contrast the seneschal's activities with those of his wife and the King: for both the husband, and his wife and his King will amuse themselves.

[40] The lady's coming (voluntarily and apparently unsolicited!) to "talk" with the King reminds us of that scene so long ago when he sent for her to come to talk with him (and we know with what result).

[41] Note that in three consecutive lines (279-81), the bed is either suggested or specifically mentioned. Yet on whose bed (*Sur le lit al seignur cucherent:* 281) are they lying? *Li reis* is always referred to as such; the husband is mentioned as *mun seignur* and *mis sire*. Since Marie has always called the husband by those terms, it may be that she could now allow herself to call him *le seignur*. Yet *seignur* could, theoretically, refer to the King who is the *seignur* of the seneschal.

Could it be that line 284 *(Pur la cuve que devant fu)* answers this question? The presence of the tub of boiling water gave them confidence? Their plan has been carried out successfully to the final stage that they themselves could prepare; nothing is lacking except for the husband to take his bath, as he had promised. It seems that Marie allows the King, at this point in the narrative, to lose all his sense and *mesure*, to commit (with the lady) the most senseless act imaginable, an act of almost allegorical implications.[42] It is artistically significant that this scene (beginning at 279) in which the lovers, so soon to die, lie embracing upon the bed[43] is the second (and last) staged scene in the narrative.

The seneschal returns to the chamber: (285-92)

>   L'un firent tenir e garder;
>   Une meschine i dut ester.
>   Li senescal hastif revint,
> 288 A l'hus buta, cele le tint;
>   Icil le fiert par tel aïr,
>   Par force li estut ovrir.
>   Le rei e sa femme ad trovez [44]
> 292 U il gisent entr'acolez.

With the opening line of this section, we feel a rapidity in the narrative movement as the dénouement begins. This rapidity will accelerate, with each successive event leading to the death of both lovers.

In 287, the word *hastif* is employed for the second time in our story. The reader may remember that the lady had said that

---

[42] In this respect, we are reminded of the blindness of the father in the OF *Alexius*, a blindness which was infra-human. And as we see Equitan lose all reason and moderation, we recall Marie's indictment in vv. 17-20: ("Cil met[ent] lur vie en nu[n]cure / Que d'amur n'unt sen e mesure; / Tels est la mesure de amer / Que nul n'i deit reisun garder."

[43] This is the first and only occasion that we actually see the lovers together in bed. They are not arguing (as during his first visit), nor are they harassing their wits (as at the second time we see them). This, the only time we see them happy and carefree, taking their pleasure in each other's company (and note the double predication of their pleasure in 282, E *deduistrent e enveiserent*) — is immediately before they are killed.

[44] The husband's discovery of the two lovers is a parallel to the *Tristan*, with two important differences: King Mark never discovers the two lovers in each other's arms, or in bed together.

she would *quickly* see to her husband's death; and now he *quickly* comes back![45] Furthermore, the adjective *hastif* is also applicable to the manner in which the seneschal acquires knowledge about the lovers: upon finding his wife in the arms of his King, he learns the truth! What is more, this term will be descriptive of the King's and the lady's demise.

In 287-90, the energy of the seneschal's actions is particularly striking;[46] we will soon see more forceful activity (cf. 303-4) on his part.

The King jumps into the tub intended for the seneschal: (293-300)

```
          Li reis garda, sil vit venir.
          Pur sa vileinie covrir
          Dedenz la cuve saut joinz pez,
    296   E il fu nuz e despuillez;
          Unques garde ne s'en dona.
          Ileoc murut [e] escauda;
          Sur lui est le mal revertiz,
    300   E cil en est sauf e gariz. [47]
```

After Equitan has lost every vestige of reason ("Unques garde ne s'en dona"), he jumps to his death into the tub of boiling water intended for the husband. We can not fail to be struck by the macabre humor of the situation, as the "courtly" King, naked (does Marie twice mention his nakedness to stress his confusion?) thus attempts to cover up his uncourtly action (*vileinie*).

Of great importance is the auctorial intervention coming directly after the presentation[48] of the King's death: "Sur lui est

---

[45] It may very well be that by this time the husband had become suspicious, and that, by his absence from the bed-chamber, he deliberately gives the lovers just time enough to be discovered together.

[46] This is the second time (cf. *Guigemar*, 587-90) that we have seen a bed-room door opened forcibly by a husband, revealing an erring wife with her lover on the bed. What an enormous difference there is between each husband's reactions!

[47] With the King's death and the husband's escape from danger, we have a third reversal.

[48] It is noteworthy that Equitan's death is presented in terms ("Ileoc murut [e] escauda") precisely identical to those in which the lady prophesies the realization of the proposed murder of her husband ("Quant mort serat e escaudez": 257).

le mal revertiz, / E cil en est sauf e gariz" (299-300). Here Marie allows us once again to see with whom her sympathies lie, and to indicate her satisfaction over the outcome.

In Marie's remark is employed the term *le mal*, one of the lay's key-words, and one which acquires different meanings in the course of the narration. In its principal use, *mal* is equated with *amur*. Our poem is the only one of Marie's lays in which this equivalence is made. And we have seen how King Equitan has become the pathological victim of his love for the lady.

In Marie's comment discussed above (299-300), *le mal* has still another meaning, that of damage or harm. It is with this signification that the word will be repeated in 309-10.

The wife is put headfirst into the tub by the seneschal: (301-6)

>   Le senescal ad bien veü
>   Coment del rei est avenu. [49]
>   Sa femme prent demeintenant,
> 304   El bain la met le chief avant. [50]
>   Issi mururent amb[e]dui,
>   Li reis avant, e ele od lui.

It is fitting that the lady, the more wicked of the two lovers, is punished by the one who was destined to die. The swift-moving events, begun when the husband returned to the door of the bed-chamber, thus cease abruptly, and with stunning finality.

In this passage's final couplet, why does Marie sum up the end of the two lovers? Just as at the close of the preceding passage Marie repeats the obvious truth that the lover suffered the

---

[49] Surely not the end which Equitan had envisioned for his adventure!

[50] In line 304 we have a problem: did the seneschal put his wife into the same tub of boiling water that the King had entered (in that case, she too, was scalded)? Surely the other tub, intended for the King to bathe in, contained water only pleasantly warm; if the lady were put there, head first, and held down, she would have drowned.

The first possibility has the greater suggestion of grim justice: both in the same tub, made to share the same fate — only, with the position of head and feet reversed, as if to make them fit better in the same tub.

Thus Marie, before Dante (cf. *Purg.* XXVI), punishes the luxurious by means of heat.

It may be noted that drowning as a punishment for adultery is mentioned in Stith Thompson, *Motif-Index of Folk Literature* (Bloomington, 1955-1958), V (1957), p. 226, among the punishments for sexual sins.

fate intended for the husband, so here she must repeat that both the lovers (and she states that twice!) did die. With this second repetition, Marie has reached the point in the story which she had already anticipated at the end of the second section ("Bien les tiendrent, must s'entr'amerent; / Puis en mururent e finerent": 183-4).

In the same moralizing mood, Marie offers this story as an *exemplum*: (307-10)

> Ki bien vodreit reisun entendre,
> 308 Ici purreit ensample prendre:
> Tel purcace le mal d'autrui [51]
> Dunt le mals [tut] revert sur lui. [52]

In the Epilogue Marie tells us that it happened as she has told, and speaks again of the Bretons: (311-14)

> Issi avient cum dit vus ai.
> 312 Li Bretun en firent un lai,
> D'Equitan, cum[ent] il fina
> E la dame que tant l'ama.

The last four lines (which begin with a repetition) remind us ironically of the Prologue telling us of the noble, courteous Bretons and their noble, courteous King.

---

[51] The verb *purcace* recalls the lady's plan to murder her husband; in exposition of the murder plot, that verb was twice used.

[52] Note that the theme of reversal of roles first stated in the couplet, 299-300, summing up Equitan's death: "Sur lui est le mal revertiz, / E cil en est sauf e gariz") is now reiterated in a moralization ("Tel purcace le mal d'autrui / Dunt le mals [tut] revert sur lui": 309-10) for everybody.

The maxim (in 309-10) that concludes the narrative reminds us that in Equitan's speech to the lady there were two maxims (163-6; and 167-8) which mentioned deserved punishments.

LE FRESNE

The lay of *Le Fresne* reveals a tripartite structure of 518 verses, containing the stories both of the heroine Le Fresne and that of her family. Of the three narrative divisions (each of which, moreover, may be subdivided into two unequal parts) the first and third are relatively equal in length, occupying vv. 3-176, and vv. 313-514, respectively. It is in these two particular sections that the family is seen; in the former, the mother is the principal character; in the latter, she will re-emerge, again to dominate the situation. In the central and shortest section (from v. 177 to v. 312), the focus is entirely upon the heroine.

In the Prologue Marie promises us one thing: (1-2)

> Le lai del Freisne vus dirai
> Sulunc le cunte que jeo sai.

In the briefest of formulas, Marie proclaims her auctorial intent, and mentions in passing, her source.

In Brittany long ago there lived two married knights: (3-18)

>   En Bretaine jadis maneient
> 4   Dui chevalier, veisin esteient;
>   Riche humme furent e manant
>   E chevalers pruz e vaillant.
>   Prochein furent, de une cuntree;
> 8   Chescun femme aveit espusee.
>   L'une des dames enceinta;
>   Al terme que ele delivra,
>   A cele feiz ot deus enfanz.
> 12 Sis sires est liez e joianz;
>   Pur la joie quë il en a
>   A sun bon veisin le manda

> Que sa femme ad deus fiz eüz,
> 16 De tanz enfanz esteit creüz;
> L'un li tramettra a lever,
> De sun nun le face nomer.

In this passage we are struck by the emergence of the note of joy out of the matter-of-fact and introductory summary of the first half (through the end of 11). The report of the double birth is immediately followed by the portrait of the doubly joyous father ("liez," "joianz"),[1] whose emotion motivates him to send word to his neighbor.

At the second knight's castle, the messenger relates the news: (19-24)

> Li riches hum sist al manger;
> 20 Atant es vus le messager![2]
> Devant le deis se agenoila,
> Tut sun message li cunta.
> Li sire en ad Deu mercïé;
> 24 Un bel cheval li ad doné.

With this section, Marie shifts from narrative summary to a dramatic staged scene (one of many in our lay). We do not see the messenger start out, we are already in the dining hall to witness his sudden and unexpected appearance ("Atant es vus le messager!") before the knight and his retinue.

The joy and happiness of the new father is echoed at the beginning of this scene: his friend gives thanks to God[3] for such good news, and handsomely rewards the servant.[4]

The knight's wife smiles at the news: (25-8)

---

[1] Although synonymic iteration is a commonplace in Medieval Romance languages, surely Marie uses it here to stress the double reason for the new father's joy. Compare the article by Robert L. Politzer, "Synonymic Repetition in Late Latin and Romance," *Language*, XXXVII (1961), 484-87.

[2] This is the first lay containing a reference to a (character specifically named) *messager*, though in *Guigemar* a message was entrusted to one of the characters.

[3] In line 23 we have the first of many references to God in this lay. As for this particular allusion, its significance for the entire poem will be pointed out later. With the many references to the Divine, and the presence of the abbess and the archbishop, a theological flavor is imparted to what is, essentially, a story of profane love.

[4] In all the lays, this messenger is the only one so handsomely rewarded.

> La femme al chevalier surist —
> Ki juste lui al manger sist —
> Kar ele ert feinte e orguilluse
> 28 E mesdisante e envïuse.

There is a forceful contrast between the wife's characterization and that of her husband (and his friend) begun twenty lines earlier. Whereas he exemplifies desirable masculine and knightly virtues, she epitomizes qualities least expected in the wife of such a worthy man. Note, too, as a recurring feature of this lay, the numerical parallel of adjectives (here, four in number) in the descriptions of the husband and wife. Although the adjectives depicting the knight are somewhat vague, those pertaining to the wife are absolutely precise; her utter meanness is left in no doubt.

In 23-8, the reader is struck by the very sudden change of mood: the new father was so happy, his friend is so happy, and with the reference to the wife's smile, we expect her happiness, too.[5] But instead, there is an abrupt cessation of this happy mood.

Now we hear her speak: (29-42)

> Ele parlat mut folement
> E dist, oant tute sa gent:
> 'Si m'aït Deus, jo m'esmerveil
> 32 U cest produm prist cest conseil
> Que il ad mandé a mun seignur
> Sa huntë e sa deshonur,
> Que sa femme ad eü deus fiz.
> 36 E il e ele en sunt huniz.
> Nus savum bien qu'il i afiert:
> Unques ne fu ne ja nen iert
> Ne n'avendrat cel' aventure
> 40 Que a une sule porteüre
> Quë une femme deus fiz eit,[6]
> Si deus hommes ne li unt feit.'[7]

---

[5] Not once in all of Marie's lays will we see a character smile out of joy.

[6] Within the entire episode at the knight's hall and in the narrative passage immediately preceding (3-42), upon five different occasions mention is made of the double birth of sons (in 11; 15; 22; 35; and in 41, respectively).

[7] For a discussion of the superstition enunciated by the lady in 41-2, cf. Ewert, p. 170, n. 42.

In the lady's spiteful words,[8] the double birth becomes a source of shame and dishonor to both parents. The shock that results from her remarks contrasts vividly with the happiness previously related. And her slanderous words accusing the new mother of adultery will kill and shatter everything.

The knight rebukes his wife for her speech: (43-8)

>   Si sires l'a mut esgardee,
> 44   Mut durement l'en ad blamee.
>   'Dame,' fet il, 'lessez ester!
>   Ne devez mie issi parler!
>   Verité est que ceste dame
> 48   Ad mut esté de bone fame.'

An effective detail is that long moment during which the knight looks at his wife before he harshly rebukes her, commanding her to drop the matter, and defending the mother's reputation.

The wife's speech is made known throughout Brittany: (49-56)

>   La gent që en la meisun erent
>   Cele parole recorderent.
>   Asez fu dite e coneüe,
> 52   Par tute Bretaine seüe:
>   Mut en fu la dame haïe,
>   Pois en dut estre maubailie;
>   Tutes les femmes ki l'oïrent,
> 56   Povres e riches, l'en haïrent.

For the first time in our narrative, we find the two motifs (so important in Marie's lays, and recurrent throughout *Le Fresne*) of remembrance (50), and of reporting and hearsay (51-2). But here there is a deeper use of reporting and hearsay: the reverberations of the lady's mean and bitter words have a very special effect. It is as if the punishment[9] of which the lady is unaware and of which she will become aware when she herself bears twins begins now, as all women who have wombs hate her.

---

[8] Note the pious oath ('Si m'aït Deus') with which she introduces her calumniating words.

[9] Is 54 ("Pois en dut estre maubailie") also anticipatory of the punishment of her own womb?

The messenger relates the scene in the dining-hall to his master: (57-64)

>   Cil que le message ot porté
>   A sun seignur ad tut cunté. [10]
>   Quant il l'oï dire e retraire,
> 60 Dolent en fu, ne sot quei faire;
>   La prode femmë en haï
>   E durement la mescreï,
>   E mut la teneit en destreit
> 64 Sanz ceo que ele nel deserveit.

At the beginning of this passage the motif of reporting is continued. The second of multiple results of the lady's slander is arresting: the father of the twin boys begins to hate his own wife. He will mistrust her, putting her unjustly into custody. [11]

Yet there is no doubt of her virtue, for we are informed of it three times (47-8; 61; and 64). Although the new father and his wife are characterized in similar terms ("cest produm": 32; "la prode femme": 61), how unworthy are his actions reported in this section.

That same year, the slanderous wife gives birth to twin girls: (65-72)

>   La dame que si mesparla
>   En l'an meïsmes enceinta,
>   De deus enfanz est enceintie;
> 68 Ore est sa veisine vengie.
>   Desque a sun terme les porta;
>   Deus filles ot; mut li pesa,
>   Mut durement en est dolente;
> 72 A sei meïsmes se desmente.

The birth of the two girls, evidently not immediately known to their father, is met with an emotion totally different from the

---

[10] This round trip is the first of five instances (*Lanval, Milun,* and two trips of different messengers in *Eliduc*) where a messenger will make such a journey. It is unusual, however, for a messenger to report back to the master or mistress; such is the case here in *Le Fresne* and in only one other lay (*Eliduc*).

[11] This situation is a further variation upon the theme of a wife who has, or who will have, a lover, and who is kept under guard by her (jealous) (old) husband.

joy resulting from the first birth: the grief of the new mother is insisted upon three times in as many lines. With the birth of twins, the first cycle is brought to an end (for she is fully punished), and a new cycle begins.

The new mother laments bitterly: (73-94)

>   'Lasse!' fet ele, 'quei ferai?
>   Jamés pris në honur n'avrai!
>   Hunie sui, c'est veritez.
> 76   Mis sire e tut si parentez,[12]
>   Certes, jamés ne me crerrunt,
>   Desque ceste aventure orrunt;
>   Kar jeo meïsmes me jugai:
> 80   De tutes femmes mesparlai.
>   Dunc [ne] dis jeo quë unc ne fu
>   Ne nus ne l'avïum veü
>   Que femme deus enfanz eüst,
> 84   Si deus humes ne coneüst?
>   Or en ai deus, ceo m'est avis,
>   Sur mei en est turné le pis.
>   Ki sur autrui mesdit e ment
> 88   Ne seit mie qu'a l'oil li pent;
>   De tel hum[me] peot l'um parler
>   Que meuz de lui fet a loër.
>   Pur mei defendre de hunir,
> 92   Un des enfanz m'estuet murdrir:
>   Muez le voil vers Deu amender
>   Que mei hunir e vergunder.'

In the presence of the women in her chamber, we hear the lady bewail the adventure that has befallen her. Here her words are those of self-reproach; but just as in her scornful speech about her neighbor's wife, their tone is remarkably authoritarian; she enjoys passing judgment! She also has an excellent memory: in her lament, emphasizing the irony of her predicament, she recalls exactly (81-4) what she had said in her accusation of the neighbor's wife. This a narrative device which Marie uses only in this one lay.

She is dissuaded from her intention: (95-116)

---

[12] That the lady mentions her husband's kinfolk (rather than her own) is understandable: they are an extension of her husband of whom she thinks first of all.

```
            Ce[le]s quë en la chambre esteient
      96    La cunfort[ou]ent e diseient
            Que eles nel suff[e]reient pas:
            De hummë ocire n'est pas gas.
              La dame aveit une meschine,
     100    Que mut esteit de franche orine;
            Lung tens l'ot gardee e nurie
            E mut amee e mut cherie.
            Cele oï sa dame plurer,
     104    Durement pleindre e doluser;
            Anguissusement li pesa.
            Ele vient, si la cunforta.
            'Dame,' fet ele, 'ne vaut rien.
     108    Lessez cest dol, si ferez bien!
            L'un des enfanz me baillez ça!
            Jeo vus en deliverai ja,
            Si que hunie ne serez
     112    Ne ke jamés ne la verrez:
            A un mustier la geterai,
            Tut sein e sauf le porterai;
            Aucun produm la trovera;
     116    Si Deu plest, nurir la f[e]ra.'
```

And the final result of her ratiocination and moralizing is the decision to murder one of her new-born children. To this woman God's anger is less to be feared than worldly shame.

In Marie's presentation of the maidservant, loved so dearly by her mistress, we learn that the lady can not be completely bad: she *is* capable of love and affection. The one to whom she had shown affection will come to her rescue, to save her from the punishment her hateful words would otherwise have brought about — and to save her from committing a crime.

The lady's continuing grief [13] reflects upon the servant who now participates in the lady's emotion. Yet, in contrast to her mistress, the maiden is immediately and completely practical.

In the maiden's words of comfort, she makes two prophetic utterances concerning the child she offers to dispose of. The first

---

[13] Notice the triple insistence upon her grief within the space of one couplet (*plurer, durement pleindre, doluser*: 103-4), followed in the next line by the report of the maiden's grief which, incidentally, is presented in an expression (*Anguissusement li pesa*: 105) echoing the first mention of the lady's grief (... *mut li pesa*: 70).

remark (*Ne ke jamés ne la verrez:* 112) will be doubly contradicted by events: the mother will see her daughter, first without recognizing her, then recognizing her. The second statement (*Aucun produm la trovera:* 115) will be fulfilled — and perhaps twice — in the course of the narrative.

The main motif of this lay now emerges. It concerns the concealment, then the gradual revelation — on more than one plane — of the daughter that the lady had just intended to murder. From 112 to the end of the first narrative division at the close of 176, emphasis will be given to the sequestration and concealment of the child. In the middle portion of the lay (177-312), the reader will note both continuing concealment of Le Fresne as well as the beginning of her gradual revelation, with total revelation and recognition of that character taking place in the final section.

The lady agrees to the plan: (117-120)

> La dame oï quei cele dist;
> Grant joie en out, si li promist
> Si cel service li feseit,
> 120 Bon guer[e]dun de li avreit.

The lady's swift transition from great grief to great joy is, after all, understandable: she believes the story is over. The detail of the reward [14] promised to the maidservant (we must assume that the promise was kept, but we will never what the gift was) serves to indicate the lady's confidence that her ordeal will soon be over.

The lady and her maidservant prepare the infant for the trip: (121-136)

> En un chief de mut bon chesil
> Envolupent l'enfant gentil [15]
> E desus un paile roé —
> 124 Ses sires l'i ot aporté
> De Costentinoble, u il fu;

---

[14] Are we meant to remember that the previous mention of a reward was for the glad tidings of the birth of twins?

[15] Although the expression *l'enfant gentil* is formulaic, it is not used here lightly: we will later learn how important nobility of birth will be in the story's development.

> Unques si bon n'orent veü.
> A une pice de sun laz
> 128 Un gros anel li lie al braz.
> De fin or i aveit un' unce;
> El chestun out une jagunce;
> La verge entur esteit lettree:
> 132 La u la meschine ert trovee,
> Bien sachent tuit vereiement
> Que ele est nee de bone gent.
> La dameisele prist l'enfant,
> 136 De la chambre s'en ist atant.

In this section we learn of two possessions destined to show the infant's noble birth. Yet why does Marie choose to tell us now the origin only of the silken cloth, [16] withholding until the end that of the magnificent ruby-set gold ring? It is not necessary for the reader to know that the husband had been to Constantinople where he got the *paile* (124-6), but it is a clever gesture on Marie's part to fill us in, toward the beginning of the baby's story, with this information known to the lady. Perhaps we are given these details now because later the mother will first see the cloth, the sight of which will lead her to wonder, then to question the damsel, and then to ask to see the ring!

The maiden travels through the night: (137-158)

> La nuit, quant tut fu aseri, [17]
> Fors de la vile s'en eissi;
> En un grant chemin est entré,
> 140 Ki en la forest l'ad mené.
> Par mi le bois sa veie tint,
> Od tut l'enfant utrë en vint;
> Unques del grant chemin ne eissi.
> 144 Bien loinz sur destre aveit oï
> Chiens abaier e coks chanter:
> Iloc purrat vile trover.
> Cele part vet a grant espleit
> 148 U la noise des chiens oieit.
> En une vile riche e bele

---

[16] In contrast to Marie's presentation of the gold ring, observe that she gives no sensuous description of the *paile roé*, but speaks only of its superlative 'goodness.'

[17] Note the emphasis on darkness and concealment.

> Est entree la dameisele.
> En la vile out une abeïe,
> 152 Durement richë e garnie; [18]
> Mun escïent noneins i ot
> E abbeesse kis guardot.
> La meschine vit le muster,
> 156 Les turs, les murs e le clocher;
> Hastivement est la venue,
> Devant l'us est areste[ü]e.

The use of precise and delicate details is continued in this section (perhaps the most beautiful descriptive passage in Marie's lays) where the maiden, under cover of night, journeys with the infant to a convent. From the reference to sound in 144-5 (the crowing of cocks far away to the right) we know that her passage through the forest must have been from dark to dawn, the length of her trip stressed by the expression *grant chemin* (139 and 143).

For the maidservant, the existence of the city is predicated upon aural perception, whereas it is by her visual perception of parts of the abbey after she has entered the city that she knows (in the dimness of pre-dawn) that the end of her journey is near. [19] And how quickly she arrives at her destination: no sooner does she perceive the outlines of the convent than she is there!

The maiden prays to God: (159-164)

> L'enfant mist jus que ele aporta,
> 160 Mut humblement se agenuila.
> Ele comence s'oreisun.
> 'Deus,' fait ele, 'par tun seint nun,
> Sire, si te vient a pleisir, [20]
> 164 Cest enfant garde de perir.'

---

[18] Observe the emphasis on wealth: both of the city and of the abbey. The "wealthy infant" must be fittingly lodged.

[19] Why does Marie intervene toward the end of this passage to tell us (153-4) that there were nuns and an abbess in the abbey? (For if there is an abbey, there would certainly be the usual inhabitants!). It is as if Marie had to come into the story not only to corroborate the girl's knowledge concerning the convent (in 113), but also to reassure the reader that there really would be someone at the convent to take care of the infant, soon to be deposited at that very place.

[20] Note how the phrasing of her request 'Deus, ... si te vient a pleisir' (162-3) is a reminiscence of her earlier statement to the lady ('Si Deu plest ...: 116).

This brief, staged scene of the maiden's prayer (whose humility and sincerity are touching) begins by reminding us that she has been carrying the baby in her arms, all night long. She must put the infant down before she kneels. How to describe the artistry of this detail (line 159)! On the one hand, it is obvious that she must have been carrying the new-born baby. But we have been allowed to forget it (we have almost forgotten the baby, concerned as we are with the maiden's preoccupations); we must be reminded of the tiny bundle — which the porter will so soon discover.

The baby is placed in the forks of the tree: (165-176)

>   Quant la prïerë out finee,
>   Ariere [sei] se est regardee.
>   Un freisne vit lé e branchu
> 168 E mut espés e bien ramu;
>   En quatre fors esteit quarré; [21]
>   Pur umbre fere i fu planté. [22]
>   Entre ses braz ad pris l'enfant,
> 172 De si que al freisne vient corant; [23]
>   Desus le mist, puis le lessa;
>   A Deu le veir le comanda.
>   La dameisele ariere vait,
> 176 Sa dame cunte qu'ele ad fait.

The brevity of the account of the maiden's return trip (resumed in one couplet) contrasts elegantly with the long description of her journey to the abbey.

The abbey's porter finds the child: (177-192)

>   En l'abbeïe ot un porter,
>   Ovrir suleit l'us del muster
>   Defors par unt la gent veneient

---

[21] In the description of the tree, note the use of *four* adjectives which corresponds with the *four* forks of the tree.

[22] With the mention of the shade of the tree (for which purpose it was planted) there is an obvious reference to obscurity. But the maiden will use the tree for a different purpose: that of revelation.

[23] Why should the maiden come running up to the tree? Has she suddenly seen or heard something that would frighten her, or make her fear for the infant's safety? In her swift movement toward the tree we may see a parallel to her rapid arrival in front of the sanctuary door. In both cases, the maidservant catches sight of something, then moves rapidly toward it, as if drawn by a magnet.

"LE FRESNE" 59

180 Que le servise oïr voleient.
    Icel[e] nuit par tens leva,
    Chandeille e lampes aluma,
    Les seins sona e l'us ovri.
184 Sur le freisne les dras choisi;
    Quidat ke aukun les eüst pris
    En larecin e ileoc mis;
    D'autre chose n'ot il regard.
188 Plus tost qu'il pot vint cele part,
    Taste, si ad l'enfant trové.
    Il en ad Deu mut mercïé,
    E puis l'ad pris, si ne l'i lait;
192 A sun ostel ariere vait.

The first part of the narrative has come to an end. Of the characters mentioned, only Le Fresne will continue into the second part. Some of the characters will disappear completely from the story;[24] others will reappear only in the third portion of our lay.[25]

With this passage, the scene changes. The opening verses 177-83 take us to the world of the convent, where everything is proceeding in order. Yet with these opening lines, there is an overlapping of time from the moment ("La dameisele ariere vait, / Sa dame cunte qu'ele ad fait": 175-6) related at the close of the first narrative division. In those two lines, the maiden is back home; but by that time, the porter, one of several new characters to enter the stage, has surely discovered the child. The smooth-functioning of the porter's duties, and his accomplishment of them, makes the discovery inevitable.

In this, and the next two sections, the before-dawn darkness in which the child was abandoned will now begin to be dispelled. On this particular night the porter arises early to light candle and lamps; he opens the door, and then comes light into the dark yard.

Both the maidservant's prayer to God and her prophetic utterance to the lady ('Aucun produm la trovera': 115) are fulfilled, as the porter discovers first the cloth, then the child. There is a

---

[24] For example, the parents of the twin sons, the messenger, and the *meschine*.
[25] The knight, his spiteful wife, and their other daughter.

building-down, as it were, in the initial part of Marie's report of his discovery: he thinks he has found only a bundle of cloth which he mistakenly believes placed in the tree by a fearful robber; then, with the sense of touch, he finds the soft, warm body of a human being. [26] The building — down has enhanced the importance of his discovery of life.

Marie tells us nothing about what must have obviously been the porter's extreme surprise at his discovery, [27] only that "he thanked God very much for it." His action of giving thanks reminds us of the knight's similar immediate reaction to his friend's good news (in 23). We are impressed by the selflessness and the sweetness of these two men, the knight and the porter.

He calls to his widowed daughter: (193-202)

>   Une fille ot que vedve esteit;
>   Si sire ert mort, enfant aveit
>   Petit en berz e aleitant.
> 196 Li produm l'apelat avant. [28]
>   'Fille,' fet il, 'levez, levez!
>   Fu e chaundelë alumez!
>   Un enfaunt ai ci aporté,
> 200 La fors el freisne l'ai trové.
>   De vostre leit le [m']alaitez,
>   Eschaufez lë e sil baignez!'

In this passage there are three details to be mentioned: the porter's excitement (which Marie has postponed reporting until he can share his astonishing news with his daughter); secondly, the fortuitous presence of a nursing mother who can feed the foundling; [29] thirdly, the increase of light (in 198).

---

[26] Line 189 ("Taste, si ad l'enfant trové") is perhaps the most poignant verse in all of Marie's twelve lays: someone touches something supposedly inanimate, only to find it living and warm.

[27] In this lay, Marie generally omits reporting the inner feelings and/or outer reactions of a character at a given moment. And when Marie does give us such information, it is unusually meaningful.

[28] The appellation *li produm* (which is rather unusual in reference to a door-keeper) is surely meant to recall the maidservant's prophetic statement in 115, "Aucun produm la trovera."

[29] Indeed, this secondary character exists only for that purpose, and for no other. Perhaps that is the reason why Marie has the porter first of all command his daughter to 'nurse the child for him.'

As the daughter fulfills her father's command, she finds the ring: (203-210)

>   Cele ad fet sun comandement:
> 204   Le feu alum' e l'enfant prent,
>   Eschaufé l'ad e bien baigné;
>   Pus l'ad de sun leit aleité.
>   Entur sun braz treve l'anel;
> 208   Le paile virent riche e bel.
>   Bien surent cil tut a scïent
>   Que ele est nee de haute gent.

In the daughter's execution of her father's commands, we may note that she does not follow the order of actions prescribed by the porter in his excitement (evidently he thinks feeding the baby is the most important, — or does he think of his daughter mainly as someone who can give milk in this emergency?); with her maternal experience she knows the baby should not be fed before being bathed.

In the last four lines (207-210) of this passage (in which Marie goes back a little in time), the mother's hopes in sending the silken cloth and the ring with the child have been fulfilled. Now everything is as it should be, according to the mother's intention.[80]

There has been one mention (and there will be more) of the *paile roé*. On all the other occasions, reference is made only to the outstanding excellence of the cloth. In her artistry, Marie has chosen to reserve the only sensuous description (albeit brief and expressed in vague terms) for the very moment when the sight of the sumptuous silken cloth will cause the greatest admiration. The silken coverlet, seen by the humble door-keeper and his daughter to be *riche e bel*,[81] corroborates the evidence of the baby's noble birth given by the gold ring.

The abbess, hearing of the door-keeper's discovery, sends for the child: (211-218)

---

[80] Notice that the couplet relating the fulfillment of the mother's desire (209-10) repeats the contents (especially of the last two lines) of the short passage telling the mother's purpose (cf. 132-4).

[81] In rapidly reading the poem, it is all too easy to overlook this small, but extremely important detail, for the reader's attention is drawn more to the events that are taking place than to the description of the cloth.

El demain aprés le servise,
212 Quant l'abbeesse eist de l'eglise,
Li portiers vet a li parler;
L'aventure li veut cunter
De l'enfant cum il le trovat.
216 L'abbeesse le comaundat
Que devaunt li seit aporté
Tut issi cum il fu trové.

The movement of revelation, begun three sections earlier (at 177) is continued here, as the door-keeper, after night is gone, reports the discovery of the child to the abbess after she had come forth from the church.[32] The outward composure of the abbess is a striking foil to the door-keeper's excitement we witnessed earlier. Why did the abbess ask that the infant be brought to her "Tut issi cum il fu trové"? Had the door-keeper told her of the manner in which the child was wrapped, and of the ring? We do not know how much information the expression *cum il le trovat* (215) includes.

The abbess decides to raise the infant as her niece: (219-230)

A sa meisun vet li portiers,
220 L'enfant aporte volenters,
Si l'ad a la dame mustré.
E el l'ad forment esgardé
E dit que nurir le fera
224 E pur sa niece la tendra.
Al porter ad bien defendu
Que il ne die cument il fu. [33]
Ele meïsmes l'ad levee.
228 Pur ceo que al freisne fu trovee,
Le Freisne li mistrent a nun,
E Le Freisne l'apelet hum.

---

[32] Through the open door which is not mentioned! From the moment when the maidservant stops in front of the door of the chapel (and that is where she kneels to pray), to the moment when the abbess leaves the church, the door of the chapel is mentioned (or suggested) four times (cf. 158; 178; 183; and now, 212). The opening of the door is a detail symbolic of the (gradual) revelation of the child.

[33] Again, the motif of concealment.

Later we will be told twice (in 241-2 and in 310-12) that no one could see Le Fresne without loving her.[34] Here in 222, the abbess looks at the infant,[35] and looks at her hard. What could she have seen in this new-born infant that inspired her to adopt it? Was this infant phenomenal, and beautiful even at birth? Or had the abbess a divinatory power? At any rate, we are meant to remember, throughout the rest of the lay (as Le Fresne is seen and loved by more and more persons), the deep, scrutinizing gaze of the abbess.

Is it possible that Marie mentions the detail of the baby's christening in 227 to remind us of the two baby boys (for one of whom Le Fresne's own father was to be god-parent, cf. 17-18) whom we may have forgotten and of whom we will never hear anything again? After all, it was the news of the twin boys' birth that provoked the lady's spiteful remarks which set our present story in motion.

In the four lines (227-230) dealing with the baby's christening, only one line is given to the ceremony itself. The last three explain carefully the reason for the choice of the name — each line containing the word *freisne*, first as common noun, then as name.[36]

The foundling attains womanhood: (231-242)

> La dame la tient pur sa niece.
> 232 Issi fu celee grant piece:[37]
> Dedenz le clos de l'abbeïe
> Fur la dameisele nurie.
> Quant [ele] vient en tel eé

---

[34] Indeed, much later in the story, the mother is ready to hate Le Fresne, but just to look at her is to love her (cf. 383-4, *Sa mere l'ad mut esgardee, / En sun qor preisie e amee*).

[35] On this second occasion when the wrapped-up infant is seen by someone, we are not told that the silken cloth was noticed. Obviously, the sight of the *paile roé* would not have the same impact upon the abbess as it had upon the humble door-keeper and his daughter.

[36] Verse 230 (*E Le Freisne l'apelet hum*) anticipates the way in which the knight's name will be given in 246: *El païs l'apelent Gurun*.

[37] This is one of the lays in which a long period of time passes by. But note here that Marie (unlike her procedure in some other lays) does not give us the duration of the time-period in years. Instead, she uses the rather vague expression *grant piece*, which, in its present context, signifies the time-span from Le Fresne's infancy to maturity.

> 236 Que nature furme beuté,
> En Bretaine ne fu si bele
> Ne tant curteise dameisele:
> Franche esteit e de bone escole
> 240 [E] en semblant e en parole;
> Nul ne la vist que ne l'amast
> E a merveille la preisast.

Although the motif of concealment is continued in this section (at the beginning we learn that Le Fresne is raised within the innermost part of the convent), Marie's authoritative declaration "Nul ne la vist que ne l'amast / E a merveille la preisast" (which ends the first division of the second large narrative portion) not only suggests the admiration she must already have inspired at the convent, but also hints at the imminent disclosure of the maiden.

Here we have the first portrait of Le Fresne's beauty and character, given in rather conventional terms.[38] The true individuality of the maiden will be allowed to display itself as the lay develops, and in a way we could not guess from this description. In no other of Marie's lays is the character of a person allowed to expand as the opportunities present themselves.

Gurun hears about the maiden: (243-256)

> A Dol aveit un bon seignur;
> 244 Unc puis në einz n'i ot meillur.
> Ici vus numerai sun nun:

---

[38] When the reader goes back over the text, the adjectives used in Le Fresne's description gain in depth (as do those in the second description in 253-4). For example, in 238, though *curteise* is a stock epithet, it is surely if not the key-word describing Le Fresne, one of the key-words. And *franche* (in 239) signifying 'noble,' then by extension, 'free,' 'open, sincere in bearing' is also heavily weighted in the context of the total poem. For a documented discussion of the semantic development of the term *franc*, see K.-J. Hollyman, *le Développement du vocabulaire féodal en France pendant le haut moyen âge* (Genève, 1957), pp. 145-50, particularly p. 150 where Hollyman mentions the twelfth-century meanings of *franc* as "généreux, sincère, affable."

Indeed, it may be stated that Le Fresne, in comparison to Marie's other heroines, represents a combination of the spiritual nobility of the wife in *Eliduc*, and of the physical beauty of the young girl Guilliadun in that same lay.

El païs l'apelent Gurun. [39]
De la pucele oï parler; [40]
248 Si la cumença a amer.
A un turneiement ala;
Par l'abbeïe returna,
La dameisele ad demandee;
252 L'abeesse li ad mustree.
Mut la vit bele e enseignee,
Sage, curteise e afeitee. [41]
Si il n[en] ad l'amur de li,
256 Mut se tendrat a maubailli.

The truth of the statement 'No one could see her without loving her' is made evident when Gurun sees Le Fresne and falls in love with her. [42]

In this section there is a further stage (beginning at 252) in the disclosure of the maiden to the world. Now the *meschine*'s prophecy is fulfilled on still another level, as the knight seeks out and finds the maiden (and will later take care of her).

The maiden is described once again, this time significantly through the eyes of her future lover. Although the first portrait stressed the heroine's moral qualities, nevertheless Marie did immediately describe her as 'bele.' And what Gurun notices first of all is her physical beauty.

The knight devises a plan whereby he may frequently visit the convent: (257-270)

Esguarez est, ne seit coment;
Kar si il repeirout sovent,
L'abeesse se aparcevreit,
260 Jamés des oilz ne la vereit. [43]

---

[39] There are only two other lays (*Chevrefoil* and *Eliduc*) where both the man and the woman of the love-pair are named.

[40] Note how Marie designates Le Fresne (before she becomes Gurun's mistress) as *la pucele*, a term used for her on only this one occasion.

[41] *Le Fresne* is one of two lays (*Milun* is the other) in which not only the protagonists fall in love after the beginning of the lay, but their first meeting is passed over.

[42] *Le Fresne* is the second of three lays where a person falls in love through reputatoin: here, and in *Equitan*, it is the man, in *Milun*, the girl.

[43] Already mentioned is the lack of individuality of the abbess. Although she is but one of the many secondary personages in our lay, her function in the narrative is, nevertheless, very important, for she plays three suc-

>   De une chose se purpensa: [44]
>   L'abeïe crestre vodra; [45]
>   De sa tere tant i dura
> 264 Dunt a tuz jurs l'amendera;
>   Kar il [i] vout aveir retur
>   E le repaire e le sejur.
>   Pur aver lur fraternité
> 268 La ad grantment del soen doné;
>   Mes il ad autrë acheisun
>   Que de receivre le pardun.

In 258 ("Kar si il repeirout sovent") [46] Gurun must be thinking hopefully of secret meetings with the maiden; — well realizing the danger that might be involved. He is not above using the subterfuge of making gifts to the abbey in order to see the girl. For as a donor, he would have a legitimate reason to be received there. (But would he have a legitimate right to keep on seeing the maiden, at these other visits?)

One humorous detail deserves comment: although we learn that for the sake of the nuns' "fraternity" [47] Gurun gives so generously of his wealth, in the closing couplet of the passage, Marie's auctorial aside clearly informs us (as if we had not already understood) that his motivation is not as pious as it would appear.

The maiden finally grants Gurun her love: (271-274)

>   Soventefeiz i repeira,
> 272 A la dameisele parla;

---

cessive roles. At first, she is the guarantee of salvation of the infant; then, she serves as a link (an unwitting go-between) between Gurun and Le Fresne; now, in the present section, she becomes (in 258-60) a danger for Gurun, should she know of those secret meetings which Gurun intends to carry out with Le Fresne.

[44] The verb *se purpensa* may well indicate that it took Gurun some time before he decided upon this particular scheme, with the risks involved.

[45] Note that the convent, already presented as rich, will become still richer.

[46] This line, where we are given Gurun's thoughts as he looks toward the future, is the precise mid-point of the number of lines in our lay. *Le Fresne* is one of the ten lays where significant subject-material is found at the precise center.

[47] The term *fraternité* is given *s. v.* by Tobler-Lommatzsch in the special sense of close association of lay persons with clerics — the first example being from our lay. But surely this word is used humorously by Marie.

> Tant li pria, tant li premist
> Que ele otria ceo kë il quist.

In the first line of this very brief passage, we learn that the visits Gurun had longed to make took place. Surely he must be seeing her alone, if he is doing the pleading predicated in 273, but how does he manage to accomplish that? Could it be through the assistance of the nuns in the cloister? Was their help perhaps anticipated in the incongruous expression *lur fraternité* (267)?

Time and events are telescoped, for in the briefest of formulas ("Tant li pria, tant li premist / Que ele otria ceo kë il quist": 273-4), Marie abruptly reports that the knight and the damsel become lovers.[48]

One day Gurun asks her to go away with him: (275-288)

>   Quant a seür fu de s'amur,
> 276 Si la mist a reisun un jur.
>   'Bele,' fet il, 'ore est issi
>   Ke de mei avez fet ami.
>   Venez vus ent del tut od mei!
> 280 Saver poëz, jol qui e crei,
>   Si votre aunte s'aparceveit,
>   Mut durement li pesereit,
>   S'entur li feussez enceintiee;
> 284 Durement sereit curuciee.
>   Si mun cunseil crere volez,
>   Ensemble od mei vus en vendrez.
>   Certes, jamés ne vus faudrai,
> 288 Richement vus cunseillerai.'

Gurun's speech is notable for several reasons. Not only is this the first (and only) occasion when we hear him speak, but it is significant that his first word to his sweetheart is 'Bele,' reminding us that her beauty was the very first of her attributes that he had

---

[48] Not only by the *tant ... que* construction, but also by the similarity of situation as well, with this particular couplet we are reminded once again of *Equitan*. The success of the king's persuasive speech and gestures in overcoming the haughty lady's objections is related ("Tant ad li reis parlé od li / E tant li ad crié merci / Que de s'amur l'aseüra, / E el sun cors li otria": 177-80) with far less delicacy, however, than the couplet under discussion in which it is said that le Fresne "granted the knight what he sought."

noted upon being presented to her (cf. 253, *Mut la vit bele...*). Moreover, the main reason he gives for urging the girl to go away with him is not, as we might expect it to be, a selfish one, but one of solicitude for her aunt: what sorrow and vexation the abbess would suffer should Le Fresne become pregnant! It is amusing that Gurun, using a subterfuge a second time, gives the reason he does. He is obviously not above playing on the girl's gentle nature and immaturity to further his own ends.

Le Fresne consents to her lover's request: (289-292)

> Cele que durement l'amot
> Bien otriat ceo que li plot:
> Ensemble od lui en est alee; [49]
> 292 A sun chastel l'en ad menee. [50]

Of this very short section, the first line is doubly interesting. We learn, for the very first time, that the girl loved Gurun, and that she loved him *durement*. Moreover, the line itself (which could be an epithet for Le Fresne) defines her essence. Just as she first granted Gurun what he sought (274), now she grants him "ceo que li plot" (290) because she loves him so very much. [51] This is the second occasion that she has done exactly as he wished. In both cases, the verb *otrier* (a feudal term) is employed to report her assent.

From 243 (when Gurun was first introduced into the narrative), up to the end of 292 (when he takes away the maiden), the knight, and not the girl, has been the point of view. Yet his role as point of view is indeed minimal: the reader gains very little insight into his feelings. Although we will learn (on a few rare occasions) some more about his feelings, from this point on in the story

---

[49] Was Le Fresne's departure, just like her trip to the nunnery, at night?

[50] The passage's concluding couplet is a narrative summary before the action really takes place.

The first line of the couplet tells of the girl's departure, the second, of her arrival at the knight's castle. Yet, in the manner in which Marie has presented this information, the artist's hand is revealed. In the first verse, it is the girl who is the agent of the action, and we somehow feel the volition of her act; in the following line, it is his volition and achievement that we sense.

[51] All her future actions will be motivated by her very great love for the knight.

Gurun will cease to exist as point of view. His place will be taken, in the final section of the lady, by the girl's mother. In her selection of the two spectators through whose eyes Le Fresne is most closely seen, Marie has chosen the two characters who have (or will have) the closest bonds with the girl, the one of physical love, the other of love based, at the beginning, on appreciation and admiration — which is later strengthened by the deeper bond of maternal love, at last allowed to bloom.

Gurun leads her to his castle: (293-306)

>   Sun paile porte e sun anel;
>   De ceo li pout estre mut bel.
>   L'abeesse li ot rendu,
> 296   E dist coment est avenu,
>   Quant primes li fu enveiee: [52]
>   Desus le freisne fu cuchee;
>   Le paile e l'anel li bailla
> 300   Cil que primes li enveia;
>   Plus de aveir ne receut od li;
>   Come sa niece la nuri.
>   La meschine ben l'esgardat,
> 304   En un cofre les afermat.
>   Le cofre fist od sei porter,
>   Nel volt lesser në ublïer. [53]

Here we find one of Marie's most important narrative procedures: the story that becomes a story to be told within the framework of the story itself, when the abbess relates to the maiden the adventure of Le Fresne's discovery and her life thereafter.

In this section, too, there is a shift in the time-sequence of the events Marie retells. In the final couplet (291-2) of the preceding passage, we had been told of Le Fresne's departure from

---

[52] The abbess was surely wise in her relationship with Le Fresne, and must have known quite a little about child psychology. In her words to the girl concerning her arrival at the convent, we may note a great tactfulness; it is as if the maiden should not be told of her abandonment and exposure as a baby. The abbess says only that the enfant was "sent" (for the purpose, unstated here, of receiving a good education and a fine upbringing). Perhaps that is why Marie had earlier said, in he description of Le Fresne, that she was "de bone escole" (in 239).

[53] With this line, it may well be that the reader is supposed to remember that the baby was abandoned, and also to believe that it was forgotten by those who had abandoned it.

the nunnery with the knight, and her arrival at his castle.[54] Now, at 293, we start to move backward in time, to learn what the abbess had said to her before she left. This shift is achieved by the device of using the pluperfect tense in the third line of the passage ("L'abeesse li ot rendu": 295) as an introduction to past events, after which Marie then continues the narrative account in the preterite ("E dist coment est avenu": 296) in the very next line, and this tense suggesting a gentle forward movement in time is continued until the end of our passage in 306, when the moment then coincides with that moment signaled in the last line (292) of the preceding section. — With respect to the structure of this particular section, it both opens and closes with allusions to the silken cloth and the ring.

The maiden is greatly loved by the knight, and by all his household: (307-312)

      Li chevalier ki l'amena
308 Mut la cheri e mut l'ama,[55]
      E tut si humme e si servant.
      N'i out un sul, petit ne grant,
      Pur sa franchise ne l'amast
312 E ne cherist e honurast.

The maiden's departure for a life at the knight's castle where she is seen by all his men and servants represents one more step toward her ultimate disclosure. With this narrative summary the second major portion of the lay comes to an end. And here we may note the parallel between the close of the first sub-division of the central narrative section (before the meeting of the maiden and her future lover, in 241-2), and the second (after the lovers' departure to Gurun's castle, in 310-12: each one is devoted to

---

[54] The lover's plan to have the girl go away with him, which is accepted by the girl and then carried out successfully, surely affords a notable contrast with a somewhat similar situation in *Les Deus Amanz*. In that lay, the lover asks the girl to elope with him; she refuses, to offer a plan of her own whose execution ends in tragedy for both the lovers.

Note that when Le Fresne leaves secretly with her lover, we are not even told that the abbess learns of the departure. The abbess fades out of the forward movement of the story, once she has played her part.

[55] In this line Marie's prophetic words of 241-2 ("Nul ne la vist que ne l'amast / E a merveille la preisast") are again fulfilled.

praising, in similar terms, Le Fresne. Moreover, the first passage predicts the esteem the maiden must enjoy ("Nul ne la vist que ne l'amast / E a merveille la preisast": 241-2), the second ("N'i out un sul, petit ne grant, / Pur sa franchise ne l'amast / E ne cherist e honurast": 310-12): fulfills (for a second time) the prediction.

Of the characters presented in the entire second narrative section, only Gurun and Le Fresne will continue. Three new individuals (the archbishop and the two chamberlains) will be introduced in the third portion of the story, and three will reappear from the first.

The knight is finally persuaded to marry: (313-330)

        Lungement ot od lui esté,
        Tant que li chevalier fiufé
        A mut grant mal li aturnerent:
316 Soventefeiz a lui parlerent
        Que une gentil femme espusast [56]
        E de cele se delivrast; [57]
        Lié serei[en]t s'il eüst heir,
320 Quë aprés lui puïst aveir
        Sa terë e sun heritage;
        Trop i avrei[en]t grant damage,
        Si il laissast pur sa suinant
324 Que de espuse n'eüst enfant;
        Jamés pur seinur nel tendrunt
        Ne volenters nel servirunt,
        Si il ne fait lur volenté.
328 Le chevalers ad graanté
        Que en lur cunseil femme prendra;
        Ore esgardent u ceo sera.

Here we find one of the situations when we are not allowed to see into Gurun's feelings: we learn nothing of his emotions when his vassals [58] talk to him of marriage, nor how he feels after

---

[56] The group of enfeoffed knights does not know, of course, of the young woman's nobility of blood. But for the reader, is not the expression "une gentil femme" intended to recall an earlier mention of Le Fresne as "l'enfant gentil"?

[57] Note that Gurun does not specifically consent to the second of his vassals' two requests, that he get rid of Le Fresne (318).

[58] This is one of Marie's lays in which a mass group of people plays an

he has finally yielded to their threats.[59] Indeed, there will be a total absence of any indication of Gurun's inner feelings until almost the end of the story. Are we meant to imagine deep anguish on his part?

In the vassals' words, there is offered a contrast between fertility and barrenness. Their suggestion that Gurun should now abandon Le Fresne because of her barrenness recalls that time when her possible pregnancy was a problem to Gurun. And this is the second time when someone would like to get rid of Le Fresne.

Gurun's vassals arrange a marriage for him with the beautiful La Codre: (331-344)

```
        'Sire,' funt il, 'ci pres de nus
332     Ad un produm, per est a vus;
        Une fille ad, quë est suen heir:
        Mut poëz tere od li aveir.
        La Codre ad nun la damesele;
336     En [tut] cest païs ne ad si bele.
        Pur le Freisne, que vus larrez, [60]
        En eschange le Codre av[r]ez.
        En la Codre ad noiz e deduiz;
340     Freisne ne portë unke fruiz.
        La pucele purchacerums;
        Si Deu plest, si la vus durums.' [61]
        Cel mariage unt purchacié
344     E de tutes parz otrïé.
```

---

important role. In addition, some members of this group will form part of the members of a later group (at the wedding, cf. 360).

Cf. Sidney Painter, *Medieval Society* (Ithaca, 1951) on the settlement of questions between vassals and their lord (p. 17), and on the interest vassals might have in the marriage of their lord (pp. 21-3).

[59] There is a partial parallel between the situation in *Le Fresne* and that in *Equitan*. In *Equitan,* the people want the king to marry (but he does not); in the lay under discussion, Gurun's enfeoffed knights want him to marry someone of gentle birth to have an heir (and he does marry).

[60] In the expression *que vus larrez,* note once more the suggestion that Gurun should abandon his sweetheart.

[61] For a second time, in reference to a hopeful prophecy, we have heard pronounced the words 'Si Deu plest' (342). It first occurred in the speech of the *meschine* to the mother about the child who is to be abandoned and exposed (" 'Si Deu plest, nurir la f[e]ra' ": 116).

In addition to the vassals' practical reasons for Gurun's marriage, they even bring in as an argument (as if it were an argument!) the metaphoric significance of the names of the two sisters. With the metaphor of the sisters' names, the problem of barrenness and fruitfulness is posed again.

As we hear the knights propose a *mariage de convenance* for Gurun, the term *la pucele* is used for the second (and last) time. Its first use, one of Marie's artistic subtleties, was discussed earlier. Here the word *la pucele* referring to La Codre is in striking opposition to the term *sa suinant* (323) by which Gurun's vassals designate Le Fresne.

Now Marie interrupts the narrative: (345-350)

> Allas! cum est [mes]avenu
> Que li [prudume] ne unt seü
> L'aventure des dameiseles,
> 348 Quë esteient serur[s] gemeles!
> Le Freisne cele fu celee;
> Sis amis ad l'autre espusee. [62]

This brief lament (one of Marie's extremely rare interruptions of this lay's narrative line) contains, in its concluding couplet, another reference to the concealment of Le Fresne.

Marie's comment upon the action of Gurun's vassals, although representing an expression of sympathy, is surely spoken with tongue in cheek. Surely Marie is only pretending to lament the situation: of course the knights' ignorance is most fortunate, since it will ultimately bring about the revelation of Le Fresne's identity. It is as if Marie pretends to know at this point only what her reader knows. This, I believe, is the only time that Marie uses such a device.

We learn of the (passive) reactions of Le Fresne to the news of Gurun's marriage: (351-358)

> Quant ele sot kë il la prist,
> 352 Unques peiur semblant ne fist:

---

[62] *Espusee* refers only to the legal contracts of marriage that have been drawn up; the religious ceremonies of the marriage will be observed later.

>   Sun seignur sert mut bonement [63]
>   E honure tute sa gent.
>   Li chevaler de la meisun
> 356   E li vadlet e li garçun
>   Merveillus dol pur li feseient
>   De ceo ke perdre la deveient.

In this description of Le Fresne's magnanimous behavior, not only do we see the maiden concealing her feelings from others (a part of her self-mastery, and her good breeding); but Marie herself refuses to reveal the girl's emotions. [64] In forceful contrast to her reserve, the reader does see the feelings of her audience; it is the servants and the members of Gurun's household who express their emotional reactions and who grieve for her.

On the wedding-day the bride is brought: (359-372)

>   Al jur des noces qu'il unt pris,
> 360   Sis sires maunde ses amis;
>   E l'erceveke[s] i esteit,
>   Cil de Dol, que de lui teneit.
>   S'espuse li unt amenee.
> 364   Sa merë est od li alee;
>   De la meschine aveit poür,
>   Vers ki sis sire ot tel amur, [65]
>   Quë a sa fille mal tenist
> 368   Vers sun seignur, s'ele poïst;
>   De sa meisun la getera,
>   A sun gendre cunseilera
>   Quë a un produm la marit;
> 372   Si s'en deliverat, ceo quit.

---

[63] The phrase *her lord* referring to Le Fresne's lover is striking, for it used almost immediately after the wedding between Gurun and La Codre has been arranged — evidently in anticipation of the fact that Gurun will later become Le Fresne's 'lord,' i. e., her husband. There will be six more instances of the expression (in 360; 366; 368; 388; 395; and 404) in the events leading up to the recognition scene.

The choice of the noun *sires (seignur)* is a subtle detail which the reader may well fail to notice.

[64] As we have already noted, this narrative device is not limited to the girl, but its use is particularly remarkable at this point. And for the rest of the story (until almost the end, at 492), Marie will not let the reader know the maiden's inner life. We must simply wonder what she must be feeling.

[65] How did the mother know ...?

In this passage, there is the movement of people coming toward the high point of the marriage, toward the ceremony we know should not take place. Among those who come is the mother of the bride. Her reappearance into the story is announced casually enough (364) but the final section is devoted to her thoughts (and she will dominate the rest of the lay).

The vulgar thinking of the mother is worthy of note: she takes it for granted that a mistress rejected must take revenge by undermining the happiness of her lover's marriage (she is still the suspicious, uncharitable person she was at the beginning); and so, before knowing anything about the character of her daughter's rival, she has already planned to dispose of her. [66]

Thus for the second time, the mother must think in terms of the elimination of Le Fresne, her daughter. And if we remember the advice of Gurun's vassals (318), the mother's present plan represents the third attempt to do away with Le Fresne.

This passage (in which the unwitting mother is trying to rid herself of her daughter for the second time) closes the first part of the third narrative division.

The wedding is held with much merry-making: (373-380)

>   Les noces tindrent richement; [67]
>   Mut i out esbanïement. [68]
>   La dameisele es chambres fu;
> 376   Unques de quanke ele ad veü
>   Ne fist semblant que li pesast
>   Ne tant que ele se curuçast;
>   Entur la dame bonement, [69]
> 380   Serveit mut afeit[ï]ement.

---

[66] What irony there is in the mother-in-law's idea of marrying off Le Fresne to a worthy man — in view of the ultimate conclusion of the narrative!

[67] It may be pointed out that this passage, as well as the preceding one (beginning at 359), opens with a reference to the wedding. This double mention of *les noces* may intentionally anticipate the second wedding ceremony and its attendant festivities that will take place toward the close of the story.

[68] The noun *esbanïement*, indicating the joy and merry-making of the wedding-guests, is conspicuous, for it ironically underlines the unmentioned grief and sadness of the two protagonists.

[69] Note the contrasting terms *la dameisele* (indicating Le Fresne, in 375) and *la dame* (referring to La Codre, as the wife of a knight, in 379).

In this brief passage there is a second exemplification of the maiden's self-abnegation: just as Le Fresne had earlier served Gurun so nicely, so does she now serve her lover's bride.

Everyone considers her behavior a miracle: (381-88)

>   A grant merveile le teneient
>   Cil e celes ki la veeient.
>   Sa mere l'ad mut esgardee,
> 384   En sun qor preisie e amee. [70]
>   Pensat e dist s'ele seüst
>   La maniere [e] kë ele fust,
>   Ja pur sa fille ne perdist,
> 388   Ne sun seignur ne li tolist.

The picture of Le Fresne's total abnegation offered in the previous section is prolonged, with another reference to those who see the maiden in the rooms after the wedding party. The merry-making has apparently subsided; in a more hushed tone, we are told how she was looked upon as a marvel. Simply to look at such perfection (*veeir:* 382; *esgarder:* 383) is enough to convince people of a marvel, a miracle (381). (There is a sort of magical quality to the events recounted here, as if it were a saint whose qualities are being recognized.) A nice touch is that the mother is brought in again at the end of the section (just as at the close of the preceding one), that even she is forced to recognize this miracle, with the result that her attitude toward the maiden is completely reversed.

At night, the maiden shows the chamberlains how to prepare the marriage-bed: (389-396)

---

[70] The couplet "Sa mere l'ad mut esgardee, / En sun qor preisie e amee" (383-4) reminds us again of that first prediction (in 241-2) concerning the maiden: "Nul ne la vist que ne l'amast / E a merveille la preisast." And perhaps we should not forget the long glance of the abbess (222: "E el l'ad forment esgardé") at the new-born baby. — No characters in the lays have been "looked at" as much as has Le Fresne.

Note the use of the term *sa mere* for Le Fresne's mother — which is of course an anticipation of the revelation of the girl's identity still to come. Is Marie also suggesting something like "le cri du sang"? If so, how elegantly done — so elegantly that the reader may have overlooked it.

> La noit, al lit aparailler,[71]
> U l'espuse deveit cucher,
> La damisele i est alee;
> 392 De sun mauntel est desfublee.
> Les chamberleins i apela,
> La maniere lur enseigna
> Cument si sires le voleit,
> 396 Kar meintefeiz veü l'aveit.

Three times in the lay, there has been reference to time of day: the night when Le Fresne was abandoned, the morning when she was found, and in our passage, the night which should be the wedding-night of her lover with another.

In this section we see the damsel directing the work of the chamberlains to prepare the bed "as her lord liked it." And she is well prepared to do so, for "meintefeiz veü l'aveit" (396).[72] Surely the expression "meintefeiz veü l'aveit" is a discrete reference to the sadness the girl must be feeling as she watches the familiar bed being prepared for her lover and his bride.

She covers the bed with the *paile roé:* (397-408)

> Quant le lit orent apresté,
> Un covertur unt sus jeté.
> Li dras esteit d'un viel bofu;
> 400 La dameisele l'ad veü;
> N'ert mie bons, ceo li sembla;
> En sun curage li pesa.
> Un cofre ovri, sun paile prist,
> 404 Sur le lit sun seignur le mist.
> Pur lui honurer le feseit;
> Kar l'erceveke[s] i esteit
> Pur eus beneistre e enseiner;
> 408 Kar c'afereit a sun mestier.

This passage contains the only explicit reference to Le Fresne's feelings of grief (*En sun curage li pesa:* 402). It is grief not for herself and her situation; she grieves that her lover can not have

---

[71] Just as Le Fresne's first adventure began at night, so will the revelation of her identity take place at that time.

[72] One would think that the two chamberlains by now would know how the bed was to be made, and would need no instructions.

a more beautiful coverlet upon the bed; here she shows not only her utter unselfishness and purity, but her aesthetic sensitivity.

For still another reason this passage is significant. Up to now, Le Fresne has shown only acquiescence. But at this moment, she does something positive, something creative, to make this night more beautiful. Since the marriage is being done perfectly (the archbishop himself has blessed the pair),[73] what the maiden can do must also be done perfectly. In her gesture of placing the silken coverlet upon the bed, her sense of propriety and beauty is exteriorized.

A brief word about the symbolic function of the coffer is in order: it is by opening it that the maiden brings forth first the cloth, then the ring, both of which in turn will reveal and establish her own identity. Of the two objects, of greater importance to the entire lay is the silken cloth, which has four successive functions. At the beginning, it is a sign of an aristocratic background (when the infant is envelopped in its folds); it next becomes a keep-sake or memento (when the maiden goes away with the knight); and now, in the present scene, it becomes a means for Le Fresne to honor her lover (405). Later (as we will see) it will become the means of recognition of her identity.

The coverlet that had been placed upon the bed by the chamberlains is depicted as "un viel bofu" (399). (And this description, which Marie did not have to give us or which she could have stated in some other manner, sounds very objective.) From the point of view of common sense, it would seem absolutely impossible not only for a chamberlain to put such a shabby coverlet on his lord's nuptial bed, but also for Gurun, a *seignur*, to have such an article in his possession.

The lady, upon bringing the bride into the empty bed-chamber, notices the silk cloth: (409-419)

        Quant la chambre fu delivree,
        La dame ad sa fille amenee.
        Ele la volt fere cuchier,
412   Si la cumande a despoilier.

---

[73] The reference to the archbishop's blessing of the nuptial bed makes us think immediately of the fact that the bed Gurun and Le Fresne had shared was not blessed. And surely she must have thought of this.

> Le paile esgarde sur le lit,
> Quë unke mes si bon ne vit [74]
> Fors sul celui que ele dona
> 416 Od sa fille ke ele cela.
> Idunc li remembra de li,
> Tut li curages li fremi;
> Le chamberlenc apele a sei.

This is the third time we have been allowed to witness the mental and emotional processes of the mother: the effect on her of this sumptuous coverlet, which stirs her memories [75] and sets her heart trembling. [76] So, after first having hated, then begun to love the young woman, the mother is next made to remember the baby she had sent away. In line 419, has the mother begun to guess, and to hope? We are reminded of the king in *Bisclavret*.

Line 414 ("Quë unke mes si bon ne vit") is surely intended to recall to us that earlier moment when the lady and her maidservant enveloped the infant in the silken cloth brought back from Constantinople by the lady's husband, and which was described in the same terms: "Unques si bon n'orent veü" (126).

Since this cloth is vital to the story-development, the use of the simple word *bon* in the relation of the lady's reaction to its sight ("...unke mes si bon ne vit": 414) is very effective, suggesting that of a connoisseur of beautiful textiles. Furthermore, the use of the adjective *bon* in the lady's appreciation of the silken cloth in 414 brings to mind Le Fresne's own evaluation of the *viel bofu* in 401, where we are told that the ugly cloth "N'ert mie bons...." [77] We see, then, that for the mother and the (yet unknown) daughter there is a common system of value and

---

[74] Just as seeing was stressed, in 382-3, by the use of verbs of visual perception in two successive lines, so is it here emphasized again by the same procedure (and incidentally, by the same two verbs, *esgarder* and *veeir*) as the lady notices the cloth which, in turn, will lead her to really see the lost child.

[75] As for 417, *Idunc il remembra de li*, could it really be that the lady had completely repressed the memory of the child she had concealed?

[76] This is the first of three instances in Marie's lays (the others are in *Yonec* and *Milun*) in which a woman experiences a *frémissement* because of the unexpected. The present example is, however, the only case of a *frémissement du cœur*.

[77] Moreover, throughout the recognition scene (from 397-450), there will be repeated use of the adjective *bon* in reference to the cloth.

appreciation. Thus it may be said that the silk coverlet has by now acquired even a fifth function in the narrative, that of serving as a standard of value, of beauty and of excellence which binds together the mother and daughter even before the bond of blood between them is revealed.

The chamberlain tells the lady who brought the cloth: (420-26)

>   420 'Di mei,' fait ele, 'par ta fei,
>   U fu cest bon paile trovez?'
>   'Dame,' fait il, 'vus le savrez:
>   La dameisele l'aporta,
>   424 Sur le covertur le geta,
>   Kar ne li sembla mie bons;[78]
>   Jeo qui que le pailë est soens.'

We now pass to a (seemingly) casual scene, in which the lady's practical question meets with a supposedly practical answer. The future tense used by the chamberlain in his reply (422) indicates his readiness and willingness to answer. For indeed, he is ready and willing to play his part in the story although he does not know what that part is: he has, obviously, no idea whatever of the significance of his reply.

As for 424, in which previously withheld information is given, the reader might have thought that the chamberlains removed the ugly coverlet, replacing it by the silken cloth. Instead, the *paile roé* was placed on top of the *viel bofu*. It may well be that Marie, in her story, put the *viel bofu* on the nuptial bed and allowed it to remain there, so that Le Fresne could make the more poetic gesture of covering it up with the precious silken cloth: covering the shabbiness of others with the beauty that is hers.

The lady calls the maiden before her: (427-442)

>   La dame l'aveit apelee,
>   428 [E] ele est devant li alee;
>   De sun mauntel se desfubla,
>   E la mere l'areisuna:
>   'Bele amie, nel me celez!
>   432 U fu cist bons pailes trovez?
>   Dunt vus vient il? Kil vus dona?

---

[78] It may be noted that this line repeats, almost verbatim, line 401.

"LE FRESNE" 81

  Kar me dites kil vus bailla!'
  La meschine li respundi:
436 'Dame, m'aunte, ke me nuri, [79]
  L'abeesse, kil me bailla,
  A garder le me comanda;
  Cest e un anel me baillerent [80]
440 Cil ki a nurir me enveierent.'
  'Bele, pois jeo veer l'anel?' [81]
  'Oïl, dame, ceo m'est [mut] bel.'

In this section, the mother addresses a series of questions to the *meschine*. (For the second time she asks: "Where was this fine cloth found?") [82] Again, there is a series of answers of factual information given by one who does not know their significance. As to what must be going on in the mother's mind as she hears the maiden's replies, this we are left to imagine.

---

[79] This is the fifth and last time that the pretended aunt-niece relationship of the abbess and the maiden will be mentioned.

That the relationship exists at all can surely be attributed in great part to the cloth and the ring, as these influenced the abbess' first look at the child. And without the genteel upbringing resulting from this relationship, Le Fresne's *aventure* could certainly not have developed in the same manner.

The first time the aunt-niece relationship is mentioned, it is mentioned as an intent, for in 223-4, we learn of the abbess that "E dit que nurir le fera / E pur sa niece la tendra." The other four times the relationship is given, it is mentioned as an accomplished fact, from four different viewpoints: from that of Marie, in 231; from that of Gurun, in 281; from that of the abbess, in 302; and from that of the maiden, in 436-7.

And as the girl tells the lady of that relationship, the mother learns for the first time that her child was actually cared for at a convent.

[80] The reader may note that whenever the two tokens are mentioned in this section, it is always in the same order, just as when they were first named when the infant was prepared for its journey, and also when the damsel went away with the knight ("Sun paile porte e sun anel": 293).

[81] For the second time (first by her lover, now by her mother) we hear Le Fresne called 'Bele,' a term which Marie uses sparingly in the direct discourse of her characters. *Le Fresne* is one of the three lays in which there is the greatest stress on beauty. In two of them (*Le Fresne* and *Eliduc*) the reader may note a spiritual response to that beauty; in the third, *Lanval*, no such reaction is present.

[82] In this scene in which the mother speaks to Le Fresne for the only time in the narrative, the lady's opening address is noteworthy for its structure: it both begins and ends with a command, encompassing three questions, — the last imperative ('Kar me dites kil vus bailla!') urgently repeating her request for the same information sought in the third question, 'Kil vus dona?'

About the girl's replies to the lady, there are several observations to be offered. This is the first and only instance in the entire narrative that Le Fresne's words to anyone (and here, they are spoken so courteously and unknowingly to her own mother!) are recorded in direct address. Thus, the first time we hear her speak, it will be to open the way to her own identification.

Furthermore, in the story that Le Fresne tells her mother (a story the abbess had partially fabricated in the first place), the maiden embroiders a bit upon its details, saying about the cloth that " 'L'abeesse, kil me bailla, / A garder le me comanda' " (437-8). That Marie allows the girl to delicately add to the information given by her "aunt" is a charming detail insightful of feminine psychology.

The lady recognizes the cloth and the ring: (443-52)

> L'anel li ad dunc aporté,
> 444 E ele l'ad mut esgardé;
> El l'ad tresbien reconeü
> E le paile ke ele ad veü. [83]
> Ne dute mes, bien seit e creit
> 448 Que ele memes sa fille esteit;
> Oiant tuz, dist, ne ceil[e] mie: [84]

---

[83] For a third time, note the use of verbs of visual perception in successive verses. In our passage where the recognition scene rises to its climax, the number of verbs of seeing (of which the mother is the subject) is increased to three (in 444-6).

Moreover, line 444 ("E ele l'ad mut esgardé") reporting the mother's intense scrutiny of the ring is a counterpart to the verse relating her earlier and equally intense look at the maiden ("Sa mere l'ad mut esgardee": 383). In addition, just as when the lady saw the silken cloth upon the bed (cf. 413) and when much earlier the abbess gazed upon the foundling (cf. 222), the verb *esgarder* is used. The use of the same verb on these four notable occasions is surely not fortuitous.

In both *Le Fresne* and *Milun*, the sight of the ring is vital to the recognition of a child, though in *Le Fresne*, the golden ring is not the only element in the recognition scene. We wonder why this ring in *Le Fresne* was so thoroughly described, and why the one in *Milun* is not.

Could it be that Marie thought it more appropriate to describe a ring destined to be worn by a woman, than to describe one which would be worn by a young man?

[84] The phrase "... ne ceil[e] mie" not only echoes the mother's initial command to the maiden (cf. 431: "'... nel me celez!"), but is surely intended as a striking contrast to the lady's previous efforts to hide the relationship.

> 'Tu es ma fille, bele amie!' [85]
> De la pité kë ele en a
> 452 Ariere cheit, si se pauma. [86]

In this passage the revelation and discovery of Le Fresne is finally accomplished: the sight of the ring corroborates the evidence of the silk cloth. Whereas so long ago, the lady, without forethought, had spoken foolishly and evilly of her neighbor in the presence of all ("Ele parlat mut folement / E dist, oant tute sa gent": 29-30), at this time, it is only after confirming her convictions concerning the girl's identity, that she proclaims openly, in the presence of all those in the bed-chamber ("Oiant tuz, dist, ne ceil[e] mie": 449) the truth.

When the lady first saw the cloth, she was deeply moved ("Tut li curages li fremi": 418). Now, at this great moment of truth, her emotion ("De la pité kë ele en a / Ariere cheit, si se pauma": 451-2) is understandably still greater.

After regaining consciousness, the lady immediately sends for her husband: (453-464)

> E quant de paumeisun leva,
> Pur sun seignur tost enveia;
> E il [i] vient tut effreez.
> 456 Quant il est en chambrë entrez,
> La dame li cheï as piez,
> Estreitement l[i] ad baisiez,
> Pardun li quert de sun mesfait.
> 460 Il ne feseit nïent del plait.
> 'Dame,' fet il, 'quei dites vus?
> Il n'ad si bien nun entre nus.
> Quanke vus plest seit pardunê!
> 464 Dites mei vostre volunté!'

---

[85] This recognition scene is the second of six such scenes in Marie's lays.

It may be pointed out that *Le Fresne* is the second of three lays in which the reader may note an abnormal family relationship. Here, the peculiar parental-child relationship is the mother's rejection of her daughter. In *Guigemar*, the abnormality is that of Guigemar's closeness to his sister and his mother. In *Les Deus Amanz* it is the relationship between the king and his daughter.

[86] An example of hysteron proteron.

The husband's presence at the wedding is not mentioned until now. Whereas his wife's emotion in 451-2 was caused by what she knew, note that his emotion of utter fright is caused by his ignorance!

The wife now begs forgiveness of her husband for her sin as she would have done of God had she murdered the child. With her request for forgiveness, she is shamed before her husband. Her act which recalls the *meschine's* first prediction ('Jeo vus en delivrerai ja, / Si que hunie ne serez...': 110-11) proves the prophecy to be incorrect. He pardons her at once, thus cancelling out, as it were, her shame.

Thus, the second time we see the father, he is still the good-hearted man, the *paterfamilias* who is only sweet and generous. But we may well wonder whether he is not also a bit obtuse and imperceptive. For we think back, first to the lady's nastiness in the opening scene, and then, to her distrust of Le Fresne, twenty or so years later. Since the wife must have been a suspicious, ungracious person in the intervening years, it is hard to imagine that their marriage was harmonious. And, given his generosity and sweetness so clearly manifest in this passage, it is doubtful whether he has really analyzed his wife's nature.

After the husband's arrival in the nuptial chamber, more and more persons (i.e., the archbishop of Dol, the knight Gurun, with probably many of the wedding guests) will gradually appear or reappear, until at the close of the narrative there will be a plenitude of characters resembling that in the narrative's opening scene. Furthermore, there will be a parallel between the harmony and joy of that opening scene, where there apparently was so much happiness (soon to be destroyed by the lady's words) and the joyousness of the final scene.

The lady relates the entire story to her husband: (465-484)

'Sire, quant pardoné l'avez,
Jel vus dirai; si m'escutez!
Jadis par ma grant vileinie
468 De ma veisine dis folie;
De ses deus enfanz mesparlai:
Vers mei meïsmes [mes]errai.
Verité est que j'enceintai,
472 Deus filles oi, l'une celai;
A un muster la fis geter

<blockquote>

E nostre paile od li porter
E l'anel que vus me donastes
476 Quant vus primes od mei parlastes.[87]
Ne vus peot mie estre celé:
Le drap e l'anel ai trové.
Nostre fille ai ci coneüe,
480 Que par ma folie oi perdue;
E ja est ceo la dameisele
Que tant est pruz e sage e bele,[88]
Ke li chevaler ad amee
484 Ki sa serur ad espusee.'

</blockquote>

The lady's final words deserve much comment. This confession (of 20 lines), accurring toward the end of the lay, forms a pendant to her earlier lament (of 22 verses) occurring toward the beginning. After publicly commanding her husband to listen (thereby imposing a sort of penance upon herself), the lady reveals for the second time the identity of her daughter.[89] Once again, we listen to a story that we know so well. As we have come to expect, the father's emotions will be left to our imagination during this, the most dramatic re-telling in all of Marie's lays.

In the first four lines of the lady's confession (467-70),[90] in which she recalls the opening scene of the lay, there is self-blame. Moreover, the words of self-accusation appear in the important end-line position, forming the rhymed list: *vileinie, folie, mesparlai, [mes]errai.*

We may also note certain verbal resonances of earlier scenes. Verse 468 ('De ma veisine dis folie') clearly echoes Marie's own assertion about the lady in 29 ("Ele parlat mut folement"). Furthermore, the following couplet ('De ses deus enfanz mesparlai: / Vers mei meismes [mes]errai': 469-70) immediately

---

[87] The husband's imperceptiveness may serve to explain why, through all these years, he had never noticed the absence of these two possessions importantly connected with him.

[88] Although Marie often uses these very adjectives to describe her characters, here they strike our ears with the full force of their meaning.

[89] In this passage where the wife reveals what she has kept secret for so long, it is interesting that the verb *celer* (used twice in the first scene of recognition, in 431 and 449) is again used two times (in 472 and 477).

[90] But notice that the lady does not confess everything to her husband. She does not mention her plan to murder her child!

reminds us of the scene when the lady blames herself before her women ('Kar jeo meïsmes jugai; / De tutes femmes mesparlai': 79-80).

One further detail may be noted in this, as well as in the next section: the concept of unity, of mutual possession with the spouse. This concept is shown linguistically by the use of the possessive adjective *nostre,* or by an expression associating the lady and her husband. [91] Both these details are involved when the lady speaks of the *paile* (in 474), of the *anel* (in 475-6), then of the daughter (479).

It was earlier mentioned that the cloth and the ring have already played different roles in the narrative. Now learn that these material possessions had once still another role. We should imagine that the father, when a young suitor, had given them to the lady, when a maiden, the ring being evidently the very first of his gifts to her (475-6). [92] In a very delicate manner we are made to think of the lady as an innocent young girl. Somehow, her figure suggests (briefly, and faintly) the sweetness of Le Fresne.

When the lady tells her husband 'Le drap e l'anel ai trové' (note that she does not go on to tell him how or where), it is very possible that he is not even looking at the bed at that moment. As his wife continues to speak, he shows no interest whatever in the silken cloth or the gold ring; is this one further instance of his lack of perception?

The last three lines (482-4) of the lady's speech are composed of relative clauses. The concentration suggested by their use is impressive, since they tell us so much. In the first, we are reminded of the beauty and the virtue of the maiden; in the second, of the deep love of the knight for her; in the third, of the event which never should have happened. [93]

---

[91] This stylistic detail is, of course, in accord with the theme of recognition by the mother and acknowledgement of the lost daughter by both parents.

[92] It is somehow fitting that Marie reserves for this moment the revelation of the origin of the ring, the token which corroborated the evidence given by the silken *paile.*

[93] Le Fresne is the second of five lays (cf. also *Equitan, Bisclavret, Laüstic, Eliduc*) in which a secondary character (here, the mother) determines the outcome of the story.

The husband joyfully acknowledges his daughter: (485-92)

>   Li sires dit: 'De ceo sui liez; [94]
>   Unques mes ne fu[i] si haitiez;
>   Quant nostre fille avum trovee,
> 488 Grant joie nus ad Deu donee, [95]
>   Ainz que li pechez fust dublez.
>   Fille,' fet il, 'avant venez!'
>   La meschine mut s'esjoï
> 492 De l'aventure ke ele oï.

Once, long ago, the husband was happy for another man who had become the father of two children; now he is happy that he has gained a second daughter. The unmistakable tone of joy in this passage (containing four references to joy) reminds us of the joy with which the lay began. Just as in the opening scene the new father's joy was doubly mentioned ("Sis sires est liez e joianz": 12), so here the second father's joy is doubly predicated *(liez; haitiez)*, with the important distinction that the second father himself speaks of his happiness. [96] Moreover, joy extends to all those present, and in a more personal way, to Le Fresne herself. At the close of her father's speech, we are permitted to know (for the second and final time in the lay) her emotional response.

---

[94] The husband, good-hearted and sweet man that he is, never reproves his wife for her action! Note, too, that we are never told whether, after hearing his wife's story, he wondered concerning her fidelity. Is the husband so overjoyed at the news (or so trusting) that this thought never occurs to him?

[95] This line recalls the first time that the knight mentioned God ("Li sire en ad Deu mercïé: 23). In both cases, he refers to God after learning of a double birth. Moreover, these references to the Divinity appear symmetrically, in almost the same position from the end of the narrative as from the beginning.

[96] In 485-6, we may note the first of three instances in Marie's lays (the others are to be found in *Milun* and *Eliduc*) of the end-line rhyme *liez / haitiez*. In all cases, the rhyme reports and stresses the deep joy of a character who either finds someone he had believed irretrievably lost, or, as in the case of the father in *Le Fresne*, who finds someone whose existence had previously been totally unknown. Of the three characters involved, the father in the present narrative is the only one whom Marie allows to personally express his happiness.

Note that Marie allows the father two lines (485-6) to talk about his own joy, followed by two lines (487-8) where he mentions both parents' joy; then come two lines (491-2) given over by Marie to the girl's joy, and several lines later, there are two lines (497-8) describing the lover's joy.

The archbishop, when informed, advises dissolution of the marriage he has just performed: (493-503)

>   Sun pere ne volt plus atendre;
>   Il meïsmes vet pur son gendre,
>   E l'erceveke i amena,
> 496 Cele aventure li cunta.
>   Li chevaler, quant il le sot,
>   Unques si grant joie nen ot. [97]
>   L'erceveke[s] ad cunseilié
> 500 Quë issi seit la noit laissié; [98]
>   El demain les departira, [99]
>   Lui e cele qu'il espusa.
>   Issi l'unt fet e graanté.

The adventure which had made the maiden so joyous must be related for a second time. The happy father, taking matters into his own hands, now tells it to his son-in-law and the archbishop. The reference to Gurun's joy ("Li chevaler, quant il le sot, / Unques si grant joie nen ot": 497-8) reflects that of the father ('Unques mes ne fu[i] si haitiez': 486).

The tone of deep happiness and the warmth of the scene begun in the preceding passage continue up to the end of 498. But at 499 the tone changes to that of dry summary. This new

---

[97] This is the second time that Marie herself uses the term *joie* in this lay in a non-erotic sense. Although in 448 it is the father talking ('Grant joie nus ad Deu donee'), it may be significant that twice (cf. 13, "Pur la joie quë il en a") in this lay she uses the noun *joie* for describing family relationships.

[98] With this decision, the reader perceives an analogy with the *Tristram* legend: the man, while loving dearly one woman, marries another (in *Le Fresne*, he is forced into marriage), and the marriage is not consummated. In our lay, the names of both wives are trees. We are reminded again of the *Tristram* story, for there both the mistress and the wife have the same name, although the wife's name is qualified by the phrase *as blanches mains*.

[99] It is certainly convenient to have present an ecclesiastic of such rank as to have the power to separate the parties of an unconsummated marriage.

It may be of interest to note that as far back as the twelfth century there began "a theological and juridical controversy" as to the possibility of the dissolution of such marriages, and as to who had the power to do so. Cf. *New Catholic Encyclopedia* (New York: McGraw-Hill Book Company, 1967), Vol. 9, "Canon Laws of Marriage: Section 11: Nonconsummated Marriage Cases," 286-7.

tone will continue until the end of the narrative. Marie, wishing to move away from the joyousness of the two lovers, thus is beginning to be deliberately prosaic, as may be seen in the practical advice of the archbishop.[100]

The two lovers are married: (504-514)

> 504 El demain furent desevré;[101]
> Après ad s'amie espusee,[102]
> E li peres li ad donee,
> Que mut ot vers li bon curage;[103]
> 508 Par mi li part sun heritage.[104]
> Il e la mere as noces furent[105]
> Od lur fille, si cum il durent.
> Quant en lur païs s'en alerent,
> 512 La Coudre lur fille menerent;
> Mut richement en lur cuntree[106]
> Fu puis la meschine donee.

In this section the 'fairy-tale' method of ending a tale may be noted. An event already foretold in the preceding passage now takes place (in the very first line), followed by the inevitable marriage of the two lovers, which in turn is followed by an apparently mechanical sequence of events recounted in rapid order. The quick summary of these events that are necessary to a happy ending serves to give closure to the story. But it also adds variety to the final movement of the narrative. First, a change of focus

---

[100] The archbishop's emotional flatness (in 499-502) is similar to that of the abbess.

[101] In the light of day, the love of Gurun and Le Fresne is sanctified.

[102] This line presenting the wedding from Gurun's point of view ("Aprés ad s'amie espusee") contrasts with line 350 ("Sis amis ad l'autre espusee") recounting the first marriage from Le Fresne's vantage-point.

[103] Here the reader may note a tiny reference to the father's new-born paternal feelings toward Le Fresne.

[104] Were the vassals disappointed that the knight Gurun received only half of the original marriage-settlement? And what of their strong objections to the barrenness of Le Fresne? The courtiers seem to have just disappeared, to have faded away; they were last mentioned in Marie's lament in 345-8.

[105] For the third time in the story, we hear of *les noces*. By these words, not only is the reader reminded of that first wedding, but also the two weddings are brought together. The parents and daughter are at the wedding, but now La Codre looks on, as did Le Fresne!

[106] Insistence again upon wealth and riches.

from the lovers [107] to Le Fresne's parents, begins in 509 ("Il e la mere as noces furent"). In that line, the parents are becoming the main personages once again. By their autonomous act reported in 512 ("La Coudre lur fille menerent") they are established as the principal characters, so that the story ends with the father and mother, just as it began. This shift of focus, surely a deliberate reminder of the beginning, is a most artistic device.

Moreover, as we move away from the scene at Gurun's castle, we have the impression of a gradual opening-out of poetic time and space, [108] contrasting strikingly with the concentration of events within a very brief time-period that began at the first wedding-scene, and came to a climax in the nuptial bed-chamber.

The passage (and the story) concludes with La Codre's marriage. [109]

---

[107] This is a departure from the traditional 'fairy-tale' ending. But, although Marie does not explicitly state of the lovers that 'they lived happily ever after,' there is that implication.

[108] That same impression, but felt to a greater degree, is received by the reader toward the close of *Bisclavret*.

[109] La Codre and her presentation throughout the narrative deserve some comment. She is treated like a thing; she is always presented in this way.

In addition, Marie mentions only what is done to her: La Codre is brought to the wedding (363-4); she is brought into the nuptial-chamber (410-12); she is separated from the man to whom she has just been married (note that in 502 she is called "the one whom he married"); she is just along with her parents at the wedding of her sister (510); she is taken home by them (512), then given away in marriage (514).

La Codre is an utterly pale and passive figure. Nowhere are her feelings mentioned, or even vaguely suggested. Nothing in which she might show preference or decision is mentioned to us. What must she have felt as she was lying undressed in the nuptial bed, hearing her mother's confession and her father's acknowledgement of the maiden who had served her so courteously at the wedding-festivities? Further, what must she have felt the night before (500), and also when she was witness to the second wedding-ceremony?

As to why the sister of Le Fresne was called La Codre, she is the "other one" (cf. 350, "Sis amis ad l'autre espusee"): not Le Fresne, but a pale copy of her sister. Thus her name must be a reflection of the other's name. Moreover, La Codre is a reflection of her twin sister in two other respects: the description of her beauty ('En [tut] cest païs ne ad si bele': 336) echoes that given earlier of Le Fresne ("En Bretaine ne fui si bele": 237), and the report of her marriage in 514 ("Fu puis la meschine donee") is predicated in the same manner as that of her sister in 510 ("E li peres li ad donee").

Le Fresne's adventure was made into a lay: (515-518)

>   Quant l'aventure fu seüe
> 516 Coment ele esteit avenue,
>   Le lai del Freisne en unt trové:
>   Pur la dame l'unt si numé. [110]

It is very fitting that Marie calls the protagonist *la dame* in the final line. For with this denomination, Le Fresne's gradual double emergence, not only in terms of character development, but also from out of the very far-off background (where she was a foundling) to the foreground (where she has attained the status and dignity of rank) is completed.

---

[110] This is the only one of Marie's twelve lays that is named after the woman of the love-pair.

The apparent naïveté of Marie's last line as an explanation to the reader can only make us smile. Can she really expect us not to know why the lay was called *Le Fresne?* It is as if she were saying "Guess why they called the lay Le Fresne," and as such, it is a light and graceful way of ending the poem.

BISCLAVRET

The lay of *Bisclavret*, 318 verses in length, prefaced by an introduction of fourteen lines and ending with a brief conclusion of four, easily divides itself into two portions of unequal length. In the first part (v. 15 to the end of 134), we learn of a knight whose *aventure* is to undergo a periodic transformation[1] into a werewolf, and how he is condemned, through his wife's treachery, to remain in the animal state. The second and longer section (135-314) relates Bisclavret's revenge upon his wife, and how he finally reassumes human form.

In the Prologue, Marie speaks of werewolves of former times, and promises to tell us the story of the Bisclavret: (1-14)

> Quant de lais faire m'entremet,
> Ne voil ublïer Bisclavret:[2]
> Bisclavret ad nun en bretan,
> 4 Garwaf l'apelent li Norman.
> Jadis le poeit hume oïr
> E sovent suleit avenir,
> Humes plusurs garual devindrent

---

[1] In only one other lay does Marie employ the metamorphosis motif (and there, the metamorphosis is not periodic). In *Yonec*, the knight Muldumarec transforms himself into a hawk, in order to leave and to return to his kingdom on his visits to a lady imprisoned in a tower by her jealous elderly husband.

[2] The word *ublier*, in the negative, must remind us of line 10 of *Equitan*, where the lay is declared to be one *ki ne fet mie a ublier*. It can be no coincidence if Marie uses the same formula for these two lays (and only for these two). In both, the wife not only becomes unfaithful but conspires with her lover to bring about her husband's undoing: his physical death in *Equitan*, his spiritual death in *Bisclavret*. And it is only in these two lays (which are not to be forgotten) that Marie condemns the unfaithful wife.

>   8 E es boscages meisun tindrent.
>   Garualf, c[eo] est beste salvage:
>   Tant cum il est en cele rage,
>   Hummes devure, grant mal fait,
>   12 Es granz forez converse e vait.
>   Cest afere les ore ester;
>   Del Bisclavret [vus] voil cunter.

Three uses of the noun *bisclavret* appear in these fourteen lines: in line 2 it refers to the title of our lay, in line 3 it designates a type of animal (for which the Norman term is immediately given us),[3] in the last line, where it appears with the article, a specific being is alluded to, for whom the word apparently serves as a proper name. After telling us about the nature of werewolves, Marie seems ready to drop the subject ("Cest afere les ore ester"), in favor of the theme of *le Bisclavret*, as if they were indeed two different themes.

In Brittany there lived a baron and his wife who loved each other: (15-23)

>   En Bretaine maneit un ber,
>   16 Merveille l'ai oï loër;
>   Beaus chevalers e bons esteit
>   E noblement se cunteneit.
>   De sun seinur esteit privez
>   20 E de tuz ses veisins amez.
>   Femme ot espuse mut vailant
>   E que mut feseit beu semblant.
>   Il amot li e ele lui;

With the opening lines of the narrative, there is a shift from the ravening animals of the forest to a married pair living in elegant society. Before the knight's qualities are described, we hear of the marvelous reputation he enjoyed,[4] and the description

---

[3] In two other lays Marie will offer a translation of her title: for *Laüstic*, as for *Bisclavret*, she chooses a Celtic word to translate into French (in the former, an English translation is also given); in *Chevrefoil* she will translate the French word into English. These are the only lays whose title does not suggest a human being, but a bird (*Laüstic*), an animal (*Bisclavret*), a plant (*Chevrefoil*).

[4] The way in which Marie refers to the knight's reputation is most curious (and has no parallel in her other lays): "Merveille l'ai oï loër."

ends with a reference to the esteem and affection he inspired in all who knew him. As for his qualities, we are told of his physical beauty, his noble behavior and of his goodness; the last represents a spiritual quality, and the first two represent traits of an exterior nature: his appearance and his relationships with others.

As for the brief analysis of the wife, the adjective *vaillant*, if it refers to her nature, is even more vague than is the *bons* applied to her husband; and it may refer merely to her social rank. This seems the more likely interpretation, given the second characterization *mut feseit beu semblant*, which surely refers to her cultivation of social graces.[5] There is a suggestion of mystery in the figure of the knight, who was loved by all who knew him and about whose nature we have been told so little, but it seems that Marie is presenting the wife simply as a superficial, worldly person.

The description of the married pair ends with a reference to their love: *il amot li, e ele lui*. This statement with its double beat would seem to guarantee reciprocity, and the coupling of husband and wife, to suggest the indissolubility of their union. Or could it be that by presenting them separately (instead, for example, of using the verb *s'entr'amer*, as she so often does of lovers), Marie has wished to introduce the nuance of separation: as if each is loving the other in his own and separate way? The lines that follow (24-8) should give the answer.

Yet one thing makes the wife unhappy: (24-8)

> 24 Mes d'une chose ert grant ennui,
> Que en la semeine le perdeit
> Treis jurs entiers, que el ne saveit

How could Marie have heard one of her own characters praised? One might assume she has "heard" the author of her source use words of praise about this character — but in this lay no source is mentioned. Is Marie, perhaps, pretending to know, if only by reputation, a certain individual, living in society, whose story she decided to tell?

[5] Such expressions as *mut feseit beu semblant* (or *noblement se cunteneit*, 18) referring to habitual activity, behavior, are not often found in Marie's character descriptions, which mainly consist of the static construction: copula plus predicative word. Since this infrequent type is used of both husband and wife, could a contrast be intended between the two kinds of behavior in question?

U deveneit në u alout,
28 Ne nul des soens nïent n'en sout.

With the *mes* ... the picture of apparent conjugal felicity becomes immediately beclouded,[6] as mention is made of the knight's regular absences from home, the purpose of which is a complete mystery to the wife, as to all the household (note the effect of the sequence of negatives in "*Ne nul* des soens *nïent* n'en sout").[7] At this point, Marie surely wants the reader to suspect a connection between the knight beloved by all, and "Le Bisclavret" of the Prologue.

Now that the background situation has been sketched for us, the narrative proper may begin. And it begins when the wife has finally decided (why had she waited so long?) to question her husband, one day when he comes back home "joyous and happy":[8] (29-41)

Une feiz esteit repeirez
A sa meisun joius e liez;[9]
Demandé li ad e enquis.
32 'Sire,' fait il, 'beau duz amis,
Une chose vus demandasse
Mut volenters, si jeo osasse;
Mes jeo creim tant vostre curuz,
36 Que nule rien tant ne redut.'
Quant il l'oï, si l'acola,
Vers lui la traist, si la beisa.
'Dame,' fait il, '[or] demandez!
40 Ja cele chose ne querrez,
Si jo la sai, ne la vus die.'

We note the respectful and affectionate way in which the wife addresses her husband ('Sire, ... beau duz amis'), and

---

[6] And note how smoothly we have passed from the public domain where the husband has his reputation, to come closer home.

[7] We shall never know whether his neighbors and his lord were aware of his absences, although it is difficult to imagine that this was not the case.

[8] How is the knight's mood to be explained? Is he happy because he has come home to his wife, has his stay away been an ordeal for him? Or is he happy because he has enjoyed himself so much in his last *fugue*? The answer to this question is of momentous importance.

[9] With the repetition here of *meisun*, are we meant to remember what Marie has told us in line 8, "E es boscages meisun tindrent"?

the circumspect manner in which she continues. One wonders whether she may not have rehearsed her words in preparation for this scene, for she hesitantly suggests her desire to ask her husband a certain question, only to draw back immediately ('Mes jeo creim tant vostre curuz'). We shall see more of this to-and-fro movement in the course of the conversation.

As for the husband's reaction to her words, his first response is a tender caress: drawing her to him, he hugs and kisses her.[10] Then, expansively, as if happily, he bids her ask whatever she wants. Why this assurance, and his ready promise? Surely he must suspect what her question will be!

But perhaps not: perhaps he has accepted his dual existence so completely (which has become, as it were, a routine, to which his wife seems to have become accustomed), that he temporarily forgets his other life when he returns home: so happy is he to return, so ready to take up again the life he leads at home and in society, that he is not prepared to be questioned about his absences. Moreover, as a husband, he has done nothing wrong.

Another interpretation is possible, and in my opinion, more likely:[11] that his foolhardy promise, like his sudden embrace, represents an outpouring of tenderness. This is his immediate response to what he may have believed was her genuine concern for, and interest in, him. At this moment, he may well have felt that he can now finally confide his secret, and that she will show him understanding and tenderness.

Reassured, she asks her question: (42-52)

    'Par fei,' fet ele, 'ore sui garie!
    Sire, jeo sui en tel effrei
44 Les jurs quant vus partez de mei,

---

[10] In Marie's lays few clear-cut physical movements are recorded (fewer than in Old French literature in general); when this does occur, the gesture must be understood as especially significant. But we will see only later how very important was the knight's movement "... vers lui la traist."

It might be added, however, that this particular gesture cannot be perfectly visualized, since the scene is completely unstaged: we do not know whether they are standing, sitting or lying.

[11] There is theoretically possible a third interpretation: that the husband is simply being smooth and clever with his wife. But this is hardly likely, given the course the dialogue is allowed to take.

> El quor en ai mut grant dolur
> E de vus perdre tel poür,
> Si jeo n'en ai hastif cunfort,
> 48 Bien tost en puis aver la mort.
> Kar me dites u vus alez,
> U vus estes, u conversez!
> Mun escïent que vus amez,
> 52 E si si est, vus meserrez.'

The wife's sigh of relief ('Par fei... ore sui gariel'), whether rehearsed or not, is unmistakable.

In her long reply of eleven lines, the first seven represent a postponement of her question. For in them, the lady releases her tension, telling of her fears and her concern of losing her husband. Not once does she mention her concern for him during his absence: she talks solely of her own feelings.

She then blurts out three questions ('Kar me dites u vus alez, / U vus estes, u conversez!': 49-50).[12] Her crude manner and urgent tone contrast strongly with the finesse and delicacy of her request to her husband.

He vehemently refuses to answer: (53-6)

> 'Dame,' fet il, 'pur Deu, merci!
> Mal m'en vendra, si jol vus di,
> Kar de m'amur vus partirai
> 56 E mei meïsmes en perdrai.'

Here there is another postponement, another backward movement in the conversation, as the husband now contradicts his promise, begging her mercy. The reason he offers takes the form of a prediction.

Yet what does 'Kar de m'amur vus partirai' mean: that he will separate her from his love for her — or from her love for him? Moreover, he does not deny that he is in love with another woman. It may well be that he thinks her suspicion is so irrelevant

---

[12] In these three questions, she seems to be asking almost the same thing. Is she trying to visualize his habitat? The last verb *converser* is very frequently found in OF in the expression *converser od* (to dwell with): this idea will be expressed in the two final lines (51-2) in which she voices her suspicion (which explains her fear of losing him) that he has found other human companionship.

that it is not even worth mentioning. [13] As for his change of mind, it may have been caused by the way his wife put her question. At any rate, his words throw more mystery than light upon the situation.

The wife continues to importune her husband: (57-66)

> Quant la dame l'ad entendu,
> Ne l'ad neent en gab tenu.
> Suventefeiz li demanda;
> 60 Tant le blandi e losenga
> Que s'aventure li cunta;
> Nule chose ne li cela.
> 'Dame, jeo devienc bisclavret:
> 64 En cele grant forest me met,
> Al plus espés de la gaudine,
> S'i vif de preie e de ravine.'

The wife, who has absolutely no sense of mystery, refuses to dismiss the matter, and shows him no mercy. She uses repeated flattery and wiles (whose mechanical aspect is denoted by the formula *tant... que*) until her husband can no longer hold out against her questions. It may well be that he, longing so much for tenderness (and even flattery), is taken in by her words.

Up to line 63 there has been no word to startle the reader in the courteous dialogue of husband and wife. But now his courteous address ('Dame') prefaces a revelation of utter horror, related in four lines of massive impact. We are also struck by the matter-of-fact manner in which he states his *aventure;* could this attitude, perhaps, be a sign of his acceptance of his dual way of life?

In these tremendous four lines (63-6) it is almost as if the husband becomes a werewolf at that moment. [14] Yet an animal would not think in terms of *preie* and *ravine;* it is as if he judges himself already. Although he does not say that he devours men,

---

[13] The *si jol vus di*, means obviously 'if I tell you where I go', *not* 'if I tell you it' (= 'whether I love another woman').

[14] Contrasting in tone with the first and last lines, which tell of his metamorphosis and the means of his existence, are the two middle verses (64-5). In them, we have a feeling of secrecy, but also of space, of expansiveness. And we recall again what Marie says in the Prologue about the 'house in the forest.'

we immediately think of what Marie had told us in the Prologue.[15]

The lady presses her husband for further details: (67-71)

> Quant il li aveit tut cunté,[16]
> 68 Enquis li ad e demaundé[17]
> S'il se despuille u vet vestu.
> 'Dame,' fet il, 'jeo vois tut nu.'
> 'Di mei, pur Deu, u sunt voz dras.'

The wife's reaction to the husband's terrible revelation is indeed amazing. There is no outburst of horror (we could hardly expect an immediate show of sympathy from her), nor does she become silent, striving to take in the import of his words. Instead she continues talking, apparently quite calmly, in her pursuit of further information about his life away from home. Has the shock been so great that her real reaction (to be described in 99-102) can only come late? Or is she possessed of superhuman self control?

Why should she be so interested in the detail of the clothing? Is she trying to force herself to visualize her husband as a hairy animal stalking through the forest? Or do her questions indicate a sort of idle curiosity: being superficial and trivial, she would

---

[15] Or is the Bisclavret to be completely different from other werewolves? Why did he become a werewolf? Was it because of a curse, or was it a punishment? Or was it that the husband, because of his wife's lack of tenderness and her failure to recognize his excessively vital nature, was forced to become one? (And was the husband's failure to explain to his wife the cause of his metamorphosis due to his hope that she herself would ask for the explanation?)

At any rate, we shall never know whether Bisclavret is to be characterized as a "constitutional werewolf" or a "werewolf by magic" — to use the distinction made by Kirby Flower Smith, "An Historical Study of the Werwolf in Literature," PMLA, IX (New Series, Vol. II) [1894], 1-42.

[16] Does the clause "Quant il aveit tut cunté..." mean that after his four-line revelation, he offers further grisly details, filling in the bare outline given there? I think not because of line 62: the statement "Nule chose ne li cela," followed by the four lines of the husband's answer, suggests that, in this answer, he has indeed told everything — that is, everything necessary for the disclosure of the hideous nature of his *aventure*.

[17] In line 68, note the second occurrence (cf. line 31) in our poem of the same two verbs of 'asking' (*enquere, demander*) used in a context of ignorance and mystery.

concern herself only with externals (this would have to mean that she has not yet taken in the significance of the revelation she has heard)? Or is there a more knowing, more sinister reason for her curiosity?

For the second time, the knight refuses to answer her question: (72-8)

> 72 'Dame, ceo ne dirai jeo pas;
> Kar si jes eüsse perduz
> E de ceo feusse aparceüz,
> Bisclavret sereie a tuz jurs;
> 76 Jamés n'avreie mes sucurs,
> De si k'il me fussent rendu.
> Pur ceo ne voil k'il seit seü.' [18]

The reason he gives for his second refusal ('... Bisclavret sereie a tuz jurs') [19] serves to make explicit the vague reason he had given for his first ('Mal m'en vendra, si jol vus di'). Now, when speaking of the terrible consequences of the loss of his clothing, the reference to his loss ('... si jes eüsse perduz') is

---

[18] Note that the knight's courteous but firm words to his wife both begin and end with a "no": 'Dame, ceo ne dirai jeo pas' (72) and '... Pur ceo ne voil k'il seit seü' (78). Yet at the end he will give in.

The husband's drawing back forms a part of the cyclical movement of this dialogue: the wife's questioning, followed by the wife's relentless pressure forcing the husband to succumb.

[19] Smith, An Historical Study of the *Werwolf*," pp. 8 and 11, discusses the necessity of repossession of the same clothes that were taken off in order to recover human form. (In reference to the wife's actions, this could mean that with her question "... u sunt voz dras" (71), she has already begun to plot.)

Smith cites (pp. 5-11) two tales older than Marie's lay in which the same necessity is made evident: the one, the werewolf story of Petronius Arbiter in which a soldier voluntarily becomes a werewolf; the other, a late Greek tale called "The Thief and the Innkeeper." Smith also mentions (p. 13) two poems which he believes related to Marie's lay, the *Histoire de Biclarel*, and the *Lai de Melion* of the fourteenth century. The same two poems are also cited by Karl Warnke, *Die Lais der Marie de France*, 3rd. ed. (Bibliotheca Normannica, III), with comparative notes by Reinhold Köhler (Halle, 1925), pp. cxxiii-cxxviii. This work will be referred to hereafter as Warnke-Köhler.

A more recent tale in which clothing is necessary to the recovery of human form is "The Wild Swans" of Hans Christian Andersen (Anne Scott, trans. *The Hans Christian Andersen Fairy Tale Book*, New York, 1959).

retouched by the strangely effective words '... E de ceo feusse aparceüz'; the Bisclavret is envisaging that moment of mental anguish when the full awareness of his loss will seize him. At the same time, however, that he thinks of his possible condemnation he is also looking ahead to the possibility of his ensuing redemption: '... De si k'il me fussent rendu.'

The lady renews her plea: (79-86)

> 'Sire,' la dame li respunt,
> 80 'Jeo vus eim plus que tut le mund:
> Nel me devez nïent celer,
> Ne [mei] de nule rien duter;
> Ne semblereit pas amisté.
> 84 Qu'ai jeo forfait? Pur queil peché
> Me dutez vus de nule rien?
> Dites [le] mei, si ferez bien!'

The seven lines of 80-6, in which the wife gives release to her emotion, are a parallel to the seven lines of 42-8 describing her anguish during his absences. But here her opening words are a forthright declaration of her love, expressed in the most absolute of terms ('Jeo vus eim plus que tut le mund'). Whereas in the first passage her fears seemed credible and her sweetness genuine (for we had no reason to believe otherwise), here, in the second appeal of seven lines her assertion 'I love you' is pure hypocrisy, as events will soon show. From this it may follow that her first appeal was also hypocritical.

The hypocritical declaration of love appears intended to dispel any doubts which her husband might have as to her trustworthiness. Moreover, she even takes it upon herself to prescribe (in a tone reminiscent of that addressed to a small and naughty child) what he must not do ('Nel me devez nïent celer, / Ne [mei] de nule rien duter': 81-2),[20] for such action would violate their love. By this admonition she attempts to shame him into revealing the final part of his secret.

Next the wife asks two rhetorical questions ('Qu'ai jeo forfait? Pur queil peché / Me dutez vus de nule rien?') in order to dispel

---

[20] Notice the use of the five negatives in the lady's advice (81-3).

any further reservations he might have, and to corroborate her good faith. She ends with a brief command 'Dites [le] mei,' softened by the persuasive 'si ferez bien.' [21]

So much does she urge him that he yields to her request: (87-96)

>   Tant l'anguissa, tant le suzprist,
> 88 Ne pout el faire, si li dist.
>   'Dame,' fet il, 'delez cel bois,
>   Lez le chemin par unt jeo vois,
>   Une vielz chapele i esteit,
> 92 Ke meintefeiz grant bien me feit:
>   La est la piere cruose e lee
>   Suz un buissun, dedenz cavee;
>   Mes dras i met suz le buissun,
> 96 Tant que jeo revi[e]nc a meisun.' [22]

Now, in a transitional couplet beginning this new section, we find the formulaic *tant... que* construction used for the second time. With respect to its first instance in 60-1 ("Tant le blandi e losenga / Que s'aventure li cunta"), it was the lady's sweetness and deceitful flattery, liberally (and repeatedly?) employed, which served to lower her husband's resistance to her questioning. But here ("Tant l'anguissa ...": 87-8) the sweetness and flattery are missing; all we see is her urgent pressing of her husband. [23]

In a passage of eight lines (numerically paralleling the wife's speech) we hear the knight give away that information which he had sworn he would never reveal. Indeed, he even tells her twice (is he aware of doing so?) of the precise location of his clothing ("suz un buisson," "suz le buisson"). The lady has finally had her question answered.

---

[21] I am taking it for granted that her command means 'tell me your secret' not 'tell me what crimes I have committed against you'; surely the wife would not end her plea on such a defiant, sarcastic note. (We are reminded of the ambiguous '... si jol vus di' of line 54, which was likewise taken to refer to the husband's secret.)

[22] Note the (generally) increasing length of the husband's replies during the entire interview.

And note that the conversation both begins (29-30) and ends (96) with a reference to *meisun*.

[23] In the verb *suzprendre* there is no indication of trickery or wiles; it simply means 'to overcome,' 'to conquer,' 'to overpower.'

Once again, the knight has pointed to the forest ("cel bois") which he had pointed out for the first time in his speech of momentous revelation ('En cele grant forest me met, / Al plus espés de la gaudine': 64-5). These two lines hardly qualify as sustained description, but in the second instance we are given quite vivid details. This lay and *Chaitivel,* I believe, are the only ones so flat in their descriptive narration: not a place, not a person, not an object, is physically described. Thus the descriptions given by the husband in his conversation are all the more noticeable. Only here (in 89-96), as we hear the knight talk to his wife, is there something for the eye to dwell upon.

When the husband indicates the woods, note that he says "delez cel bois," the border of the forest. This symbolizes the borderline of his two natures and his two worlds: the place where the man becomes a werewolf (then to go off into the thickest part of the forest), and the werewolf (later) a man again. [24]

The wife is terrified by the *aventure* of Bisclavret: (97-102)

        La dame oï cele merveille, [25]
        De poür fu tute vermeille;
        De l'aventure se esfrea.
100   E[n] maint endreit se purpensa
        Cum ele s'en puïst partir ;
        Ne voleit mes lez lui gisir.

---

[24] Why does Marie choose to have him mention the old chapel? Why this suggestion of the religious? Moreover, what is this mysterious reference to the chapel's help? Could this mean that he seeks refuge there from hunters while in his animal form?

Although this interpretation is a possibility, the chapel's help may be explained in the following manner. Since *la piere* refers to the material out of which the chapel is built, Bisclavret buries his clothing in the stone wall of the chapel underneath a bush where the stone is crumbly and hollow. How ironical it is that he says the chapel serves him well, for he will lose his humanity there; by burying his garments, it is as if he were burying his body (or his soul).

[25] With this expression, *cele merveille,* we may note the second use of the noun *merveille* which will recur several other times during the lay, always referring to the knight whether in human or animal form. It is most likely that the first instance (line 16) of this noun, used quite conventionally ("Merveille l'ai oï löer"), is meant to anticipate this line in the present section.

Only now that the husband's story has come to an end, do we learn of the wife's reaction [26] (and of its physiological manifestation as well) [27] — a reaction which probably began much earlier. But why does Marie choose to wait until this moment, after the lady has heard the entire extraordinary tale, far more terrifying than any infidelity? Once again, in a scene containing an equally dramatic revelation, Marie will use much the same technique.

Just as the lady reacted to her husband's absences by considering only herself, so does she react here. After hearing that he is a werewolf *(cele merveille)*, she thinks simply of ridding herself of him, even if this means the destruction of her husband as a human being. And we might point out that the reactions to her husband are erotic: in the first part of the interview scene, she suspected that he was in love with another woman; here, it is the desire never to lie with him (she does not want to sleep with a monster) that motivates her actions. [28]

In the lines "E[n] maint endreit se purpensa / Cume ele s'en puïst partir" (100-1) we learn of the wife's gradually growing inquiry into the means of ridding herself of the man's body she does not want to sleep with. Yet "E[n] maint endreit," as well as the intensive "se purpensa," seems preposterous: is the reader to believe that it takes her a long, long time and much hard thinking, to arrive at the idea (already made obvious by her husband's remarks) of having him deprived of his clothing?

She must be thinking of the detail of *who* will take the clothes. The idea of removing them herself evidently did not appeal to her. It may be a kind of repugnance: her physical repulsion pertaining to his body (102) might also have extended to a repugnance of his clothes, a desire not to touch them.

Another possible explanation of her lengthy thinking is that she may be afraid: afraid of the forest, afraid of Bisclavret, of

---

[26] The two verses telling us of the lady's fear (doubly mentioned in 98-9) and the one line (102) revealing her sexual estrangement from her husband represent all we will ever know of the wife's deepest feelings.

[27] For the color red as a sign of fear, cf. *Guigemar*, 271-2: "Si ele ad poür n'est merveille. / Tute en fu sa face vermeille." Note that in both lays the rhyme-scheme of the couplet is identical.

[28] Yet she too, by her actions, will become monstrous, more monstrous to the reader than her husband.

what he might do if he caught her in her act of treachery. It may also be a question of struggling with her conscience: she may have wished to devise a plan in which her guilt would be somewhat minimized.

We do not know at what precise point in the story the lady started plotting. Did her disgust begin after line 70, when she heard her husband tell of his wolfish nakedness? Or already at line 63, when she learned that he became a werewolf? And at lines 87-8 ("Tant l'anguissa, tant le suzprist, / Ne pout el faire, si li dist"), did the wife already have her plan in mind which would have been suggested to her by Bisclavret's words 'Bisclavret sereie a tuz jurs'?

She sends word to a knight of the region: (103-10)

> Un chevaler de la cuntree,
> 104 Que lungement l'aveit amee
> E mut preié' e mut requise
> E mut duné en sun servise—
> Ele ne l'aveit unc amé
> 108 Ne de s'amur aseüré—
> Celui manda par sun message,
> Si li descovri sun curage.

Only at the very end does the lady think [29] of the one who, we are told, loved her very much. The sudden revelation of his existence (which, of course, means that Marie has to give a very rapid summary) is very surprising. We ask ourselves, *what* knight? For it seems as though he comes into existence now only to fulfill the lady's need; he is, as it were, improvised at the moment.

The piling-up of information to bring us up to date quickly as well as to establish the admirer's place in the narrative creates a humorous, although heavy touch in this passage. The *celui* of 109 is weighted down by the preceding five lines (104-8) of breathless summary, yet of those lines, verses 107-8 ("Ele ne l'aveit unc amé / Ne de s'amur aseüré—") almost blot out the knight. And, of course, in lines 104-6 we can not see the knight doing the things mentioned; we are only told of them afterward.

---

[29] As for *E[n] maint endreit* (100), did she perhaps think of using different servants (which plan she would finally reject)?

It is as though the *chevaler de la cuntree* is pulled, even dragged, into the story, by the use of the verb *manda* in 109; with *manda*, we have evidence of the lady's will. Moreover, with *manda*, not only is the previously rejected suitor now established as a character in the lay, but his physical presence is assured: it is taken for granted that, when summoned, he comes.

Furthermore, the spatial and psychological distantiation between the 'knight of the region' and the lady is shown linguistically. The recipient of the lady's message (*un chevaler*, 103) is separated, by both a lengthy relative clause (104-6) and a parenthetical remark (107-8), from the verb *manda* (in 109) relating the lady's act of sending the message. In the final line of this passage ("Si li descovri sun curage") we may note a telescoping of time, as a result of which the previously spurned admirer is immediately in the lady's presence. We are not even told *that* he came; we simply hear her speaking to him.

She promises him her love and her body: (111-19)

'Amis,' fet ele, 'seez leéz! [30]
112 Ceo dunt vus estes travaillez
Vus otri jeo sanz nul respit:
Ja n'i avrez nul cuntredit;
M'amur e mun cors vus otrei, [31]
116 Vostre drue fetes de mei!'
Cil l'en mercie bonement
E la fiance de li prent;
E el le met par serement.

Now that her decision is made, the wife is determined to carry out her plan as quickly as possible. As examples of this, note her elimination of all obstacles *(nul contredit)*, and the rapidity *(sanz nul repit)* with which she grants her suitor her favors.

We are chilled by the matter-of-fact, blunt and loveless way in which she bestows her favors (particularly when she says,

---

[30] We hear the faithless wife address her admirer at once with the very same expression ('Amis') she had previously reserved for her husband (cf. 32, at the opening of the fateful conversation with the latter).

[31] It is pertinent to note the parallel examples of the phrase *otrïer son cors* in *Equitan*, 180 and *Bisclavret*, 115, both times referring to a treacherous wife.

'M'amur e mun cors vus otrei'). [32] For this is the only one of Marie's lays in which no love is born between a man and a woman. Rather, we see here a falling-out of love (if it can be said that the lady loved her husband), even a negation of love. Just as the lady had been insensitive to her husband's experience, so she is insensitive to the *chevaler de la cuntree;* her childish statement 'Be happy!' is crude and joyless. [33]

Of the knight's inner reactions to the lady's words telling him he could have her body, Marie gives no hint whatsoever. [34] Nor do we hear his answer, for in keeping with his secondary role of lover-accomplice, he is never shown speaking directly to the lady. We know only of his blind obedience to her will.

Notable is the manner in which Marie recounts the giving of pledges. Whereas she could have said, most simply, 'they exchanged their pledge,' she presents this action in more detail. First, the lady's pledge (a simple verbal promise) is related from the knight's point of view ("Cil ... la fiance de li prent"), then his pledge, from hers. The strong wording of "... ele le met par serement" (i.e. 'she binds him by an oath') is arresting: for only after having assured herself of the knight's complete fidelity and service will the wife reveal her husband's secret.

Bisclavret is betrayed: (120-26)

```
120  Puis li cunta cumfaitement
     Ses sire ala e k'il devint;
     Tute la veie kë il tint
     Vers la forest l[i] enseigna;
124  Pur sa despuille l'enveia. [35]
```

---

[32] Because of the lady's physical revulsion toward her husband, she now replaces his body by another male body. Moreover, she does not really give the knight her love, for she has none to give; she is absolutely incapable of loving.

[33] Furthermore, note the circularity of the lady's speech: her words begin and end with a command, each completing the other: 'Be happy,' 'make me your sweetheart.'

[34] Marie tells us only that 'he thanks her nicely.'

[35] Whereas the verb *se despuiller* refers to the quite normal action of undressing ("S'il se despuille u vet vestu": 69), the noun *despuille* has a more sinister meaning: 'clothing or armor taken off, sometimes in battle,' 'removed booty or captured materiel.' The substantive *despuille* is used in our lay only after the husband's betrayal has taken place; *despuille* recurs

Issi fu Bisclavret trahiz
E par sa femme maubailiz. [36]

The words we had once heard the baron speak to his wife are now summed up by her as she speaks to her lover: the story within the story has become again a story. In 120-21 ("Puis li cunta cumfaitement / Ses sire ala e k'il devint") is summarized by the husband's first disclosure (cf. 63-6); in 213, his final secret of the hiding-place for his clothes is revealed. As for *tute la veie* of 122, although the Bisclavret had not described the road to his wife, she knew the *chemin* (90) and the forest (64 and 89).

Just as we never knew what the lover's feelings were when the lady granted him her love, we never learn what his feelings are when she tells him her husband's secret and what she wants. The absolute nullity of this person who is simply a means to the ends of the lady (herself shrewd and selfishly scheming) is extraordinary. With just one exception (the sister *La Codre* who comes into existence only to complete the set of twins forming the mother's punishment in *Le Fresne*), there is no character so characterless in any of Marie's lays. [37]

And when we see the lover later in the narrative, he is only one among the group of anonymous nobles summoned to the king's celebration. At that *feste,* we will see him pulled along like a bundle of straw. Much later, he will be seized and held at the king's command.

Now we learn of three events resulting from the husband's disappearance: (127-34)

---

in 268, 275 (and is repeated by the pronoun in 277, 278, 279) and in 290.

Note that when the lady asks her husband the fateful question 'Di mei, pur Deu, u sunt voz dras' (71), she does not employ the term *despuille*. The noun *dras* will be used again, in 271 and 285, where it is a question of the baron's humanity.

[36] In the concluding couplet (125-6) of this section, Marie once more interrupts the narrative line, first to designate the wife's act as treachery, then to condemn indirectly the person whom one might expect to have shown the greatest sympathy and understanding.

[37] What an opposition between the absolute emptiness of the lover and the ardent, dramatic nature of the husband!

>   Pur ceo que hum le perdeit sovent
> 128 Quidouent tuz communalment [38]
>   Que dunc s'en fust del tut alez.
>   Asez fu quis e demandez, [39]
>   Mes n'en porent mie trover;
> 132 Si lur estuit lesser ester.
>   La dame ad cil dunc espusee,
>   Que lungement aveit amee.

In this brief passage of narrative summary, we learn why the baron's disappearance (in spite of the search) was so readily and casually accepted. Yet 127-9 are curious: if the husband used to go away so often, why then was he sought for? [40]

Here we have a perfunctory search, creating not too much stir: a mass of indefinite people (indicated by the third person plural impersonal verbs in 128 and 131) are looking for a man whom they can never find, [41] and who, in a sense, has ceased to exist altogether. And what about the wife and her lover? Did they look for him? Of the feelings of the guilty pair while the search is going on, we are told nothing. The falling note at the end of the search ("Si lur estuit lesser ester") reminds us of Marie's auctorial intervention ("Cest afere les ore ester": 13) at the close of the Prologue.

The passage ends with a couplet [42] relating the inevitable marriage of the wife to her lover. Their marriage is presented

---

[38] From 127 on, the reader (in contrast to the *tuz* of 128) will enjoy more and more the privileged position of knowing what the mystery was. We have knowledge about the beast and past events which the king and his retinue do not (as yet) possess (and which the knight's retainers will never have). The unfolding of events leading up to their acquisition of this knowledge comprises the remainder of our poem.

[39] These are practically the same verbs that were used when the lady started to question her husband in 31 and 68. There is some similarity between the three situations: each time, the husband is being pursued in some way, people are trying to pin him down.

[40] Was it a search instigated by his king? Or perhaps the lady, in order to save her reputation, had her husband looked for.

[41] Indeed, in 131 we learn that they could not find a single bit of him (not even his clothes!).

[42] The couplet's final line (*Que lungement aveit amee*) is an almost perfect echo of 104 (*Que lungement l'aveit amee*) which introduces the lover in a relative clause; each of these relative clauses has the same contents, but not the same structure. In 134 there is a delicate variation,

in the same mechanical and joyless manner as war her offer of love. We wonder how long they had to wait for the search to come to an end before their marriage (whose inevitability is heightened by the forceful *dunc* in 133). [43]

With the end of this passage we have come to the close of the first part of the narrative, in which the wife has been our (main) point of view.

Now we shift to the king, who loved Bisclavret: [44] (135-48)

>   Issi remist un an entier,
> 136 Tant que li reis ala chacier;
>   A la forest ala tut dreit,
>   La u li Bisclavret esteit.
>   Quant li chiens furent descuplé,
> 140 Le Bisclavret unt encuntré;
>   A lui cururent tutejur
>   E li chien e li veneür,
>   Tant que pur poi ne l'eurent pris
> 144 E tut deciré e maumis,
>   De si qu'il ad le rei choisi;
>   Vers lui curut quere merci.
>   Il l'aveit pris par sun estrié,
> 148 La jambe li baise e le pié. [45]

The lull toward the end of the preceding section ("Si lur estuit lesser ester") is echoed (and prolonged) at the very beginning of this passage: "Issi remist un an entier." Then in the following line the formulaic *tant ... que* indicates that the narrative movement will once again go forward. (But a year has passed, a year

---

for the relative clause describes the lady. And with this clause in 134, both the lover and the lady are dismissed, as it were, for a while from the narrative.

[43] In the events concerning the lady and the *chevaler de la cuntree* in this first part of the lay, a sort of chiasmus may be seen. For the lady's words to her admirer begin with talk of love; then she reveals her plan; next, her plain is carried out (by the knight); finally, they are wed. And in a somewhat ironic tone, Marie tells us that the lady, conventional and proper as we know her to be, is legally married.

[44] This shift surely implies a contrastive parallel between the wicked wife and the good king, a parallel which the remainder of the poem will bear out.

[45] The action related in this verse will have a counterpart later in the king's kiss of the Bisclavret.

of horror for Bisclavret in the forest — which the reader must imagine for himself, as he was forced to imagine Bisclavret's feelings at the instant when he perceived that the hollowed stone was empty.)

When the hunting-dogs are unleashed, they find the Bisclavret. [46] In the following four lines (141-4), the hero's fortunes are at their lowest ebb. [47] Not only is Bisclavret reduced to bestiality by his wife's action, his life is in danger. And if he had been killed by the dogs, she would have been guilty of his death.

Just as the shift to the king was sudden, so is Bisclavret's appearance: his flight takes direction when, upon seeing the king, he runs toward him, after the huntsmen and dogs have been going toward the Bisclavret.

In lines 146-8 describing Bisclavret's disclosure of human traits, [48] the rising movement of the lay is already prepared for. As for "Vers lui curut quere merci" (146), [49] is the reader not meant to see in this line a reflection of the knight's pleas to his wife (in 53) not to be pursued by further questions? Moreover, how could the king know that Bisclavret was seeking mercy? Is the king so perceptive?

And why do the dogs not jump on Bisclavret at this moment? Do they understand Bisclavret's gestures to the king?

The king reacts to Bisclavret's gestures: (149-60)

---

[46] With the verb *encuntrer* (140), we are reminded of the unsuccessful search for the lost Bisclavret in human form.

[47] *Tutejur* (in 141), although usually meaning 'all day long,' can also mean 'repeatedly,' 'continuously' (cf. Peter Rickard, "Toute jour, tout le jour, et toute la journée en français médiéval," Romania, LXXXV (1964), 145-80); this is probably the meaning here: the king had not been hunting all day long if he decides to call off the hunt.

[48] Is Marie's omission of any attempt on Bisclavret's part to hurt or kill the hunters and the dogs pursuing him an intentional anticipation of the revelation of his human qualities?

[49] If Bisclavret could run away from the dogs toward the king, why did he not run away before? Was he going to let the dogs tear him to pieces before he caught sight of the ruler?

In our lay, as has been said, physical gestures are extremely important. Indeed, there is more violent physical movement in this poem than in any other of Marie's lays. In 146 ("Vers lui curut quere merci") we may note the first of three running movements that Bisclavret will make.

>   Li reis le vit, grant poür ad;
>   Ses cumpainuns tuz apelad. [50]
>   'Seignurs,' fet il, 'avant venez!
> 152 Ceste merveillë esgardez,
>   Cum ceste beste se humilie!
>   Ele ad sen de hume, merci crie.
>   Chacez mei tuz ces chiens arere,
> 156 Si gardez që hum ne la fiere!
>   Ceste beste ad entente e sen.
>   Espleitez vus! Alum nus en!
>   A la beste durrai ma pes;
> 160 Kar jeo ne chacerai hui mes.'

For the second time, Bisclavret is presented as the cause of fright.[51] Between the account of the king's reaction to the appearance of Bisclavret, and that of the wife to the revelation he has offered her, there is an unmistakably clear parallel. In both cases, the noun *merveille* is used: for the wife, the "marvel" (line 97) is the revelation of animality in a human being; for the king (in his excited appeal to his companions in 152), it is the revelation of humanity in a beast. Thus, in both cases, the emotion of fear leads to quite different attitudes: in the wife, to hatred and loathing, in the king (as we will see), to compassion and veneration. The words "grant poür ad" surely afford insight into his nature. Where we might have expected him to be afraid, he shows no fear whatever, but then when he has seen something marvellous (the beast's humanity, gentleness and humility) he shows fear and awe of the miraculous.

It is significant that the king's first words are *not* (as the reader might expect them to be) 'Chase those dogs back.' It is as if the king had ample time to share his wonderment with his companions, and as if the dogs were miraculously immobilized. Only after he has spoken of his amazement does he seem to remember the hunting-hounds' presence.

---

[50] Contrary to the ancient belief that a man becomes instantly (and temporarily) mute if a wolf sees him first, the king is not rendered speechless. For a discussion of this belief, cf. Salvatore Battaglia, "Lupus in Fabula," *Filologia Romanza*, III (1956), 292-95.

[51] This is one of the very rare references to emotional reactions in our poem.

We are struck by the swiftness and vigor of the king's subsequent reaction, for in a brief speech (the only one we are allowed to hear him utter, 151-60) he gives six commands to his companions (including measures to insure the animal's safety and protection). The forceful manner in which these commands are delivered imparts great energy to the rising movement of the narrative. In the king's address, not only do we notice his authority, but an acute perception of what he sees.

The moment of the king's recognition of the beast's humanity (149 ff.) is a transcendent one. In his assertion, 'Ele a sen de hume, merci crie' (154) [52] is there not something Christian? [53] For man asks for mercy from God, to balance the human and the animal in his nature, to beg mercy for his sins. There is surely some connection between Bisclavret's being pressed and pursued by questions, and his being pursued and hunted; this connection must somehow relate to the dual nature of man.

After his third set of commands ('Espleitez vus! Alum nus en!') [54] the ruler states his decision to "give his peace" [55] to the beast and to hunt no more that day. With these words, Bisclavret receives the mercy which he had sought (and which was denied to him by his wife). [56] Furthermore, note that because of the king's decision, mercy is extended to the other beasts in the forest.

There has been dramatic tension in the last few lines. We have seen Bisclavret's life in danger; we have seen his reactions and his revelation of his human qualities; we have seen his life spared. And the story could have ended there. But with the king's

---

[52] This line is perhaps the most epigrammatic verse in all of Marie's lays.

[53] The puzzling religious note given by Bisclavret's reference to the "old chapel" has already been pointed out. Perhaps the chapel can stand for a religious symbol of marriage. And it is *nearby* a chapel (with an emphasis on the chapel) that the dissolution of his matrimonial state takes place, that he becomes a *bisclavret*.

[54] Why is the king in such a hurry?

[55] A feudal term; it is the lord who 'gives his peace' to his vassal.

[56] The king's perspicacious decision to save the life of the beast becomes even more significant when we notice that it is expressed in the line ending the first of the lay (159). From this moment on, the beast will no longer be a hunted animal. Moreover, in the following line (160) beginning the second half, a situation paralleling that of Bisclavret may be noted.

Bisclavret is one of the ten lays of Marie in which significant subject material is found at the precise center of the poem.

recognition of the animal's humanity, and his order that the beast not be killed, we have the first stage of Bisclavret's return to mankind.

Bisclavret follows the king to the palace: (161-74)

>   Li reis s'en est turné atant.
>   Le Bisclavret li vet siwant;
>   Mut se tint pres, n'en vout partir,
> 164 Il n'ad cure de lui guerpir.
>   Li reis l'en meine en sun chastel;
>   Mut en fu liez, mut li est bel,
>   Kar unke mes tel n'ot veü;
> 168 A grant merveille l'ot tenu
>   E mut le tient a grant chierté.
>   A tuz les suens ad comaundé
>   Que sur s'amur le gardent bien
> 172 E li ne mesfacent de rien,
>   Ne par nul de eus ne seit feruz;
>   Bien seit abevreiz e peüz.

The beast's manifestation of his desire for human companionship is movingly presented: not only does he decide to follow the king (who had already turned away) to his castle, but he stays close, very close to him (note the three-fold insistence on his desire for closeness: 163-4). We are told nothing whatsoever of his feelings,[57] but surely we can assume that the tenderness and insight the king had just shown him (and which he had failed to find in his wife) answered a deep craving in his nature. We can also understand his desire to live, once again, in human society: for a year he had endured an enforced, uninterrupted bestiality. Once the "rage" had passed (which was always of short duration with him), this bestiality became something alien to his nature, something loathesome to the very important human side of Bisclavret's nature — which now, thanks to the king, he could, if only in a limited way, express. And he may have hoped, or dimly believed, that human companionship might lead to the recovery of his human form, if his behavior would warrant it.

---

[57] Except for the casual reference in line 29 to his happy, joyful return home, never are Bisclavret's emotional reactions analyzed.

From line 170 to 184, there is given an idyllic picture of life at the court. Just as the king recognized the human in Bisclavret (and marvelled thereat) when he begged for mercy, so does he now recognize the marvel (167-8) in the animal's act of following him.[58] The king is now loving Bisclavret in animal form as he once had loved him in human form. (Does he hold the beast in such tenderness because the animal wanted to be so close to him?) The sovereign's commands to the members of his household (170-4) are an expansion of his order to his servants in the preceding section (151-60). In this second set of orders, three details may impress the reader: the feudal flavor of the phrase *sur s'amur*, the king's insistence that the beast should not be struck,[59] and the lofty tone of the last command ("Bien seit abreveiz e peüz").[60]

Bisclavret lives harmoniously with the king and his retainers: (175-84)

        Cil le garderent volenters;
176   Tuz jurs entre les chevalers
        E pres del rei se alout cuchier.
        N'i ad celui que ne l'ad chier;
        Tant esteit franc e deboneire,
180   Unques ne volt a rien mesfeire.
        U ke li reis deüst errer,
        Il n'out cure de desevrer;

---

[58] 167-8 are significant in still another respect: they anticipate the words of the wise man in 259-60.

[59] This is the second time (cf. 156) that the king issues the very same command. In his words reported in 172, "E li ne mesfacent de rien," the *de rien* should include everything, but then in 173, with the order not to hit the animal ("Ne par nul de eus ne seit feruz"), the sovereign reminds his household members in case they might forget. It is as if the king feels the indignity of such an act toward such an animal.

[60] This is the second of four lays where food and drink are important. Two instances have to do with animals (here, in *Bisclavret*, and in *Milun*), and two with persons (*Guigemar* and *Les Deus Amanz*).

In three cases the same verbs, *abevrer* and *paistre*, are used, of which one rare instance pertains to a human being.

Here in *Bisclavret*, this is the second time that a protagonist is coddled (cf. Marie's comment about the wounded Guigemar "Bien est peüz e abrevez": 378, *Guigemar*). In both instances, before Marie gives the reader specific details of the care of the knight (*Guigemar*, 365-78) and of the beast (*Bisclavret*, 161-74), she uses a similar expression to report the concern of others for the protagonist: 'to hold someone dear.'

Ensemble od lui tuz jurs alout:
184 Bien s'aperceit qüe il l'amout. [61]

The beast is now surrounded by tenderness and loving concern, [62] for the royal retainers gladly carry out the king's orders.

By day, Bisclavret is the king's constant companion; at night, he sleeps among the knights close to the king. Unlike the baron's wife (cf. 102, "Ne voleit mes lez lui gisir"), the ruler is never afraid to sleep near the werewolf. [63] Marie tells us four times (in this and the preceding passage) of the animal's unwillingness to separate himself from the king.

In this entire section, Bisclavret is coming closer and closer to humanity; people are already treating him as a human being. The beast (when at the court) is the same kind of being as he was a man, courteous and gentle. The description of Bisclavret given now ("Tant esteit franc e deboneire, / Unques ne volt a rien mesfaire": 179-80) [64] corresponds with the portrait of the

---

[61] This line (Bien s'aparceit qüe il l'amout") deserves our attention for several reasons. First, could *s'aparceveir* (a verb of mental perception) pertain to an animal? Could the subject of *s'aparceit* (for which no subject is given, as is also true for *alout* in the preceding line) be the pronoun *il*, clearly designating Bisclavret, and given at the beginning of the clause in 182? In this case, the one who perceived such love would be Bisclavret. (Indeed, he had experienced the fact that his wife did not love him in human form; now, he experiences the fact that the king does love him in animal form.)

If we accept this reading, then "Bien s'aparceit qüe il l'amout" is most assuredly the complement of a line in the preceding passage ("E mut le tient a grant chierté": 169) describing the king's attitude toward the animal. Thus we are given a picture of reciprocal affection and mutual trust between the king and the beast.

Yet the subject of *s'aparceit* could also be indicated by the antecedent *lui* in 183, where *lui* unequivocally refers to the king. This further instance of ambiguity stresses all the more that this is the most mysterious of Marie's lays.

[62] When Bisclavret is at the court, emphasis is given to the compassion and perception, commingled with tenderness, which the king and his servants show to him. From this situation, and from Bisclavret's reactions to it, it is quite obvious that Bisclavret did not want only the sexual (and we might recall that the wife's reaction to her husband's experience was only sexual, never compassionate).

[63] Moreover, when Bisclavret is later found (in human form) by the king, he will be sleeping — on the king's bed!

[64] In 180, the verb *mesfeire* (used, quite normally, in 172 to refer to a human being's act against social and ethical codes) is repeated, with the

baron given in the most general terms at the beginning of the story ("Beaus chevalers e bons esteit / E noblement se cunteneit": 17-18).

Furthermore, the same situation obtains for Bisclavret as an animal as when he was knight: everyone loved him (178).[65] Here it is a reciprocal situation whose reason is mentioned two lines later: He does not want to harm anyone.

The wife's lover comes to court: (185-95)

>   Oëz aprés cument avint.
>   A une curt ke li rei tint
>   Tuz les baruns aveit mandez,
> 188   Ceus ki furent de lui chasez,
>   Pur aider sa feste a tenir.
>   E lui plus beal faire servir.
>   Li chevaler i est alez,[66]
> 192   Richement e bien aturnez,
>   Ki la femme Bisclavret ot.[67]
>   Il ne saveit ne ne quidot
>   Que il le deüst trover si pres.

Marie now interrupts the narrative line to give a vague indication *(aprés)* of the passing of time. At the close of this section, she will interrupt once again, to remark omnisciently about the wife's lover: "Il ne saveit ne ne quidot / Que il le deüst trover si pres." These two lines, in which the lover and Bisclavret are linked together linguistically, are an anticipation of, as well as a

---

subtle result that it now applies to the act of a beast! This is the only example in Tobler-Lommatzsch of the verb being used of an animal.

In addition to this delicate variation in the use of *mesfeire*, line 180 ("Unques ne volt a rien mesfeire") points ahead to Bisclavret's attack upon the lover, and his revenge upon his wife.

[65] The expression 'everyone loved him' reminds us of a similar statement made about another protagonist in a previous lay. About the maiden Le Fresne, we learn that "N'i out un sul, petit ne grant, / Pur sa franchise ne l'amast / E ne cherist e honurast" (*Le Fresne*, 310-12). Of all the protagonists in Marie's lays, it is significant that Bisclavret and Le Fresne are the only ones to be characterized as 'loved by everyone.'

[66] Nothing is said in the lay of rumor spreading about the animal which constantly accompanies the king. Had the knight, before he went to court, heard about Bisclavret?

[67] Note that the woman he married is still called "la femme Bisclavret."

transition to, the physical clash that will be recounted in the next passage.

The lover has never been described physically. Here we are told about his clothes ("Richement e bien aturnez") but they are not pictured, merely indicated by a verb signifying 'to put on clothing.' The knight's fine appearance fulfills the king's command for his barons' presence [68] in order to "lui plus beal faire servir." Yet the result of mentioning the lover's clothing is as if he were a faceless man, all dressed up.

The lover is attacked by Bisclavret: (196-203)

> 196 Si tost cum il vint al paleis
> E le Bisclavret le aparceut,
> De plain esleis vers lui curut;
> As denz le prist, vers lui le trait.
> 200 Ja li eüst mut grant leid fait, [69]
> Ne fust li reis ki l'apela,
> De une verge le manaça.
> Deus feiz le vout mordrë al jur.

The idyllic life of harmony and repose at the castle, of mutual trustfulness between the beast and those around him, is now abruptly shattered. For Bisclavret, upon perceiving the knight, in a sudden rush of activity, runs headlong toward him. In a ferocious movement ("As denz le prist..."), [70] Bisclavret drags

---

[68] The only other time (in *Yonec*) that a noble is ordered to attend a feast, it may be noted that he is to attend with his friends, bringing along his wife and son.
Here in *Bisclavret*, only the barons themselves were summoned. It is also notable that it was the fief (rightfully belonging to Bisclavret) which made the lover's presence at the court mandatory.
Had the wife been ordered to accompany her husband to court (in *Bisclavret*), and had the lady (and her son) remained at home (in *Yonec*), what a difference there would be in the two plots!

[69] "Ja li eüst mut grant leid fait" recalls the scene when the dogs would have torn Bisclavret to pieces (cf. 143-4).

[70] With this savage gesture, the reader is reminded of what Bisclavret could have done (but did not do) when he seized the king's stirrup.
In this lay there may be seen, according to Salvatore Battaglia, "Il mito del licantropo nel 'Bisclavret' di Maria di Francia," *Filologia Romanza*, III (1956), 229-53, the fusion of two myths, that of the lycanthrope, and that of the faithful yet vindictive dog.

the knight toward himself. Recalling again Marie's words in the Prologue ("Garualf, c[eo] est beste salvage: / Tant cum il est en cele rage, / Hummes devure, grant mal fait": 9-11), we wonder if Bisclavret would have devoured the lover had he not been prevented. That same day he attacked the lover at least once more ("Deus feiz le vout mordrë al jur": 203).

The reader is struck by Bisclavret's swift, ferocious attack.[71] Moreover, his running attack upon the lover [72] may be contrasted with the time we saw him run to the king to beg for mercy (146-8). There is an unmistakable parallel between the two episodes, for each has a threefold movement.

From 199 ("As denz le prist, vers lui le trait") it appears that the animal, in order to drag the lover toward him, has caught hold of his clothing — that is, he seizes (with his teeth) the clothing of the person who had stolen his clothes. The ferocious movement indicated by "... vers lui le trait" (199) recalls the first (and very different) situation where we saw the baron make the same gesture, as a manifestation of tenderness toward his wife (cf. 37-8, "Quant il l'oï, si l'acola, / *Vers lui la traist*, si la beisa.")

By the animal's totally unexpected brutality, the joyful dignity of a feast at court has been marred. For the first time since the beast left the forest, threats of physical violence are necessary to subdue him to obedience. For the first time, too, the king is compelled to act toward the beast in a manner differing from his customary courtesy.[73] (Yet the sovereign still acts as one would toward a pet who had attacked a guest.)[74]

---

[71] In this poem, we are forced to visualize many physical movements occurring at precise moments. We are, however, rarely told from where the characters move. In the present scene, only a vague stage-setting of 'at the palace' (196) is given, after which the beast springs into action, from where we do not know.

[72] Did Bisclavret know that the baron had taken his clothes? Had he seen the lover do that? Or had he heard at court that this was his wife's new husband? (And what of Bisclavret's feelings upon hearing of his wife's second marriage?)

[73] Now, for the second time, Bisclavret is in danger of experiencing physical violence.

[74] The king chases Bisclavret away from the lover, just as he had chased the dogs off Bisclavret.

The assembly of knights is amazed: (204-10)

> 204 Mut s'esmerveillent li plusur;
> Kar unkes tel semblant ne fist
> Vers nul hume kë il veïst.
> Ceo dïent tut par la meisun
> 208 Ke il nel fet mie sanz reisun:
> Mesfait li ad, coment que seit;
> Kar volenters se vengereit.

The verb *s'esmerveiller* must be deliberately intended to recall the noun *(cele merveille)* used twice before in reference to Bisclavret. Just as his wife was amazed at the revelation of the animal in a human, just as all had been amazed at the revelation of the human in an animal, the assembly is amazed at Bisclavret's savage attack (the revelation of the animal in an animal!).

The barons' amazement gives way to their suspicion that Bisclavret's behavior must have been a legitimate attempt at vengeance. This correct guess about what we, in our privileged position, know to be a fact represents the first stage in the revelation of Bisclavret's story.

In addition, the final couplet ("Mesfait li ad, coment que seit; / Kar volenters se vengereit": 209-10) [75] may be considered as a dual anticipation: of the vengeance (which will take place first), and of the denouement, in which the king and his entourage will learn what misdeed the lover and Bisclavret's wife had done to the beast. [76]

The feast comes to an end: (211-18)

> A cele feiz remist issi,
> 212 Tant que la feste departi
> E li barun unt pris cungé;

---

[75] In 209, there is the third instance of *mesfeire*, this time again relevant to a human's act against social and ethical codes.

In the last three lines of this passage, note the sudden shift of subject without warning, from the *il* of 208 clearly referring to Bisclavret, to the verb *Mesfait li ad* (209) relating the lover's action, and back again to Bisclavret in 210.

[76] Notice that the passage 207-10 begins with indirect discourse and ends with *discours indirect libre*.

"BISCLAVRET" 121

>A lur meisun sunt repeiré.
>Alez s'en est li chevaliers,
>216 Mien escïent tut as premers,
>Que le Bisclavret asailli;
>N'est merveille s'il le haï.

For the third time (cf. 13 and 32) a mysterious situation is dismissed ("A cele feiz remist issi"). This same formula ("Issi remist un an entier, / Tant que li reis ala chacier": 135-6) began the section following the subsidence in the action after the husband's betrayal and the wife's remarriage. Here, after Bisclavret's unsuccessful attempt at retribution, there also is a lull in the activity.

Activity is resumed again, as the barons take their leave at the close of the feast. Of this brief section, five lines are devoted to their departure: first, we see the barons leave, as it were, in a body; then attention is focused upon the lover who, we learn only now, was among the first to leave.[77]

A slight humor is discernible in the line "Mien escïent tut as premers" (216), for this verse makes us think of the lover's situation. Surely the knight must have been poised for escape, to reach the security of his home.[78] At least twice his life had been endangered by a wild beast; we are led to imagine his state of nerves. Also, he has been made to realize that he did not have the sympathy of those present at the feast. His feelings, of course, are not mentioned; once more we become aware of the relative scarcity of personal reactions and emotions reported in this narrative.

The king goes again to the forest: (219-26)

---

[77] This is a subtle variant of *hysteron proteron*.

[78] In the elegantly constructed compound sentence concluding the episode at the king's court, not only is there a second linguistic association of the knight and the beast ("Alez s'en est li chevaliers, / Mien escïent tut as premers, / Que le Bisclavret asailli: / N'est merveille s'il le haï": 215-18), but also two parenthetical remarks by Marie. The humor of the first auctorial observation (216) has already been pointed out.

Perhaps more significant (in view of the paucity of personal feelings given us) is Marie's declaration of Bisclavret's hatred of the lover. Yet why should Marie insist upon this emotion which has already been vividly manifested? Is it to remaind us of a situation which we have been privileged to know, and which those present at the feast have not?

>   Ne fu puis gueres lungement,
> 220   Ceo m'est avis, si cum j'entent, [79]
>   Que a la forest ala li reis,
>   Que tant fu sages e curteis, [80]
>   U li Bisclavret fu trovez;
> 224   E il i est od lui alez.
>   La nuit quant il s'en repeira, [81]
>   En la cuntree herberga.

The narrative rhythm will once more begin to accelerate, as the king returns to the forest where Bisclavret was found. (This time his purpose of hunting is not specified; we are meant to take it for granted.) Moreover, this time the hunt is not broken off, as it was before. What must have been Bisclavret's fears (and reactions) as he watches the other animals being destroyed? [82]

The next day Bisclavret's wife comes to the king's quarters: (227-30)

>   La femme Bisclavret le sot; [83]
> 228   Avenantment se appareilot.

---

[79] Why does Marie, at the beginning of this section which introduces the poem's final episode, parenthetically remark "Ceo m'est avis, si cum j'entent"? Her tone here is so casual, perhaps even indifferent.

[80] The parenthetical clause ("Que tant fu sages e curteis") describing the king is worthy of note: we are told for the first time of qualities of character previously revealed through the king's actions. It may be that this simple phrase *sages e curteis* is introduced at this point in the narrative to anticipate the second important occasion on which these virtues of the king will be shown.

Since *Equitan* and *Bisclavret* are the only two lays in which the king plays so important a role, it may be significant to compare the two figures, and their treatment by Marie. In *Bisclavret* we have noted the delay in the characterization of the sovereign: the king's sagacity and courtesy are shown first, then he is described later. Whereas in *Equitan*, the king is described first (as one of the noble and courteous Bretons), then he acts. And in *Equitan*, Marie suggests very soon that the king's character is not what we believe it to be. Incidentally, both King Equitan and the anonymous king in Bisclavret are hunters.

[81] Evidently the king hunts all day; that is why he takes lodging for the night in the countryside, instead of returning to his castle.

[82] To imagine him as suffering anguish would heighten the impression of his fidelity demonstrated by the beast's presence at the king's side (about which Marie does not fail to remind us, in 224).

[83] Again (cf. 193), the faithless wife, married to her lover, is called *la femme Bisclavret*. The first such reminder precedes immediately Bisclavret's attack on the lover; the second, his attack on the faithless wife.

> Al demain vait al rei parler,
> Riche present li fait porter. [84]

The wife's decision to visit the king and to pay him her respects, is, in itself, understandable; entirely in keeping with her character (cf. "... mut feseit beu semblant": 22) is her wish to impress the king. Not only does she bring him a rich present, but (like her husband at the time of his court appearance) she is beautifully arrayed. Are we meant to see her as just a dressed-up figure?

Bisclavret leaps upon the wife: (231-6)

>   Quant Bisclavret la veit venir,
> 232   Nul hum nel poeit retenir;
>   Vers li curut cum enragiez.
>   Oiez cum il est bien vengiez!
>   Le neis li esracha del vis.
> 236   Quei li peüst il faire pis?

This is the third occasion when the reader is told 'When Bisclavret sees so-and-so, he runs': the first time, to the king (146); then, toward the lover (198); and now, toward his wife (233). The reader feels that Marie has deliberately shifted from the events she is recounting to Bisclavret, in the last two instances without previously letting us know of his presence on the scene. Each time the transition to the animal takes place, Marie tells us of his visual perception (*choisir*, 146; *aparceveir*, 197; *veeir*, 231), then his immediate reaction. We, in turn, see him spring into action.

In the first attack, we were very clearly given to understand that Bisclavret wanted to go farther, and had to be (at least twice) restrained. But, here, in the second case, we see that the beast's initial act represented all that he wanted to do. That such was the total revenge intended by Bisclavret is evident from Marie's personal interjections preceding ("Oiez cum il est bien

---

[84] The expression *riche present*, a stock phrase in a description of an act of reverence, is notable here as one of the very rare references to material objects in our poem; even so, it is impossible to visualize the lady's gift.

vengiez!": 234)[85] and following ("Quei li peüst il faire pis?": 236) his revenge. But why should he rip off his wife's nose?[86]

Although never allowed to see the beast's ravening nature, here we do witness an act of bestiality. By this act of savagery he has destroyed her beauty in which she took such pride and which her lover adored, and — with her noseless face — has given her an animal-like appearance.

Threatened on all sides, Bisclavret is saved by the words of a wise man: (237-60)

```
       De tutes parz l'unt manacié;
       Ja l'eüssent tut depescié,
       Quant un sages hum dist al rei:
240    'Sire,' fet il, 'entent a mei!
       Ceste beste ad esté od vus;
       N'i ad ore celui de nus
       Que ne l'eit veü lungement
244    E pres de lui alé sovent;
       Unke mes humme ne tucha
       Ne felunie ne mustra,
       Fors a la dame que ici vei.
248    Par cele fei ke jeo vus dei,
       Aukun curuz ad il vers li,
       E vers sun seignur autresi.
       Ceo est la femme al chevaler
252    Que taunt par suliez aveir chier,
       Que lung tens ad esté perduz,
       Ne seümes qu'est devenuz.
       Kar metez la dame en destreit,
256    S'aucune chose vus direit,
       Pur quei ceste beste la heit;
```

---

[85] This comment reminds us of Marie's first announcement ("Oëz aprés cument avint": 185), at the very beginning of the lay's second section where the action rises to the climax of the first unsuccessful attack.

[86] In this lay where so many astonishing events take place, once again Marie omits telling us the reactions or feelings of a certain character. We are never told the lady's feelings, or even her physical reactions, when her nose is bitten off; we can easily imagine them.

In connection with Bisclavret's second attack, it may be pertinent to cite from *The Bestiary: A Book of Beasts*, being a translation from a Latin Bestiary of the twelfth century, trans. and ed. T. H. White, Capricorn Books edition (New York, 1960), pp. 56-7, concerning the beast called *Lupus*: "Wolves are known for their rapacity.... Moreover, a wolf ... keeps his strength in his chest and jaws: in his loins there is really very little."

>   Fetes li dire s'el le seit!
>   Meinte merveille avum veü
> 260 Quë en Bretaigne est avenu.'

Just as when Bisclavret was surrounded by dogs in the forest, so he is again in danger of dismemberment. Just as when Bisclavret attacked the lover, so again he is threatened.[87] Furthermore, just as he was saved in the forest by the wisdom of the king, again he will be saved by the words of another wise man.

Yet why does the wise man speak only to the king, and not to the men around him? For not once does he tell them to get away from the werewolf, as the king had done to the hunters in the forest. There is some parallel between this, and the situation where the hunting-dogs have been following Bisclavret in the forest. In both cases, everything is suspended, except the words ("die lösende Wörter") that flow!

Again, the reader is startled by a sudden emergence: a wise man claims the center of the stage. From his words ("N'i ad ore celui de nus / Que ne l'eit veü lungement / E pres de lui alé sovent": 242-4) it may be supposed that the sage is a member of the king's household who obviously accompanied the king on his recent hunting-trip. This is the very first time we have seen him, or known of his existence, yet he is as essential to the plot development as is the king. This wise man is the *deus ex machina* whose action of stopping this murder by words of advice will lead to the denouement.

He exemplifies a second type of wisdom and perception in our poem. For unlike the sovereign's instantaneous recognition of the beast's human traits, the wise man's insight is the result of long observation, recollection and careful thought. It is he who perceives not only the relationship between the two attacks, but the possible connection that these two might have with the missing knight.

The wise man's speech (the longest one in direct address in our lay) may be analyzed for the careful development of his argument, in the following manner:

---

[87] There is also another parallel between the two attacks on Bisclavret: first, he is threatened by the king, then by all. This is the fifth (and last) time that Bisclavret is pursued or threatened.

He summarizes the animal's conduct up to the present time, and comes to the obvious conclusion: (240-50)

>240 'Sire,' fet il, 'entent a mei'.
>　　 Ceste beste ad esté od vus;
>　　 N'i ad ore celui de nus
>　　 Que ne l'eit veü lungement
>244 E pres de lui alé sovent;
>　　 Unke mes humme ne tucha
>　　 Ne felunie ne mustra,
>　　 Fors a la dame que ici vei. [88]
>248 Par cele fei ke jeo vus dei,
>　　 Aukun curuz ad il vers li,
>　　 E vers sun seignur autresi.

The word *felunie* is extremely important, revealing the point of view from which the wise man (as well as the king and his entourage) considers the animal. For *felunie* is a feudal term refering to an act of a human being, of noble class. According to Carl Stephenson, "very generally any action unbefitting a feudal gentleman might be called felonious." [89]

The striking force of the wise man's words in 247 when he looks at the lady ("Fors a la dame que ici vei") should be pointed out. [90] Marie has chosen (and I believe, deliberately) not to mention the wife's bloody face which we immediately and easily

---

[88] The sage's asseveration ('Unke mes humme ne tucha / Ne felunie ne mustra, / Fors a la dame que ici vei') is debatable. Precisely what is meant by 'touched'? To harm the person of an individual? If so, then his declaration is true. But, in another sense, the beast had 'touched' the knight when he seized the latter's clothing in his teeth. And indeed, Bisclavret's attack upon the lady and its result are so horrible that the wise man momentarily forgets the earlier attack upon the lover.

[89] *Medieval Feudalism* (Ithaca, 1956: Great Seal Books), p. 34.

K.-J. Hollyman states in *le Développement du vocabulaire féodal en France pendant le haut moyen âge* (Genève, 1957), p. 152, that the term *felon* was associated with *traistre*. In the situation under discussion, the reader well knows that it is not Bisclavret who is a traitor, and that he justifiably attacks the two individuals who had betrayed him.

[90] The wise man's words "Fors a la dame *que ici vei*" are not only striking; they are puzzling as well. Why does he say that? The lady is not a stranger to him, for he will very soon identify her (in 251-4). For the wise man, the lady is an object of vision; it is her noseless and bleeding face that he sees.

visualize. Arresting, too, is the implicit contrast between the splendidly garbed yet faceless knight of the animal's first attack and the wife whose maimed face is dripping blood upon her fine attire.

For the second time in the narrative (up to the end of 247), the story could have ended. But why did it not? And we recall the first instance when the king gives the animal his peace, where the story continued because the animal followed the king.

Now, once again, Bisclavret's life is saved by the words of a wise man; once again, the story continues. The wise man says "Ceo est la femme al chevaler" (251), for he has already started to guess. He has begun to suspect the truth.

He reminds the king that the lady was the wife of the lost knight: (251-4)

>   Ceo est la femme al chevaler
> 252 Que taunt par suliez aveir chier,
>   Que lung tens ad esté perduz,
>   Ne seümes qu'est devenuz. [91]

We, the readers, who know all the facts of Bisclavret's *aventure*, listen to the wise man who is completely ignorant of this and who is on his way to suspecting the truth. Particularly important are his words ("Que taunt par suliez aveir chier") dramatically ironic to the reader. What then must have been the sage's feelings as he spoke to the king of the knight as "(the one) whom you *used to love* so dearly," beginning to realize as he spoke that this love might be continuing into the present?

He counsels the king to question the lady: (255-60)

>   Kar metez la dame en destreit, [92]
> 256 S'aucune chose vus direit,

---

[91] The phrase *Ne seümes qu'est devenuz* recalls one of the lady's first questions ("... el ne saveit / U deveneit ...": 26-7) about her husband's repeated absences.

[92] Although the sage had begun his words to the king with the familiar form of address ("Sire, ... entent a mei!") most certainly due to his excitement and a sudden insight he wished to communicate at once, he now, after the lengthy explanation (which allows him to regain a certain composure), shifts to the polite command form *(metez; fetes)*.

> Pur quei ceste beste la heit;
> Fetes li dire s'el le seit!
> Meinte merveille avum veü
> 260 Quë en Bretaigne est avenu.'

In this passage once again there is the note of mystery, once again the attempt to find the answer. With the word *merveille* (used previously only in reference to the protagonist's dual nature), Marie makes it clear that the wise man has guessed the truth. In this lay where Marie insists so often upon the truth of what she is telling, she very subtly allows one of the characters in the story to say 'Many a marvel we have seen in Brittany.'

What composure the sage has, and how prudent he is not to state already what he has (hopefully) guessed. How long Marie makes us wait before even this possibility is mentioned (in his second speech, in its very last line). The slow way of gradually building up to his revelation of the truth (in 292), as well as the total omission of the king's reactions to the wise man's words, creates, maintains and even heightens the suspense of his listeners, a suspense to be relieved only by the king's discovery reported in 299. With the wise man's words in 259-60 ("Mainte merveille avum veü / Quë en Bretaigne est avenu"), had the king begun to guess? Surely he must be wondering, but Marie, in keeping with the rest of the lay, most carefully refrains from telling us anything of his thoughts or his emotions.[93]

The lady confesses everything: (261-74)

> Li reis ad sun cunseil creü:
> Le chevaler ad retenu;
> De l'autre part la dame ad prise
> 264 E en mut grant destresce mise.[94]

As for his advice in 255 ("Kar metez la dame en destreit"), the noun *destreit* may signify 'narrow dungeon' or 'keep' (Tobler-Lonmatzsch, II, cols. 1801-3). Yet Tobler-Lommatzsch quotes the line under discussion as an example of the word's figurative use, in the expression *metre en destreit*, meaning 'to press somebody,' 'to urge somebody.' We must note, however, that the precise means employed are not specified.

[93] The king's lack of reaction to the wise man's story reminds the reader of the wife's lack of reaction to the horrifying words of her husband.

[94] Tobler-Lommatzsch (II, cols. 1790-91) is right in his interpretation of 264-5 ("Um ein Geständnis zu erreichen"), but very probably wrong when he sees in *destresce* a reference to the lady's emotions.

>   Tant par destresce e par poür [95]
>   Tut li cunta de sun seignur:
>   Comment ele l'aveit trahi
> 268 E sa despoille li toli,
>   L'aventure qu'il cunta,
>   E quei devint e u ala;
>   Puis que ses dras li ot toluz,
> 272 Ne fud en sun païs veüz;
>   Tresbien quidat e bien creeit
>   Que la beste Bisclavret seit.

For the third time, the reader hears the *aventure* that Bisclavret, under pressure, told his wife, which she related to her lover, and which she now retells to the king.[96] As to her motives, while in the first instance it was her urgent desire to rid herself of her husband, in the present situation she wishes to justify her action, perhaps even to exculpate herself.

But by now, of course, the *aventure* has developed: for she must also tell the part she has played, and its result. It is significant that in the wife's account (in which she tells the king everything about her husband)[97] she mentions at once (267) her act of treachery. But why should Marie stress the wife's certainty ("Tresbien *quidat* e bien creeit") of the animal's identity? Is Marie being intentionally ironic, as if, after all the wife has disclosed, there could be any doubt remaining? Or is the wife so eager to be freed from further questioning and 'destresce' that she identifies the beast in a most positive manner?

What was the 'distress' to which the lady was subjected? Although *destresce* is vague, the first possible meanings of the word that could apply here would indicate force or compulsion. In the questioning of the wife there is a parallel to (and punishment of) her relentless interrogation of her husband. This is the only one of Marie's lays where people are pressed to give information, to tell the truth.

[95] For the second and last time we are told of the lady's fear. And did her fear cause her to flush as it did the first time? We would not see it, for now her face is already red, with gore!

[96] In her account to the king of her husband's *aventure* (summarized in just one verse, "E quei devint e u ala": 270), note the formula (repeated for the third and last time) of 'what he became and where he went.'

[97] Verse 266 ("Tut li cunta de sun seignur") clearly echoes 67 ("Quant il li aveit tut cunté") although 67 follows the husband's revelation of his *aventure,* whereas 266 precedes the lady's rehearsal of events.

Bisclavret's garments are brought before him: (275-80)

>
> Le reis demande la despoille; [98]
> 276 U bel li seit u pas nel voille,
> Ariere la fet aporter,
> Al Bisclavret la fist doner. [99]
> Quant il l'urent devant lui mise,
> 280 Ne se prist garde en nule guise.

At this moment, the king's only reaction to the lady's story that is known to us is his command (spoken most peremptorily, to be sure: "U bel li seit u pas ne voille": 276) that the stolen clothing [100] be sent for. Note that he now needs no suggestion from the wise man; hir order shows that he has already guessed what the latter had suspected. At this portentous moment we are again left in ignorance of the king's feelings. Neither are we told of Bisclavret's feelings when he sees before him the means by which he may regain humanity, if he chooses, nor are we told the reason for Bisclavret's refusal of his clothes. The animal's nobility of bearing is arresting: he is now as impassive as the king.

Once again, the sage counsels the king: (281-92)

>
> Li produm le rei apela,
> Cil ki primes le cunseilla:
> 'Sire, ne fetes mie bien:
> 284 Cist nel fereit pur nule rien,
> Que devant vus ses dras reveste
> Ne mut la semblance de beste.
> Ne savez mie que ceo munte:
> 288 Mut durement en ad grant hunte.

---

[98] It is surely notable that when the king asks for the clothing symbolic of Bisclavret's humanity, *la despoille* repeats the term used earlier in the relation of the guilty pair's betrayal ("Pur sa despuille l'enveia": 124).

[99] Notice that the sovereign does not comment upon the lady's treachery or even call her wicked. His reaction to the part she played in her husband's *aventure* is delayed until a later moment.

[100] But why did the lady keep her husband's clothes? She should have burned them. For they were not just any garments, but those the knight had worn when he disappeared from human society. The wife's lack of forethought in this matter corresponds to her lack of forethought in going to see the king.

> En tes chambres le fai mener [101]
> E la despoille od lui porter;
> Une grant piece l'i laissums.
> 292 S'il devient hum, bien le verums.'

Up to this moment, the wise man's remarks have been based upon observation and memory. But now, like the king when he first gazed upon Bisclavret in the forest, the sage speaks from pure intuition. We are struck by the beauty and solemnity of his words.

He begins by rebuking the king. As we hear him talk, he seems to know what it would be like to be a werewolf. His words bespeak grave assurance ('Ne savez mie que ceo munte: / Mut durement en ad grant hunte': 287-8), [102] as was also true of the king's words 'Ceste beste ad entente e sen' (157). Once again, Bisclavret's true nature has been understood.

That is the point of the lay: that tenderness, and *curteisie*, and understanding of his true nature is what Bisclavret had lacked, yet craved and needed. It is conceivable that a person could become enraged because he could not receive the tender understanding of his true nature from his wife. Now that Bisclavret has this understanding and tenderness, it is probable that he will never again become a werewolf.

It was earlier stated that the sage must have begun to suspect the truth at least by verse 251. Yet in his first speech he gave not the slightest hint of the possibility he had envisaged. The only reason given for his advice about the lady was that 'Many a marvel have we seen in Brittany.' When he speaks to rebuke the king, the hint we are waiting for comes, although in negative

---

[101] For the second time, we observe a shift in the forms of address (from *vos* to *tu*) in the wise man's speech. Note that with *tes chambres* (the king's chambres in the residence where he spent the previous night), the wise man even anticipates the *tu* of the verb form which is, incidentally, the only imperative in this particular speech.

Why should this shift take place? Its effect is that of intimacy and privacy, coupled with that of magnificence and solemnity created by the plural *chambres*. Just as Bisclavret slept among the knights near the king, so will he now sleep on the king's bed.

[102] Observe that the wise man ends his speech with the word *hunte*, conspicuous for its overtones of purity, delicacy and feeling of guilt.

terms, in 286 ('Ne mut la semblance de beste'). Only in the last line ('S'il devient hum, bien le verums': 292) is there any explicit mention of the animal-to-man transformation possible through the retrievement of the clothing. And there, the desired outcome is foretold, in a conditional sentence [103] (as if it were too miraculous to talk about bluntly). It is upon the materialization of this condition that the final part of the retribution will depend. The king had long recognized human traits in Bisclavret, but it remained for the wise man to recognize the true situation. This is emphasized by the fact that, in spite of evidence that the animal has some special relationship to the couple, the king either has to have the whole situation pointed out to him, or, after beginning to suspect the truth, keeps his silence to allow the wise man to confirm the ruler's suspicions.

For the second time, the wise man is obeyed: (293-301)

>   Li reis meïsmes le mena [104]
>   E tuz les hus sur lui ferma.
>   Al chief de piece i est alez, [105]
> 296   Deus baruns ad od lui menez;
>   En la chambrë entrent tut trei.
>   Sur le demeine lit al rei
>   Truevent dormant le chevaler.
> 300   Li reis le curut enbracier,
>   Plus de cent feiz l'acole e baise. [106]

---

[103] At least three times in the narrative Marie could have said 'Maybe the animal will become a man, if he has his clothes': through the wife, in her confession; through the king when he sends for Bisclavret's clothing; finally, when Bisclavret pays to attention whatever to his clothes. When the wise man finally does mention this possibility, it is voiced in such an (apparently) casual tone, as if the possibility had been present all the time.

[104] With the verb *mena* we are reminded of the scene in the forest, although there (165) the king's original intention, evidently, was not to lead the beast to his palace.

[105] The wise man had recommended that the beast be left alone *une grant piece* (291); from the expression *al chef de piece* it appears that he knew that the transformation could not have taken place immediately.

[106] In 300-1 there may be noted not only the fourth instance of running at a given moment (cf. the runs of Bisclavret toward the king, 146; toward the lover, 198; and toward the wife, 233), but also the third instance of an embrace (cf. Bisclavret's embrace of his wife, 37-8; and his embrace of the king, 147-8).

It may be noted that *Bisclavret* is the second (the first is *Guigemar*) of three lays in which a character is revived, or regains consciousness naturally.

The intensity of the king's interest in the entire matter is clear from his decision (although prompted by the wise man's remark) to personally conduct the beast into the royal chambers and to lock all the doors. The shutting of all the doors (as if the beast had been led into a *sanctum sanctorum*) is suggestive of the secrecy and intimacy of the transformation itself. Furthermore, as the king now gives to the animal the esteem he gave to him as a knight, we may recall that the beginning of the lay the knight was characterized as *privez* (19) of his lord.

In this passage dealing with Bisclavret's salvation, the reader is forced (by now he should not be surprised) to imagine the hopes and fears of everyone, especially while they are waiting. At the moment when the king, bringing with him two barons, [107] enters the bed-chamber, [108] the suspense of those who are waiting is at its highest.

Only when the sovereign perceives the baron sleeping upon the royal bed [109] does he lose his impassivity and his regal bearing, running to him and overwhelming him with embraces. [110] It is understandable why Marie says of the king's joyous welcome of the lost knight, "Plus de cent feiz l'acole e baise": his long pent-up emotions are now released.

In the phase *le demeine lit al rei* (298), [111] where royalty is twice suggested as well as intimacy with royalty, the bed must

---

[107] The two barons, who represent the king's household and who are members of Bisclavret's own class as well, accompany the king for at least two reasons: to welcome Bisclavret, and also to witness the solemnity of what the sovereign hoped to see. It may also be that the king is a bit uneasy about going into that bed-chamber alone, and feels the need of human solidarity.

[108] It should be pointed out that Marie does not mention here the unlocking of the doors symbolic of revelation, of discovery.

[109] The baron's recumbent figure, symbolizing death, also anticipates his coming resurrection (which we shall not witness). According to Sabine Baring-Gould, *The Book of Were-wolves* (London, 1865), pp. 47, 72, the transformation from animal to human form is followed by extreme lassitude, the creature needing to take to his bed (sometimes for a sleep of several days).

[110] Although the king's welcome will certainly awaken Bisclavret, the reader is not allowed to see the baron again in a state of consciousness.

[111] This is the third (and final) descriptive reference to concrete objects in our lay. In the expressions *riche present* (230) and *le demeine lit al rei,*

recall the marriage bed. For the king has assumed the role that Bisclavret's wife refused, in that he has given him the understanding of his nature, the courtesy and tenderness which she could not. And note that the lay begins with the intimacy of Bisclavret with the king, and ends (in so far as Bisclavret is concerned) with the king's tender embraces. In the presentation of the two men's relationship, there has been a movement from the abstract to the concrete, to the more immediate. The king has loved Bisclavret as a man, as an animal, and then, as a man again. As such, Bisclavret's story has the structure of an *aria da capo*.

Since Marie tells us nothing more about Bisclavret, what are we to believe about his future behavior? Did he go back to being a werewolf once again? It is also possible that, by Bisclavret's act of leaving the mark of the beast upon his wife, he is freed from his curse (perhaps visited upon him by one of his ancestors) which he has thus transmitted to her, and which, in the external manifestation of noselessness, she in turn transmits to successive generations of female progeny. I think we can be sure that his story will not repeat itself, not his year-long condemnation to that bestial life with apparently no hope for recovery of his human form.

The king metes out reward and punishment: (302-14) [112]

>   Si tost cum il pot aver aise,
>   Tute sa tere li rendi;
> 304   Plus li duna ke jeo ne di.

---

neither adjective is meant to aid in visualization, but is only suggestive of value, tone and atmosphere.

In this lay, the few concrete objects that are mentioned are described in such a way as not to invite visualization, not in a sensuous way. There is, in the narrative, no sensuous description whatever of any place in the interior or the out-of-doors. The lack of visualizable physical description of the characters, the absence of sensuous description of concrete objets, and the lack of precise décor serve to focus our attention upon the actions, gestures and speech of the personages. (In a way, this reminds me of a technique in the contemporary French theatre, where the stage is bare, the backdrop only vaguely indicated, the actors' clothing the simplest.)

[112] Once again the kings in *Equitan* and *Bisclavret* may be contrasted. In *Equitan*, where we are told immediately at the beginning that the king dispenses justice, he not only does not do so, but hands over his duties to his seneschal whenever he, the king, feels like hunting or wenching.

> La femme ad del païs ostee
> E chacie de la cuntree.
> Cil s'en alat ensemble od li,
> 308 Pur ki sun seignur ot trahi.
> Enfanz en ad asés eüz, [113]
> Puis unt esté bien cuneüz
> [E] del semblant e del visage:
> 312 Plusurs [des] femmes del lignage,
> C'est verité, senz nes sunt nees
> E si viveient esnasees.

Before we are allowed to see the baron rise from his bed, Marie now shifts to narrative summary, with *Tute sa tere li rendi* (a lengthy legal action); we learn that Bisclavret is restored to the same feudal state as he was at the beginning of his story. In fact, he is given even more than before. The expansive words "Plus li duna ke jeo ne di" [114] are a reminder of the lavishness of line 301 which described the king's embrace and which closed the final staged scene.

The last time we see the shadowy forms of the wife and her lover, her predominance is insisted upon once again. In 305-6 [115] where she is the object of the king's action, [116] her exile is twice predicated. The lover, who had served as her tool (*Pur ki sun seignur ot trahi:* 308) is presented as merely following her, to share in *her* banishment.

Why does Marie choose banishment as the punishment for the guilty pair of lovers? One reason could be that they had

---

[113] Just as the preceding lay in ms. H. *(Le Fresne)* opened with the birth of children (first twin sons, followed shortly by the birth of twin daughters), so does Bisclavret close with the birth of children (whose sex at first is not specified), followed by information pertaining to female offspring.

[114] Marie's interpolation is enigmatic. Is she simply being humorous (for she has not even told us what the king gave), or does she wish to imply something else?

[115] Among the types of punishment for adultery listed by Stith Thompson, *Motif-Index of Folk Literature* (6 vols.; rev. and enlarged ed.; Bloomington: 1955-1958), are the cutting-off of the nose, and banishment (V (1957), 231 and 227); banishment is also mentioned as a punishment for treachery (V (1957), 226).

[116] The use of the verb *chacier* may recall to the reader that earlier scene in the forest when the king had ordered the dogs driven away from Bisclavret.

sought to banish, with much more horrible consequences, the husband. Thus, just as in *Equitan,* where also the wife betrays her good husband with a lover and seeks to rid herself of him, the guilty pair would be made to suffer a fate similar to the one they had intended for her husband. [117]

---

[117] As to the fate suffered only by the wife, the similarity of her punishment by Bisclavret who marks her as a beast, and her crime committed against him, has already been pointed out.

There may well have been another reason for Marie's choice of punishment. In English medieval law the wolf was associated with the ceremony of outlawry. The sentence passed upon the outlaw contained the formula 'let him bear (he wears) the head of a wolf'; it is found in the laws of Canute (7, 3): "Lupinum enim gerit caput quod anglice *wulfes heâfod dicitur*"), and continues in use in the thirteenth century. — See Smith, *op. cit.,* pp. 26-7; Frederick Pollock and Frederic W. Maitland, *The History of English Law before the time of Edward I* (2nd. ed., Cambridge, England, 1898), I, 476.

It is true that banishment and outlawry represent different procedures. There is, however, enough in common between them to have suggested to Marie as penalty for the guilty pair who had sought to make a wolf forever of Bisclavret, a punishment similar, at least, to that which confers the status of a wolf on the condemned man. And indeed Marie's use of the verb *chacier* in 306 describing the king's punitive action might faintly recall the form of sentence quoted by Baring-Gould, *op. cit.,* p. 49): "he [the outlaw] shall be driven away as a wolf, and chased so far as men chase wolves farthest."

It would seem that, by the time of Marie, the two penalties were almost indistinguishable. Cf. André Réville, "L'Abjuratio Regni,' Histoire d'une institution anglaise," *Revue Historique,* 1892 (50), 1-42, who says:

> Où pouvait vivre l'*outlaw*? Pour échapper à la mort, il devait se soustraire aux regards de ses compatriotes, se réfugier au sein des forêts ou en des régions marécageuses et inhabitées. Déjà c'était, sous une forme déguisée, le bannissement, l'expulsion hors du cercle des vivants. Mais en autre il arriva peu à peu, à mesure que les conquérants saxons et danois se fixèrent à demeure sur le sol anglais et s'y multiplièrent, que les forêts furent entamées, défrichées ou sillonnées de sentiers, les marécages lentement desséchés; alors, pour vivre, l'*outlaw* dut fuir dans les royaumes voisins. Ainsi la mise hors la loi fut fatalement doublée de l'exil. Cette transformation logique se manifeste clairement dans les textes eux-mêmes. Être un *outlaw,* au temps d'Edgar, c'est être exilé; rentrer en grâce, c'est revenir dans la patrie: "Sit utlaga, id est exul vel exlex, nisi rex ei patriam concedat." Dans les lois d'Aethelred, dans celles de Canut, les mots d'*utlah* et de *forisbannitus* paraissent concurremment, dans les mêmes textes et avec le même sens. Enfin Canut ordonnait formellement de quitter le pays à tous ceux qui avaient subi cette condamnation: "Praecipimus ut... apostatae et utlagae Dei et hominum patriam exeant, si non resipuerint et digne poeniteant." Entre la peine de

Now we learn that the disfigurement inflicted by the beast is not limited to the wife alone; [118] it is transmitted to some of the couple's female offspring; thus the children themselves will be a punishment of the wife. [119] We may, then, discern three stages in the wife's punishment: first, the ripping off of her nose; next, the expulsion from the kingdom; and then, for good measure, the noseless children. [120] From the use of *plusurs* and *del lignage,* we have the feeling that this punishment will go on for countless generations. [121]

In the brief space of the thirteen lines of this section, Marie has moved very far ahead in time, from the given moment of the king's embrace [122] which ends the story of Bisclavret, to

---

l'abjuration, qui entraînait l'exil perpétuel, la mort civile, la confiscation des biens, et la mise hors la loi qui, au temps des Anglo-Saxons, produisait tous les mêmes effets, il y avait, on l'avouera, de singulières analogies. (p. 7)

[118] Why should Marie tell us (in 309) that it was the wife who had children (and not the couple)? Somehow, we are reminded of the expulsion of Adam and Eve from Paradise, after which she is to bear children in pain. And why should the couple wait to have children? Is it because the wife has to have the mark of the beast upon her before her motherhood could become a curse?

[119] Note the couplet 313-14 devoted to stressing the veracity of Marie's account of this most unlikely curse.

[120] That the wife's punishment is three-fold, in contrast to that of the lover, may be due not only to the fact that, in the act of treachery committed against Bisclavret, her guilt was by far the greater — but also because her sin may have been three-fold, if we were right in condemning her for her heartless reaction to Bisclavret's confession, and right in suspecting that it was her lack of understanding that drove him periodically into the forest.

[121] Why is the wife's noseless condition passed on only to her female progeny? Is Marie suggesting that the wife's was a particularly female sin?

[122] Perhaps now we may point to the rather delicate atmosphere of the king's caress while Bisclavret is lying sleeping upon the king's bed. Was Bisclavret's fatal flaw, after all, one of homosexuality? For this is the only lay where we see two men embrace. And we may remember that Bisclavret slept "close to the king." (Also, could the phrase 'to devour men', used in the Prologue, v. 11, hint at such a relationship?)

Yet if it were such a terrible thing to be a homosexual (and Marie would surely condemn it), then why does Marie not have the king become a werewolf, too?

A very interesting verbal similarity between the reference to Bisclavret's animal body and Dante's depiction of the sodomites in the *Inferno* (Canto XVI) has been pointed out to me by Professor Mark Musa.

the timeless repetition of the curse upon the wife's female descendants. With the final word of the narrative *(esnasees)*, there is a graphic suggestion of noseless women, generation after generation. Nor have we moved ahead only in time; we have also moved away in space, from the staged scene in the king's royal chamber within a human dwelling to beyond the confines of the realm away from any human habitation or human being, to nowhere.

In the Epilogue, Marie insists upon the veracity of the entire *aventure:* (315-18)

> L'aventure ke avez oïe
> 316 Veraie fu, n'en dutez mie.
> De Bisclavret fu fet li lais
> Pur remembrance a tutdis mais.

The opening couplet echoes Marie's assertion in the closing couplet of the preceding passage: what we have heard is true. The final couplet, with the phrase "Pur remembrance" thematically parallels the opening couplet in the Prologue ("Quant de lais faire m'entremet, / Ne voil ublïer Bisclavret"). What Marie wished not to forget others must remember forever. With this double affirmation of the purpose of remembrance, the 'memory-frame' of the lay is formed.

We have already heard the lady ask her husband "S'il se despuille u vet vestu," and heard his courteous reply, "'Dame,' fet il, 'jeo vois tut nu'" (69-70). The three shades whom Dante meets (in Canto XVI) have already been described as "nudi" (v. 22); their naked condition is stressed, when we hear Jacopo Rusticucci talk (in v. 35) of the second member of the group of three as he who "'Tutto che nudo e dipelato vada'."

LES DEUS AMANZ

Les Deus Amanz, one of Marie's shorter lays (244 verses), represents a departure from her usual tri-partite narrative structure. The bi-partite form of this lay, introduced by a Prologue of six lines and concluding with an Epilogue of four, is, moreover, assymetrical: its first section of 42 verses is followed by a second of almost five times its length.

In the first narrative division (7-48), a widower-king, comforted in his loss by his daughter, devises a situation to keep her to himself. In the second part (49-240),[1] a youth at the court falls in love with the princess. Advised by her, he prepares for the test which all her suitors must undergo. The boy successfully fulfills the conditions, but his lack of moderation brings about his tragic death. The damsel, her heart touched by grief, dies almost immediately thereafter. On the mountain-top where they died, the two children are buried.

In the Prologue the story of two children of which the Bretons made a lay is summarized: (1-6)

>   Jadis avint en Normendie
>   Une aventure mut oïe
>   De deus enfanz que s'entr'amerent;
> 4 Par amur ambedeus finerent.[2]

---

[1] This much longer second part (the love of the two protagonists and its consequences) could be broken down into three sections: 49-120, the coming of the youth; 121-66, the preparations followed by the boy and the girl for the test; 167-240, the test and its consequences.

[2] The striking rhyme *s'entr'amerent / finerent* in lines 3-4 is surely intended to recall to the reader a couplet in *Equitan* (*Bien les tiendrent*,

Un lai en firent li Bretun:
De Deus Amanz recuilt le nun.

In this Prologue, the only one in which Marie's auctorial voice is absent, the very first sentence (1-4) briefly states the entire story we are to hear. [3]

The expression *deus enfanz* in line 3 (and again in 10) is surely meant to stress the innocence and youth of the protagonists. In 3-4, the juxtaposition of *enfanz* with the phrase *par amur* is notable: one does not normally associate the adult emotion of love with innocent children. Furthermore, one does not expect children to die.

On the high mountain in Normandy the two children lie: (7-20)

>   Verité est kë en Neustrie,
>   8 Que nus apelum Normendie,
>   Ad un haut munt merveilles grant:
>   La sus gisent li dui enfant. [4]
>   Pres de cel munt a une part
>   12 Par grant cunseil e par esgart
>   Une cité fist faire uns reis
>   Quë esteit sire de Pistreis;
>   Des Pistreins la fist [il] numer
>   16 E Pistre la fist apeler.
>   Tuz jurs ad puis duré li nuns;
>   Uncore i ad vile e maisuns.

---

mut s'entr'amerent; / Puis en mururent e finerent: 183-4). Between these two a parallel may be drawn, significant for the contrast as well as for the similarity offered.

On the one hand, the pairs of protagonists in these two lays are diametrically opposite in character (the lecherous king and his possessive, sensual mistress in *Equitan*, the innocent, unawakened youth and the princess in *Les Deus Amanz*); on the other, the youth in *Les Deus Amanz* is as guilty of *desmesure* as are the lovers in *Equitan*.

[3] Still another parallel between *Les Deus Amanz* and *Equitan* may be noted. These are the only two of Marie's lays in whose Prologue she refrains from stating her intention to tell a certain story; she gently slips into the tale.

[4] *Les Deus Amanz* is the first of four lays (*Yonec*, *Laüstic*, and *Eliduc*) where a tomb (or variant thereof) will be specifically mentioned. The presence of a tomb is suggested here at the beginning of the story; at the end, we see it constructed.

> Nus savum bien de la contree,
> 20   Li vals de Pistrë est nomee. [5]

Not only in the Prologue, but here in the opening lines (7-10) of the narrative Marie tells of the end of the story, thus allowing the very beginning of the tale to echo its prologue. This is the only time that Marie has used the procedure of fusing prologue with narrative.

In these opening lines, moreover, not only does Marie tell the reader (in the present tense, line 10) that the two children are really dead, she even points to the place where they are. They (and the reader, too) are going to go up that high mountain where they are lying, somehow, already dead. Thus, even before any narration ever occurs in this lay where so great an emphasis is given to topography, it is extremely meaningful that this place is immediately mentioned. The mountain that casts its shadow over the whole lay will become the locus of the most significant events in the narrative.

In line 11, Marie gently starts to shift to the past where she remains only through 16. It is true that whenever one speaks of the foundation of a city and its naming,[6] there is a suggestion of remoteness. The reader has already been prepared for the touch of antiquity by *jadis* in line 1, and *Neustrie*[7] in line 7. Because of the shift to the preterite tense (13), it sounds as though the king had built that city (and what a fine city it must have been, built *par grant cunseil e par esgart*)[8] beside the mountain with the two children already lying there in their grave. And

---

[5] Marie's mention of the valley is apparently superfluous (there is always a valley where there is a mountain!). But perhaps she alludes to it now by way of anticipating its later function as a sort of stage-setting.

[6] The naming of the city, as given by Marie in 15-16, is obviously false, given the simplex *Pistre*, and the derivative *Pistreis*; it is basically the same device as that of 'eponymous hero'.

[7] For a discussion of Marie's concern with archaisms in the lays as a whole, see Ernest Hoepffner, "La géographie et l'histoire dans les Lais de Marie de France," *Romania*, LVI (1930), 1-32, and for *Les Deus Amanz* in particular, 5-6.

[8] In line 12, there is the first of the many frequent uses of *cunseil*, used here in the sense of 'thought,' 'reflection,' 'plan.' Throughout the entire lay there will be very great stress on giving counsel and seeking advice.

does Marie have the city built to afford a contrast between nature and man's creation?

In 17-20 where is a shift back to the present, Marie's tone is that of 'I'm telling you the truth; you can see the city and its houses for yourself in Normandy.' [9] And now that the background has been given, the story itself may begin.

The widowed king is comforted by his daugter: (21-26)

> Li reis ot one fille bele [10]
> [E] mut curteise dameisele. [11]
> Cunfortez fu par la meschine, [12]
> 24 Puis que perdue ot la reïne.
> Plusurs a mal li aturnerent, [13]
> Li suen meïsme le blamerent.

Beginning at 21 (where there is again a shift to the past, but only to the "past" of the story) the situation concerning the king and his daughter is introduced. Because of the way the daughter (mentioned together with her father in both 21 and 23) is brought into the narrative, she could theoretically be a new character, and not necessarily one of the two lovers already mentioned.

The affection between the king and his daughter (although we shall never know whether the perversion of a normal father-daughter relationship ever went as far as incest) has become a scandal.

---

[9] This is somewhat reminiscent of a passage in *Le Fresne* where Marie intervenes in her auctorial competence to assure the reader that an abbey already mentioned really did exist, complete with abbess and nuns.

[10] Is the king in 13 the same as in 21? Normally, we would expect this to be so, given the normal shift from the use of the indefinite article (*a* king, 13) to the definite (*the* king, 21). But perhaps not: perhaps the shift to the past involved centuries.

[11] In the description of the daughter, no physical details are given; she is presented as *bele e curteise,* as vague a description as could be offered. Yet these qualities (one physical, the other spiritual) which now seem so weightless will increase in significance as the tale progresses.

[12] Note that it is the daughter who initiates the relationship.

[13] The pronoun *plusurs* is the first of many references to crowds or masses of people which will so impress the reader because of the limited number of individual characters (of whom there will be four, one of whom the reader will not see).

In juxtaposition to *plusurs* (a vague people who are in some kind of contact with the king) is *li suen* (the king's own servants, perhaps even his vassals). Do the latter reprove him merely because he does not try hard to marry off his daughter?[14] Or do they suspect something else?

We learn of the king's double response to the reproach: (27-48)

      Quant il oï que hum en parla,
28 Mut fu dolent, mut li pesa;
      Cumença sei a purpenser
      Cument s'en purrat delivrer
      Que nul sa fille ne quesist.[15]
32 [E] luinz e pres manda e dist:[16]
      Ki sa fille vodreit aveir,
      Une chose seüst de veir:
      Sortit esteit e destiné,
36 Desur le munt fors la cité[17]
      Entre ses braz la portereit,[18]
      Si que ne se reposereit.
      Quant la nuvelë est seüe
40 E par la cuntree espandue,
      Asez plusurs s'i asaierent,[19]
      Que nule rien n'i espleiterent.
      Teus [i ot] que tant s'esforçouent
44 Quë en mi le munt la portoënt;

---

[14] This interpretation is offered by Ewert, p. 178, n. 25.

[15] Yet the applicants *will* ask for his daughter in marriage.

[16] With *luinz e pres*, we find the first instance of many of the 'far and near' motifs. Each recurrence is in relation to public opinion which is so important in this story.

[17] Note that whereas in 11-13 the city was secondary to the mountain, now the mountain is presented merely as a point outside the city.

[18] Surely it is not unimportant that in the king's plan, the suitor is to carry the princess *entre ses braz*. In OF as well as in ModF, the expression has the same connotation of the sexual. The use of this phrase (of which this is the first example of five) is particularly appropriate in a lay where will be an awakening of sexuality.

[19] Where the throngs (*asez plusurs*) come from we do not know, but there are many references to 'far and near,' 'throughout the country' (e.g., *par la cuntree*, 40) in the story. There is some connection between the blurry crowds and the blurry references to 'far and near.'

There is no lay with a fewer number of characters than *Les Deus Amanz*. It may well be that the indefinite mass of indefinite people is intended as a contrast to the three characters who come on stage.

> Ne poeient avant aler,
> Iloec l'esteut laissier ester.
> Lung tens remist cele a doner,
> 48 Que nul ne la volt demander.

Is the king unhappy because people are talking, or at the idea that he should be deprived of his daugther? In his desire to keep her for himself, the king is surely anti-nature.[20]

In 35-8, the king's decision [21] is doubly remarkable. Although it is a step taken because of the advice of his courtiers, would it really satisfy them? Just as in *Le Fresne* (where a character also acts in response to the urging of others), we will not hear any more about the courtiers' reaction to the king's behavior. It is as if the king's people were there simply to start up the movement in the story.

Secondly, the scheme announced by the king has something fatalistic about it; it is as if the king himself were speaking for the gods. This is noted in the unusual language of 35, *Sortit esteit e destiné,* [22] preceding the summary of his plan.

The king's challenge attracts many applicants (41-2). And this is rather like a fairy-tale: [23] as though because there was a proclamation, there would be applicants to try their luck. As the king's plan is carried out, we forget about his daughter for a while. She has been de-personalized to a 'thing,' a burden to be carried up a hill. This de-personalization is stressed by the lack of information about the girl's feelings as each suitor, holding her in his arms, tried his luck.

---

[20] Perhaps the king has also thwarted natural instincts on the part of his daughter (i.e., her ability to love someone else). It may be that he has become emotionally dependent on her, and that he has made her (to a certain degree) emotionally dependent on him.

[21] The king's test has some resemblance to a combat, except that the suitor has to compete not with a supernatural adversary so often noted in the fairy-story (cf. Stith Thompson, *The Folktale* (New York, 1946), p. 24), but with a force of nature.

[22] His decision reminds us somewhat of the OF epic oath that boomerangs. For what was invented by the king to preserve the present situation will, of course, destroy it.

[23] Here, at the beginning of *Les Deus Amanz,* just as at the end of *Le Fresne,* Marie's narrative technique is reminiscent of that of the fairy-story.

Although some of the applicants are successful in arriving half-way up the mountain, [24] in line 46 there is a let-down *(Ileoc l'esteut laissier ester).* [25] This means that, sooner or later, each suitor must stop trying to carry out the conditions of the test decreed by the king. While this let-down is taking place, there is evidently a return to the original situation: the king is being comforted by his daughter.

The change of tempo indicated in 46 continues in 47-8: the situation, now at a stalemate, goes on for a long time. This exemplifies Marie's tendency to pass over a period of time, saying 'nothing new happened' (whether it means a relapse to the previous situation or not). This detail within the narrative gives the reader a chance to catch his breath. Yet this pause for us to rest also warns that something is going to happen. This temporal detail of Marie's narrative art is significant in two repects: it is the way she works ahead to the dénouement, and it represents a kind of manipulation of time, a sort of *slow* versus *quick* rhythm.

It is remarkable that in the space of so few lines (7-48), there is a reference to the present time of the reader (10) which involves the end of the lay (that is, the future), plus the preparation for the opening situation, plus the opening situation (which begins at 21), plus the new situation which the king decreed *(sortit e destiné,* 35), plus a relapse to the present situation (the king being comforted by his daughter), [26] and perhaps the overlapping of the second great narrative division (the presence of the youth at court). [27] In no other lay in so brief a space is there such a compression of situations, or such a curious blending of time-levels. Of

---

[24] The mountain, an impersonal force of nature, has, in a way, become the ally of the king.

[25] The wording used in the reference to the "let-down" in this lay is somewhat reminiscent of *Bisclavret,* 132 *(Si lur estuit lesser ester),* with the very significant difference that in *Bisclavret* there is no return to the original situation presented at the beginning of the story.

[26] Thus the present situation, like the second great section of the story, is seen to contain three parts.

[27] The youth may have been there at the court as early as 39, although Marie does not introduce him into the story until 49. Because the present situation falls into three parts (which may be designated ABA'), that facilitates the overlapping of the second really new part (beginning at 49 with the youth) which is like B'.

all of Marie's lays, this is the only one in which the present situation has a twist or gimmick (the king's proclamation).

A youth falls in love with the princess: (49-62)

> Al païs ot un damisel, [28]
> Fiz a un cunte, gent e bel; [29]
> De bien faire pur aveir pris
> 52 Sur tuz autres s'est entremis.
> En la curt le rei conversot,
> Asez sovent i surjurnot;
> [E] la fillë al rei ama,
> 56 E meintefeiz l'areisuna
> Que ele s'amur li otriast
> E par drüerie l'amast.
> Pur ceo ke pruz fu e curteis [30]
> 60 E que mut le presot li reis,
> [Li otria sa drüerie, [31]
> E cil humblement l'en mercie.]

At line 49, with the appearance of a new character, *un damisel* (note the casualness of Marie's tone as she introduces him, 'In the country there was a youth'), we are getting ready for the action to start of the second great division of the lay.

After one line where both the youth's social condition and his general physical appearance are given, [32] two verses (51-2) are devoted to his character. He is ambitious; he wants to be the best and the first. (And it will be his desire to succeed that will cause his death.)

Following two references in 54-5 to the boy's habitual propinquity, we are told that he falls in love with the king's daughter

---

[28] Because of the emphasis that will be placed upon youth (and innocence), it is meaningful that Marie uses only substantives denoting a young man *(damisel, danzeus, vallez)* to name the character who will become the second of the two lovers. And here in 49, *li damisel* indicates the protagonist's youthfulness, and his noble blood.

[29] A parallel with *Lanval* may be noted, for in both lays the father of the protagonist (in *Lanval*, a king, here in *Les Deus Amanz*, a count) is mentioned incidentally, in order to give the son a social rank.

[30] Like the maiden, the youth too is 'courteous.'

[31] With this pair of lovers, we have the third instance (cf. *Le Fresne* and *Lanval*) where both lovers are unmarried.

[32] The boy's description *(gent e bel)* is as vague as was that of the princess *(bele e curteise)* at the beginning.

(although we do not know when). Marie seems to be telling us that he would have loved anybody; he was there at the court, and so was she.[33] As for why she loved him, it is both because of propinquity (he was *pruz e curteis*, not too meaningful a description), and because of her father's approval of the boy.[34] Moreover, although we are told that he loved her (in 55), never once will we be told explicitly that she loved him.

Although the youth's conversations with the princess are mentioned in the present section (and several times later), we are unable to visualize the young people together: we do not know where they are. Their conversations are unstaged, with one notable exception. The bareness of staging in this lay reminds us not only of *Equitan* (indeed, *Les Deus Amanz* may be even barer than *Equitan*), but the unstaged conversations recall the unstaged conversation (although the basic situation is so different!) of the husband and wife at the opening of *Bisclavret*.

It is a nice touch than when the girl grants the boy her *drüerie*,[35] he thanks her humbly:[36] he is so *curteis*! (And we recall his desire to succeed, to be the first.)

The boy and the girl are prudent in their love: (63-71)

> Ensemble parlerent sovent
> 64 E s'entr'amerent lëaument [37]
> E celerent a lur poeir,

---

[33] It may also be that he falls in love with the princess because he wants to be the first, and she is the very best.

[34] Still another parallel may be drawn between this lay and *Laüstic*. In both narratives, the female protagonist falls in love for two reasons. Whenever Marie offers two reasons why someone falls in love, the reader will suspect that the love is not too deep.

[35] *Drüerie*, used for the first time in the boy's request in 58, and now again in the girl's assent in 61, does not necessarily refer to physical consumation. Indeed, a range of meanings is possible; the word, according to Tobler-Lommatzsch, can signify 'diversion,' 'amusement'; 'friendship'; 'love' and 'illicit love'; and finally, 'love-token.' *Drüerie*, used in this lay where the reader will feel that there is no physical consummation, will be used again in *Eliduc*, 575-80, where there is definitely no consummation of love.

[36] The youth's expression of gratitude for her love reminds the reader of the empty lover in *Bisclavret*, who too thanked the lady.

[37] Note the repetition of the *s'entr'amerent* of the Prologue.

> Que hum nes puïst aparceveir.
> La suffrance mut lur greva;
> 68 Mes li vallez se purpensa [38]
> Que meuz en volt les maus suffrir
> Que trop haster e dunc faillir.
> Mut fu pur li amer destreiz.

We are given such a minimal description of their loving each other! We do not feel them, as lovers, to be individuals: [39] both negatively, in that Marie does not talk about their inner feelings, and positively, for Marie uses joint predications to summarize their love-relationship.

The plurality indicated by the joint predications in 63-5 is suggested in 67 by the pronoun *lur* [40] and in 68 by *nes*, after which there is a shift, for three lines (68-9 and 71), to singular verbs whose subject is the boy.

That the youth's decision to hold back (in 68-70) is framed by a reference to grief, in 67 *(La suffrance mut lur greva)* and in 71 *(Mut fu pur li amer destreiz)* is striking; it is as if that alternation were what was going on in his mind. As for *destreiz*, it is surely not the average word for 'sad.' Given the background of tightness, one justifiably thinks of the connotation of being hard-pressed, of psychological strain. [41]

---

[38] Marie's designation of the protagonist as *li vallez* is conspicuous; not only does this term emphasize his youth, but more importantly, it clearly indicates what he was doing at the king's court. (Cf. *FEW*, for the entry "*vassellitus junger edelmann*," with two meanings for the substantive: "Fr. vaslet, valet, vallet, jeune gentilhomme non encore armé chevalier," and "jeune noble placé en service auprès d'un seigneur pour faire une sorte d'apprentissage de chevalerie."

[39] Not only are the boy and the girl not individualized as lovers, they have been characterized (and they will be later) by the use of the very same adjectives.

[40] It is interesting that Marie should say *La suffrance mut lur greva*, for usually love's suffering is depicted for just one person at a time.

The meanings given for *suffrance* by Godefroy, as 'action de supporter, souffrir'; 'patience, humilité'; may well confirm the additional idea of *continence* for line 67.

[41] The suggestion of strain in 71 is repeated later, but with a difference, in 164, where, with the use of the very same verb *(Mut se destreint...)* we are told of the girl's physical strain.

In his practicality, even cautiousness,[42] of what precipitous act on his part ("…. trop haster e dunc faillir") could he be fearing? Could he be already thinking of the girl's running away with him? Yet it would be very rash to run away with the king's daughter: he could be found, and perhaps killed.

The boy proposes a plan to his sweetheart: (72-83)

> 72 Puis avient si que a une feiz
> Que a s'amie vient li danzeus,
> Que tant est sages, pruz e beus;
> Sa pleinte li mustrat e dist:
> 76 Anguissusement li requist [43]
> Que s'en alast ensemble od lui,
> Ne poeit mes suffrir l'enui;
> S'a sun pere la demandot,
> 80 Il saveit bien que tant l'amot
> Que pas ne li vodreit doner,
> Si il ne la puïst porter
> Entre ses braz en sum le munt.

The action of the lovers' story really begins at 72, as the youth, at the breaking point, goes to talk with the girl.

It is a nice detail that this one time, when he comes to suggest so rash a plan, Marie describes him, in a relative clause, as *sages, pruz e beus* (74). Of the attributes enumerated, at least *sages* (never used before of the boy) is ironic.

In his speech,[44] the youth impetuously abandons his decision announced earlier in 68-70. The forward movement of his ambition and impulsiveness can no longer be held in check; indeed, his holding back is a kind of torture for him *(Ne poeit mes suffrir l'enui)*.[45] His impatience is stressed more than his prudence. It is as though he were impatient for the machinery of the story to be set into motion (and we know that the two lovers are already together at the top of the mountain!).

---

[42] But lines 69-70 *(Que meuz en volt les maus suffrir / Que trop haster e dunc faillir)* where incidentally, the *suffrance* of 67 is picked up, anticipate what the boy will finally do, in spite of his desire to be cautious.

[43] With *anguissusement*, there is another suggestion of restraint and force.

[44] With just one striking exception, all the boy's speeches are reported in indirect address.

[45] This line is the third reference to the boy's suffering.

The princess rejects the boy's idea, offering a plan of her own: (84-116)

```
84   La damisele li respunt:
     'Amis,' fait ele, 'jeo sai bien,
     Ne m'i porterïez pur rien: ⁴⁶
     N'estes mie si vertuus.
88   Si jo m'en vois ensemble od vus,
     Mis pere avreit e doel e ire,
     Ne vivreit mie sanz martire, ⁴⁷
     Certes, tant l'eim e si l'ai chier,
92   Jeo nel vodreie curucier.
     Autre cunseil vus estuet prendre, ⁴⁸
     Kar cest ne voil jeo pas entendre.
     En Salerne ai une parente,
96   Riche femme, mut ad grant rente;
     Plus de trente anz i ad esté.
     L'art de phisike ad tant usé
     Que mut est saives de mescines:
100  Tant cunust herbes e racines,
     Si vus a li volez aler
     E mes lettres od vus porter
     E mustrer li vostre aventure,
104  Ele en prendra cunseil e cure;
     Teus lettuaires vus durat
     E teus beivres vus baillerat
     Que tut vus recunforterunt
108  E bone vertu vus durrunt.
     Quant en cest païs revendrez,
     A mun pere me requerez;
     Il vus en tendrat pur enfant,
```

---

[46] Although this line is but a partial summary of the father's conditions, yet it is the third time that they are mentioned.

[47] Whereas the youth had referred to his own suffering (*l'enui*) in 78, the girl refers to her father's. Does the noun *martire* suggest *Liebesqual* (one of the meanings given by Tobler-Lommatzsch)? It may be that Marie has used this word deliberately, with its amatory sense suggesting to the reader that the father is the lover of the girl. Then, in the following line (91), Marie has the girl declare 'I love him so much.'

Note that the girl's declaration "I love him so much" compliments the boy's statement in 80 concerning the father's love for his daughter ('... he loved her so much').

[48] This is the second instance of the word *cunseil*, which will appear many times in the lay.

112 Si vus dirat le cuvenant
Que a nul humme ne me durrat,
Ja cele peine n'il mettrat,
S'al munt ne me peüst porter
116 Entre ses braz sanz resposer.'

Although we really have known nothing of the girl up to now, she suddenly opens up in her long answer to the boy. Her lengthy speech of 32 lines has two parts: the rejection of her lover's suggestion (85-94), and her counter-proposal which may be divided into the instructions concerning his journey (95-108), and what he is to do upon his return (109-116). We may wonder at the order in which the girl answers him; one would think that she would reply first to his proposal of elopement. But instead, she begins by agreeing (in 85-7) with what the boy takes for granted: that he (who wants to be the first and the best) could not successfully perform the test!

At what precise moment did she think of the *autre cunseil?* From 93-4, it seems that the horror of his suggestion has forced her to think of something else. But why does she wait until the boy proposes his plan to tell him (beginning only at 95) of her *parente* and of her powers which she knows about? [49] Why does she wait until she sees he really is at the breaking-point? [50]

Perhaps her delay in giving the boy such helpful information is due to her enjoyment of the best of two possible worlds: although the attentions of a suitor please her, so does the warm,

---

[49] It is curious that the girl herself does not speak of her relative as an aunt, but calls her only *une parente*. *Les Deus Amanz* is the second of four lays (*Le Fresne, Yonec,* and *Milun*) in which there is an aunt, real or supposed. In three lays the aunt is helpful to her niece or nephew.

[50] If it is true that the girl mentions her relative and thinks of sending the boy there because she feels he is at the breaking-point, it may also be that for the same reason she gave into his frequent requests and granted him her love.

It is probable that if the girl sees someone in a terrible plight, needing her, she gives in. She is, therefore, not as cold an individual as we had first thought her to be. Her rôle seems to be that of a mother to men: first, as a comfort to her father, then, with her assistance to the lad to prepare for the test.

demanding affection of her father.[51] For we recall that she fell in love partly because of her father's approval of the boy. We surely do not feel the love of these two young people very deeply; there is no real passion, no real warmth of emotion.

The passage (98-108) in which the girl proposes seeking her relative's assistance is so much longer than necessary.[52] Surely the way she talks in such detail about her aunt is calculated to impress the boy, and to inspire his confidence in the latter's professional expertise. And when she says of her, *Ele en prendra cunseil e cure,*[53] it is as if all the preparations for the youth's *aventure* can not possibly fail.

In her closing words (109-116), not only does the princess predict her father's inevitable attitude toward her suitor when he will have returned (*Il vus en tendrat pur enfant,* 111), she also repeats in detail the conditions of the test (112-116).[54] Suddenly the reader realizes that this is the fourth time that the king's proclamation is formulated. It may well be that Marie deliberately creates the girl's prolixity so that the narrative device of its reiteration is not so immediately obvious. The artistic purpose of the constant reiteration of the father's decree in so short a lay must be to emphasize the important influence of public opinion, which, of course, obliged the king to make his decision.

The youth accepts the girl's plan: (117-21)

---

[51] The girl's words in 88-92 may also exemplify her *curteisie,* i.e., she is simply being considerate of her father's feelings. (Yet it may be argued that she could have been considerate of her lover's feelings before now.)

[52] This is the first of three instances (cf. *Yonec* and *Milun*) where a lover will give his or her sweetheart lengthy, detailed instructions. This is the only case, however, where the lover is needlessly loquacious.

[53] Although *prendre cunseil* is a fixed expression, no example other than this line from *Les Deus Amanz* is cited in Tobler-Lommatzsch for the phrase *prendre cunseil e cure.* Could it be that Marie herself has coined this expression (as she has done, for example, in the case of some *s'entr'* verbs)?

[54] Instead of having the girl tell her lover 'when you come back, you will be able to carry me up the mountain,' it is clever that Marie makes her say 'when you come back, my father will tell you that you won't succeed.' For of course the king will not know of the youth's stay in Salerno. Thus, Marie can then have the girl (just as the boy did earlier) summarize the king's decision.

>   Li vallez oï la novele
>   E le cunseil a la pucele; [55]
>   Mut en fu liez, si l'en mercie;
> 120 Cungé demandë a s'amie,
>   En sa cuntree en est alez.

At first reading the summary in 117-18 seems unnecessary, but perhaps it serves to bring the lad back into the story, reminding us that there really was a listener to that flow of words.

Only after the boy has heard the girl tell him of a plan whereby the success of his undertaking appears completely certain, does Marie tell us of any happiness on his part. And it is an effective detail that Marie predicates in the same verse both his happiness and his gratitude toward the girl: as once before, he does not forget to be polite!

The boy goes to Salerno: (122-45)

>   Hastivement s'est aturnez [56]
>   De riche[s] dras e de deniers,
> 124 De palefreiz e de sumers;
>   De ses hummes les plus privez
>   Ad li danzeus od sei menez.
>   A Salerne vait surjurner,
> 128 A l'aunte s'amie parler. [57]
>   De sa part li dunat un brief.
>   Quant el l'ot lit de chief en chief,
>   Ensemble od li l'a retenu
> 132 Tant que sun estre ad tut seü.
>   Par mescines l'ad esforcié,
>   Un tel beivre li ad baillié,
>   Ja ne serat tant travaillez
> 136 Ne si ateint ne si chargiez,
>   Ne li resfreschist tut le cors,
>   Neïs les vaines ne les os,
>   E qu'il nen ait tute vertu,

---

[55] The noun *pucele* (the first of two instances in the narrative) must be intended to remind the reader that theirs is a chaste relationship.

[56] This line, the precise numerical mid-point of the lay, is meaningful not only because the forward movement of the story starts up once again, but also because of the reference to the boy's eagerness (*hastivement*) which will be the cause of his downfall.

[57] The only individual subordinate character in this lay whom we do not see is the aunt.

140 Si tost cum il l'avra beü.
     Puis le remeine en sun païs. [58]
     Le beivre ad en un vessel mis.
     Li damiseus, joius e liez,
144 Quant ariere fu repeiriez,
     Ne surjurnat pas en la tere.

It may be that the detailed preparations for the youth's trip (122-6) which seem, at first, inappropriate (for he is, after all, only going to consult a physician) are expressly calculated to impress the aunt, just as the girl's details about her *parente* were designed to impress the youth. It may be too that the boy's arrival in style at Salerno is in compensation for his being a stripling.

Of his journey to Salerno the two specific stages of the beginning and the end are not specified. The five lines 121-26, beginning with *s'est aturnez*, are given to a description of his preparations, yet with the last word *menez*, the lad is already on his way. But we do not see him start: the *vait* of 127 (the only verb of pure movement) is simply an explanation of his intention. And after this explanation, with the reference to the aunt (128) — the lad is already in her presence, having handed over to her "a letter." The telescoping of time and events in 127-9 is extraordinary. Marie treats his return trip in the same manner, the boy's departure from Salerno and his arrival home not being specifically mentioned. Verse 141 is a one-line summary of his trip (the one-line summary is a frequent device of Marie), and it is only in the dependent *quant* clause of 144 that his return is mentioned — as a fact already known. It is clever that Marie predicates only what the youth took with him to Salerno, and what he takes away. The narration of his trip to and from Salerno serves to heighten the reader's impression of the boy's impetuousness.

What the girl has said the aunt will do is summarized in 133-4. Moreover, what the aunt does for the lad is probably requested explicitly by the girl in her letter. [59] In this way, Marie

---

[58] According to Godefroy, *remeiner* is mainly used with animate object; he lists only one other case with thing-object.

In 141-2 we may note a sort of variant of hysteron proteron: it is a fine detail that the act more important to the lad (the bringing back of the potion) is mentioned first.

[59] This letter of instructions will find a double parallel in *Milun*.

does not have to mention either the writing of the letter, or its contents — only the fact that it was delivered, and read.

In 134-40 there is a lengthy, insistent description of the efficacy of the *beivre*.[60] Because of its absolute virtues,[61] of course it must succeed — as soon as it is drunk: this last line, assuring us of the immediate action of the drug, also takes for granted that, of course, it will be used for the purpose for which it is intended! The two lines that follow (141-2) seem to stress the obvious: obviously, the boy is not going to leave the potion behind. But, at least, we are made to feel that everything will be all right. And this is corroborated by the reference in the next line to the boy's great happiness.[62]

The youth asks the king for his daughter: (146-66)

```
          Al rei alat sa fille quere,
          Qu'il li donast, il la prendreit,
148       En sum le munt la portereit.
          Li reis ne l'en escundist mie;
          Mes mut le tint a grant folie,
          Pur ceo qu'il iert de jeofne eage:
152       Tant produm[e] vaillant e sage 63
          Unt asaié icel afaire
          Ki n'en purent a nul chef traire.
          Terme li ad numé e pris,
156       Ses humme[s] mande e ses amis
          E tuz ceus k'il poeit aveir:
          N'en i laissa nul remaneir.
          Pur sa fille [e] pur le vallet, 64
```

---

[60] In 135-40, are these the aunt's words to the boy, or is Marie talking to the reader?

[61] Notice a reference, once again, to the lad's strength (*tute vertu*, 139).

[62] In 143-4, the rhyme-scheme *liez / repeiriez* is used for the second time in Marie's lays. There seems to be some connection between its use here and in *Bisclavret*, 29-30, for in both cases, the happiness of the principal character will be shattered.

Line 145 (*Ne surjurnat pas en la tere*) refers to the youth's impatience. Although he is just as eager to return to the king's country as he was to be on his way to Salerno, he has to return home first to leave all his equipment.

[63] The king's use of *sage* recalls the ironic context of its first appearance in Marie's characterization of the boy (cf. 74).

[64] The term *le vallet*, used for the second and final time in the story immediately preceding the test, deliberately reminds us of the boy's youth and inexperience.

> 160 Ki en aventure se met
> De li porter en sum le munt,
> De tutes parz venuz i sunt. [65]
> La dameisele s'aturna:
> 164 Mut se destreint, mut jeüna [66]
> A sun manger pur alegier,
> Que a sun ami voleit aidier.

In the boy's request, the king's stipulation is alluded to for the fifth and final time (146-8). And just as the girl had predicted (cf. 111), her father mentions the suitor's youth (*jeofne eage*, 151) which, with its suggestion of weakness and inexperience, is juxtaposed with the strength and experience of those (*Tant produm[e] vaillant e sage*, 152) who were nevertheless unsuccessful in their attempt. Yet, in spite of the boy's youth, the father does grant his request.

Could the preparations for assembling a great number of people indicate a sadistic streak on the king's part (i.e., that he wants everyone to see the lad fail in his test)? Yet it also may well be that this large crowd has gathered every time an applicant has tempted fortune, and we are being reminded of it at this moment for the first time.

After having given us all the details about the youth, and his preparations, and bringing us up to the moment when the people are about to gather for the test, at 163 Marie goes back in time, to speak (for only four lines!) about the girl's preparations. Whereas the boy's program of gaining strength (and probably weight) was prescribed by the girl's aunt, the girl's simultaneous program of slimming needed no one's directions but her own. [67] Since the purpose of her diet is to lessen the weight of the burden her lover will have to carry, it may be that she thinks of herself

---

[65] Now in 162, as earlier in 156-8, note the instance of the 'far and near' motif.

[66] The girl's constriction (*Mut se destreint...*), unlike that of the boy pointed out earlier, is physical.

[67] This is the third (cf. *Guigemar* and *Bisclavret*) out of four lays in which specific mention is made of food and drink. The strengthening of the boy and the starving of the girl in *Les Deus Amanz* may well anticipate the feeding and starving the reader will note in *Milun*.

only as a body — as, earlier, she had thought of him only in terms of his lack of bodily strength.

With the end of this passage, the second narrative division is concluded.

On the day when all come to the meadow... : (167-79)

>   Al jur quant tuz furent venu,
> 168 Li damisels primer i fu; [68]
>   Sun beivre n'i ublia mie. [69]
>   Devers Seigne en la praerie
>   En la grant gent tut asemblee [70]
> 172 Li reis ad sa fille menee.
>   N'ot drap vestu fors la chemise;
>   Entre ses braz l'aveit cil prise.
>   La fiolete od tut sun beivre—
> 176 Bien seit que el nel vout pas deceivre—
>   En sa mein [a] porter li baille;
>   Mes jo creim que poi [ne] li vaille,
>   Kar n'ot en lui point de mesure.

From this point on, the narrative acquires a new density. We feel in this concluding section a development toward which everything that has preceded has been leading: as if only now do things begin to happen, when "all were assembled in the meadow."

This group of people is, in all probability, the group which had earlier criticized the king. Yet this is the first time we see them gathered, in the meadow which is a kind of stage setting. The people are there as an audience, for the test itself is rather like a sports event, with the audience acting as umpires, to pass judgment on the performance.

In 174, the real *aventure* (anticipated five times previously) begins — when the youth, in the presence of the mass of faceless people and the king, takes the princess "entre ses braz."

---

[68] Notice how eager the boy is to begin his *aventure*.

[69] This line is cruelly humorous, for it sounds as if the story were going to turn out well. But of course we know, from the very beginning, how it ends.

[70] With *la grant gent,* there is another reference to an indefinite mass of people who may well have come from 'far and near.'

In 178-9, for the first time in the narrative Marie intervenes in her own voice, indirectly informing the reader of the end (even before the lad has taken his first step!).

The boy starts out: (180-205)

```
180  Od li s'en veit grant aleüre,
     Le munt munta de si qu'en mi.
     Pur la joie qu'il ot de li ⁷¹
     De sun beivre ne li membra. ⁷²
184  Ele senti qu'il alassa.
     'Amis,' fet ele, 'kar bevez!
     Jeo sai bien que vus [a]lassez:
     Si recuvrez vostre vertu!'
188  Li damisel ad respundu:
     'Bele, jo sent tut fort mun quer:
     Ne m'arestereie a nul fuer
     Si lungement que jeo beüsse,
192  Pur quei treis pas aler peüsse.
     Ceste gent nus escrïereient,
     De lur noise m'esturdireient;
     Tost me purreient desturber.
196  Jo ne voil pas ci arester.'
     Quant les deus parz fu munté sus,
     Pur un petit qu'il ne chiet jus.
     Sovent li prie la meschine:
200  'Ami, bevez vostre mescine!'
     Ja ne la volt oïr ne creire;
     A grant anguisse od tut l[i] eire.
     Sur le munt vint, tant se greva,
204  Ileoc cheï, puis ne leva
     Li quors del ventre s'en parti.
```

---

[71] This is the first and only instance in our lay of the term *joie;* cf. the Provençal use of *joie*, which is practically always synonymous with 'love,' with, mainly, sensuous connotations.

There surely must be an erotic context to the use of *joie* in *Les Deus Amanz*, for the boy is holding his sweetheart in his arms. Note, too, that she has nothing on but her *chemise* (cf. 173), although we are not reminded of that detail in line 182. The awakening in the boy of sensuous love is very delicately presented in 182-3.

[72] What a great change of attitude there is in so few lines, from *Sun beivre n'i ublia mie* of 169, to *De sun beivre ne li membra* of 183. Arriving half-way up the hill and not using the potion does not yet, however, indicate hybris, but simply forgetfulness, because of awakening sensuality.

For all we know, the love between the boy and the girl has been absolutely chaste (cf. the use of *la pucele* in 118, plus the fact that we are never told that the lovers kissed).

The only movement fixed in time and space that we are allowed to see is that which begins when the lad starts up the mountain with his sweetheart, and ends with his death. And when he begins his task in 180, then the visualization of the lovers (which up to now had been lacking) comes into effect. Indeed, from 180 to the end of 205, there is a cinematic effect of the zoom lens, as we move closer and closer to the bodies of the two lovers while traveling up the mountain with them.

How eagerly and with what energy *(grant aleüre)* the boy starts out. Note that Marie, in just one line, allows him to go half-way up the hill (which is as far as the brawny unsuccessful applicants could ever strain themselves to go).

Earlier we were struck by the omission of verbs of explicit movement in the account of the youth's trip to Salerno and back. As a vivid contrast, the narration of the test of going up the mountain contains not only verbs of movement through space (*s'en veit*, 180; *munta*, 181) but also verbs of bodily movement (*cheï; leva*, 204). In addition to details that invite to visualization in this passage, we are given in line 184 details of sensuous feeling.[73] In a way, we seem to get inside the bodies of the lovers, when Marie tells us that the girl (whom the lad is holding in his arms) feels his body to be weakening.[74]

Just as all the girl ever really talked about in her long speech was the *mescine* (the *mescine* which will be of no use whatever), this is all she talks about while being carried up the mountain. It is an effective touch that the half-naked burden the boy is carrying in his arms becomes the voice we hear (185; 200) urging her lover[75] to drink the strength-restoring potion.

In harmony with the emphasis given to the physical in this poem, notice that the first and only time we hear the boy speak

---

[73] The verb *sentir* is used here for the second time in Marie's lays. Although in both *Lanval* and *Les Deus Amanz* there is great emphasis upon the physical, what a difference there is between the use of *sentir* in *Lanval* (where the protagonist, in erotic reverie, longs to hold his mistress in his arms and make love to her, cf. 254-6), and its use here.

[74] How does she feel his fatigue? Is it by the way he holds her? Do his arms weaken? Or is it the fatigue of his body that she feels? Does he proceed at a slower pace?

[75] Notice that every time her words to the youth are reproduced in direct address, they begin with the word 'Amis.'

to the girl is when he is carrying her. It is significant that he addresses her as 'Bele'; surely he is erotically excited. This is probably the longest time that he has ever held her in his arms.

The lad's boast ('...jo sent tut fort mun quer'), although anticipatory of what will happen about his heart, is nevertheless not a commonplace assertion of strength. His 'heart' must be also his love for the girl; since he feels this to be strong, he would transfer his emotional strength to the physical plane. (Yet it will be his physical heart which is mentioned in 205).

There is something odd in the boy's reply to her request: twice (190 and 196) he refuses to stop, although the girl had *not* asked him to stop to drink. In fact, this would not have been necessary: the girl could hold the vessel to his lips as he is carrying her. Moreover, it was not said in the king's decree that the aspirant could not slow down a bit; only resting is forbidden (cf. 38).

The explanation is that his lack of *mesure* is the result of holding the girl in his arms; he begins to feel like a man. The boy has a few minutes of happiness (anticipating what he could have when he has married her) and this causes him to forget completely what he has to do in order to have her forever. During the trip up the mountain where there is awakening of the senses of the two lovers, the youth, in a way, *has* had her.

In 193-5, we feel the boy's continuing, desperate concentration as he strains everything to reach the top. The peculiar statement in 193 ('Ceste gent nus escrïereient') indicates his fear that, if he (like an athlete) were reminded of anything from the outside world, that would unnerve him. Then, too, these people have some kind of authority; they represent public opinion. And *if* they should shout at him, then he would have been doing something that he ought not to have done!

Whereas for the other suitors Marie at the beginning of the story had marked the mountain in two parts, in 197 she marks it into thirds for the young lover. At this point in his endeavor, his fatigue, which the girl had already felt before her first request to him, has, understandably, increased to almost utter exhaustion.

The continuous framework *(sovent)* of his activity suggested in 199-202 becomes a given moment in 203-4, when the boy arrives at the top with his burden. The five-fold movement of his arrival should be pointed out. In 203, Marie has effectively shifted the order of the clauses, putting the anticipatory *tant se greva* (with ellipsis of *que*) in second place, beginning the line with the triumphant statement of the boy's arrival at his destination. Then comes his fall, immediately following the *tant se greva;* and we see that this reference to great effort explains not only his success, but his collapse — which will be final *(puis ne leva),* for "the heart in his belly has burst."

The girl's body, so slight and light at first, and which seemed to be a source of strength to the boy, becomes during the trip just a weight that grows and grows, until his heart gives out.

The girl misunderstands what has happened: (206-28)

>   La pucele vit sun ami,
>   Quida k'il fust en paumeisuns;
> 208   Lez lui se met en genuilluns,
>   Sun beivre li voleit doner;
>   Mes il ne pout od li parler.
>   Issi murut cum jeo vus di.
> 212   Ele le pleint a mut haut cri;
>   Puis ad geté e espaundu
>   Li veissel u le beivre fu.
>   Li muns en fu bien arusez,
> 216   Mut en ad esté amendez
>   Tut le païs e la cuntree:
>   Meinte bone herbe i unt trovee,
>   Ki del beivrë orent racine.
> 220   Or vus dirai de la meschine:
>   Puis que sun ami ot perdu,
>   Unkes si dolente ne fu;
>   Lez lui se cuchë e estent,
> 224   Entre ses braz l'estreint e prent, [76]
>   Suvent li baisë oilz e buche; [77]

---

[76] The girl's embrace of her dead lover contrasts with the action of Eliduc in the lay of the same name. For when Eliduc laments in front of the maiden he is leaving for dead, he does *not* take her into his arms (cf. *Eliduc,* 931-7).

[77] Yet there is a parallel between the action of the princess and Eliduc, for both kiss the beloved. The girl kisses her dead lover's eyes and mouth (225, *Les Deus Amanz);* Eliduc kisses Guilliadun's eyes and face (*Eliduc,* 937).

>   Li dols de lui al quor la tuche. [78]
>   Ilec murut la dameisele,
> 228   Que tant ert pruz e sage e bele.

That Marie opens this new section, where the girl is allowed to grow more and more because of her awakening sensations and emotions, by naming the princess, for the second and final time, *la pucele,* is indeed meaningful.

At 208, the girl (who must have fallen with her lover) now gets to her knees. And in that position, she does three things: she first tries to put the flask to her lover's lips (209); then, when she realizes he is dead, she screams (212);[79] finally, in a concentrated physical act, she throws away the flask (213-14).

In 209-10, the juxtaposition of the *beivre* with the boy's mouth that could no longer talk (but which had talked to refuse the potion) is arresting. Moreover, what a forceful contrast there is between the lover's silent mouth (whose lower jaw is probably slack) and the girl's screaming mouth.

After the girl throws away the potion, in the next five lines of digression (215-19)[80] we go ahead in time; it is as if the maiden

---

[78] The emphasis upon the body in this lay of physical chastity where the lovers are two children is stronger than in *Lanval,* which is the most sensuous of the lays. For example, the bodies of the two lovers are prepared for the test; then the test itself takes place; next, the violent death of the lover occurs; and finally, the girl embraces her dead lover.

[79] We do not hear her lament in words; her lament is simply given in narrative summary in 212 ("Ele le pleint a mut haut cri").
This is the first of two instances when the girl (or woman) screams because of the loss of her lover. Here, in *Les Deus Amanz* the lover is actually dead; in *Yonec,* the lady knows that the lover is mortally wounded.

[80] For a discussion of the symbol in the *Lais* of Marie de France, see Anna G. Hatcher, "Le lai du Chievrefueil," *Romania,* LXXI (1950), 330-44, especially 339-40.

> ... The evolution of the *bastun* [in *Chievrefueil*] ... is in harmony with Marie's procedure of choosing a specific, concrete object as the centre of her *lai* which shall develop, within the poem, new varieties of symbolic content.... *Les Dous Amans* centers about the magic potion, which represents, supposedly, a means, and a necessary means to the fulfillment of the lovers' desire; as the boy, however, attains the top of the mountain without its aid, it seems to become superfluous; then, in the end, sprinkled like an oblation upon the grass, it symbolizes love's frustration — its virtue serving, finally, to feed the "meinte bone herbe": the memorial to the dead lovers (p. 339).

had been cancelled out. In 215-17 we are told of the immediate result of her act. The herbs, made by the aunt in Salerno into a potion which was not to be used, return to their original nature (218-19). [81] In these five lines, Marie has thrown something ahead in time: flowers will bloom in the future. And the mountain with which the story began will be forever different.

At 220, Marie, in her auctorial competence, suddenly returns to the girl and the present moment. We had seen the girl earlier kneel beside her lover; now she slips down beside him where she had first fallen, and takes him "entre ses braz" — the final use of this phrase, which has so increased in meaning. At this moment when she would lament, all we note are her physical gestures (223-5) which are maternal, as well as those of a lover. For here, in the awakening of all her emotions, she becomes a woman. She is the only one of the two lovers who achieves a real completion in her growth. [82]

When the girl clasps her dead lover in her arms (in the most graphic and most detailed of all the love-making scenes in Marie's lays, yet between chaste lovers), this gesture represents the love-making she will never have; similarly, when the boy held her in his arms, while carrying her up the mountain, that was the love-making he will never have. [83]

Whereas it had been the boy's physical heart that suffered, it is the girl's emotional heart that suffers. And whereas we had been made to feel the full force of the boy's death, here the girl's death is delicately subdued *(Li dols de lui al quor la tuche).* [84]

The citation above is also quoted by Sühela Bayrav, *Symbolisme médiéval: Béroul, Marie, Chrétien* (Paris, 1957), p. 66, in a discussion of Marie's use of symbols and emblems.

[81] As for 218-19, do people go up there to look at the tomb?

[82] *Les Deus Amanz* is the only lay where we feel the simultaneous growth of two individuals. As we have seen, this takes place during the trip up the mountain.

[83] *Les Deus Amanz* is the first of four lays in which there is unconsummated love. The situation of unconsummated love is clear-cut in this lay, as well as in *Laüstic* and *Chaitivel*. That in *Eliduc* is halfway between the loves that are and are not consummated, for as lovers, before their marriage, Eliduc and Guilliadun did not consummate their love.

[84] The girl's death after her lover is comparable to a *Liebestod,* and in fact, makes us think of Thomas d'Angleterre's *Roman de Tristan*. I am

The relative clause in 228 ending this passage is meaningful. Now, after the girl's death, she is described (*Que tant ert pruz e sage e bele:* 228) in precisely the same terms as had been her lover (*Que tant est sages, pruz e beus:* 74) when he came to her to suggest his rash plan. Thus, with this descriptive clause the lover is brought back into the focus of our attention. That this particular clause appears before the beginning, and after the end, of the events that have culminated in the two tragic deaths is an elegant detail.

---

convinced that Marie wanted to remind us of Tristan and Iseut in this lay, for there are several notable parallels as well as several equally notable contrasts.

In *Les Deus Amanz,* the potion, in conspicuous contrast to the Tristan story, is not drunk. Whereas in the Tristan story, the potion is the source of the couple's love and their erotic relationship, in *Les Deus Amanz,* the potion, if used, would have been a source of physical strength for the youth which would have allowed him to marry the girl and thereby, would have made possible an erotic relationship.

Whereas we do not hear the words of the girl's lament over her lover's body, we do hear Iseut grieve (for 31 lines in Thomas' work). Yet the girl's gesture of taking her dead lover in her arms, then lying down beside him where she dies, parallels that of Iseut (although Thomas treats Iseut's death at greater length). A comparison of the death scenes of the two heroines is interesting for reason of their similarities:

Les Deus Amanz

220   Or vus dirai de la meschine
        Puis que sun ami ot perdu,
        Unkes si dolent ne fu;
        Lez lui se cuchë e estent,
224   Entre ses braz l'estreint e prent,
        Suvent li baisë oilz e buche;
        Li dols de lui al quor la tuche.
        Ilec murut la dameisele,
228   Que tant ert pruz e sage e bele.

After Iseut's lengthy lament, we are told of her that:

        Embrace le e si s'estent,
3115   Baise li la buche e la face
        E molt estreit a li l'enbrace,
        Cors a cors, buche a buche estent,
        Sun esprit a itant rent,
        E murt dejuste lui issi
3120   Pur la dolur de sun ami.
        Tristrans murut pur sun desir,
        Ysolt, qu'a tens n'i pout venir.
        Tristrans murut pur sue amur,
        E la bele Ysolt pur tendrur.

The king and those who had waited climb to the top of the mountain: (229-34)

>Li reis e cil kis atendeient,
>Quant unt veü qu'il ne veneient,
>Vunt aprés eus, sis unt trovez.
>232 Li reis chiet a tere paumez.
>Quant pot parler, grant dol demeine,
>E si firent la gent foreine. [85]

The story of the lovers' fate must end with the father who had devised the original situation; he must be made to discover the disastrous consequences of his decision. For the third time the mountain must be climbed.

In a sense, the father participates in the death of the two children, for he falls in a faint [86] to lie beside their bodies (reminding us of the youth who had seemed to be lying in a faint). When he can speak (is not 233 meant to remind us (210) of the youth who could not speak?) the king, like his daughter, voices his grief (in which the mass of people, who had shared in the discovery of the lovers, participate). But, unlike her, he will not die of grief.

The lovers are mourned for three days: (235-40)

>Treis jurs les unt tenu sur tere.
>236 Sarcu de marbre firent quere,
>Les deus enfanz unt mis dedenz,
>Par le cunseil de cele genz
>[De]sur le munt les enfuïrent,
>240 E puis atant se departirent.

For three days the lovers' bodies remain above ground while a sarcophagus is prepared for them. Then, on the advice of the

---

[85] The phrase *la gent foreine* is significant: there is no more distinction between the various groups mentioned throughout the story; suddenly there is only the king and *la gent foreine*. Could it be that to the king, in his grief, suddenly everyone is *foreine*?

[86] Although in OF epics men will fall in a faint, this is the only time in Marie's lays that such an event will happen.

people (the story ends, as it began, with the king taking counsel!) the lovers are buried on the spot where they died. [87]

In the final line of this passage which ends the narrative, everybody departs; it is as if they know that the story is over. Indeed, their dispersal may be likened to an odd cloud-like formation: they just melt or drift away. [88] The king himself, whom we see for the last time in 232-3, has become at the end simply one of the indefinite mass of persons whose actions are indicated in 235-40.

The mountain is named for the two lovers: (241-44)

>   Pur l'aventure des enfaunz
>   Ad nun li munz des Deus Amanz.
>   Issi avint cum dit vus ai;
> 244 Li Bretun en firent un lai.

Just as in the Prologue Marie had told us that a Breton lay was named for the two lovers, in the Epilogue she tells us for whom the mountain was named.

The phrase *l'aventure des enfaunz* in 241 deliberately recalls lines 2-4 of the Prologue: *Une aventure mut oïe / De deus enfanz que s'entr'amerent; / Par amur ambedeus finerent.* The substantive *enfanz*, used in 3 and again in 10 to stress the innocence of the lovers, is repeated in 241 for that same reason, as well as to emphasize the premature conclusion of their lives.

Moreover, the phrase *par amur* of line 4, whose application to "children" may have seemed unfitting at the beginning of the

---

[87] *Les Deus Amanz* is the first of two lays where the lovers are placed together in a tomb at the end of the story. Here, the tomb has been there on the mountain-top from the very beginning; in *Yonec*, the tomb at the end has been at least prefigured.

[88] *Les Deus Amanz* is one of Marie's rare narratives that come to an end rather quickly. Once the crowd is assembled in the meadow, and the boy takes in his arms the princess who had been led there by her father, the action moves swiftly and inevitably to a close.

At this point, it may be pertinent to note some further similarities and contrasts between *Les Deus Amanz* and *Laüstic*. Not only is love unconsummated in both lays, there is also something left over: the *meinte bone herbe* in the present narrative, the decaying body of the bird in *Laüstic*.

An obvious contrast is that of the fate of the lovers in these two lays: whereas the two lovers in *Les Deus Amanz* are dead, and the *herbe* alive and flourishing, in *Laüstic* the lovers are alive, and the bird is dead.

lay, has, in the course of the narrative, acquired significant overtones and reverberations. Since we have seen the expansion of the children's innocence into desire during the journey up the mountainside, the phrase *par amur* seems, in retrospect, entirely just.[89]

The concluding line of the Epilogue *(Li Bretun en firent un lai)*[90] repeats, with almost the same structure, the contents of line 5 of the Prologue *(Un lai en firent li Bretun)*. Yet we may wonder *if* the Bretons ever did compose such a lay; there is nothing specifically Celtic in the story Marie has just recounted.[91] I very much suspect that Marie twice cites a Breton lay as an authority, to give a tradition to the lay she herself has elaborated, perhaps on the basis of other sources.

---

[89] The retrospective appropriateness of this phrase is still another instance of the subtleties of Marie's artistry.

[90] It is as if anything that happens should be recorded in poetry.

[91] For a discussion of Marie's sources for this narrative, see O. M. Johnston, "Sources of the Lay of the *Two Lovers*," MLN, XXI (1906), 34-9. Although Johnston's summary of Marie's plot (p. 34) contains several inaccuracies (a situation I have found most frequently in the critical literature on Marie's lays!), his study of two closely related groups of stories leads him to assert that "neither of the two legends used in the composition of the lay of the *Two Lovers* shows any special evidences of Celtic origin." He further claims that in the light of his study, "there seems to be no special reason for supposing that the lay of the *Two Lovers* contains any Celtic material" (p. 38).

Ewert supports an opposite point of view, stating that "it is also possible that Marie is telling the truth (ll. 5 and 243-4), that Breton jongleurs got to know of it [i.e., the legend of the two lovers] and appropriated it as part of their stock in trade, and that she owes it to them" (p. 177).

YONEC

A careful examination of the lay of *Yonec* discloses a bi-partite external structure of 554 lines, containing both the stories of *li chevaler* and *la dame*, the parents of Yonec, and that of Yonec himself. Joined together by a transition passage of eight lines, the two sections of the lay, forming a diptych and serving as a pendant to each other, are nevertheless disproportionate in length: the principal narrative is that of the knight Muldumarec and *la dame*, occupying vv. 11-456. The *récit* of Yonec takes up less than 100 lines, from v. 465 to v. 550.

In the Prologue Marie promises to tell us two things: (1-10)

> Puis que des lais ai comencé,
> Ja n'iert par mun travail laissé:
> Les aventures que j'en sai
> 4 Tut par rime les cunterai.
> En pensé ai e en talent
> Que d'Iwenec vus die avant,
> Dunt il fu nez, e de sun pere
> 8 Cum il vint primes a sa mere;
> Cil ki engendra Yuuenec
> Aveit a nun Muldumarec.

In the prelude to this lay Marie has promised to tell us two things: concerning Yonec, she will tell us of whom he was born, i.e., who his father was; concerning his father, she will tell us how he first came to the mother. By the singling out of Yonec and his father, Marie would seem to indicate that these are the two main characters (for they are the only ones named in the total narrative). The mother is only the one-to-whom-the-father-came.

The Prologue offers the reader two problems. Before the Prologue comes to an end, Marie has already answered the first of her two questions; in 9-10, we are told who Yonec's father was.[1] But why should Marie answer one of her two questions in the Prologue?

Since Marie has already told us the first thing she promised, there is nothing left to tell in the whole lay except the second: how Muldumarec came to Yonec's mother. Yet, most obviously, we are told more than that, three other things: we are told how the lady came to Yonec's father; about Yonec's birth and growth; and also about his final vengeance. Why does Marie, in the course of the narrative, tell us so much more than she had promised?

A wealthy old man marries a beautiful girl for the sake of an heir: (11-36)

> En Bretain[e] maneit jadis [2]
> 12 Un riches hum viel e antis;
> De Carwent fu avouez

---

[1] One wonders what the *dire avant* of line 6 means; could this explain why Marie tells us *immediately* the name of the father?

[2] For a contemporary example of the bi-partition of a verse-narrative in which the story of two lovers precedes that of their son, for whom the *roman* is named, cf. *Cligés* of Chrétien de Troyes, which Reto Roberto Bezzola cites in *Le sens de l'aventure et de l'amour: Chrétien de Troyes* (Paris, 1947, p. 81). The predilection for genealogies is not new in either Marie or Chrétien, for as Jessie Crosland remarks in *Medieval French Literature* (Oxford, 1956, p. 109), it is found in "Welsh chroniclers" by whom such genealogies were "so loved." Cf. also Edmond Faral, *Les Arts poétiques du 12e et du 13e siècles, Recherches et Documents sur la Technique littéraire du Moyen-Age* (Paris, 1927), in *Bibliothèque de l'Ecole des Hautes-Études*, CCXXXVIII, 60. There Faral speaks of some formulae already made that were offered to all craftsmen; for example, the establishment of "le type du roman qu'on pourrait appeler généalogique, où l'histoire des deux héros est précédée de celle de leurs parents: *Tristan, Cligés, L'Escoufle*, etc."

Within the four narratives in question, of greater importance is the gradation of space given over to the story of the parents. In the *Tristan*, the parents' story is the briefest of introductions, whereas in the *Cligés*, and in *L'Escoufle*, the parents' story is developed at length: in the *Cligés*, some two thousand lines are devoted to recounting the tale of Cligés' parents, a tale which is independent of the main action; for *L'Escoufle*, slightly more than fifteen hundred verses go by before the son is born, whose own story will be told at greater length. In contrast to these three narratives is the *Yonec*: there the principal story is that of the parents, for the son exists

E del païs sire clamez.
La cite siet sur Düelas;
16 Jadis i ot de nes trespas.
Mut fu trespassez en eage.
Pur ceo k'il ot bon heritage,
Femme prist pur enfanz aveir,
20 Qüe aprés lui fuissent si heir.
De haute gent fu la pucele,
Sage, curteise e forment bele,
Qüe al riche hume fu donee.
24 Pur sa beauté l'ad mut amee.
De ceo kë ele ert bele e gente,
En li garder mist mut s'entente:
Dedenz sa tur l'ad enserree
28 En une grant chambre pavee.
Il ot une sue serur,
Veillë e vedve, sanz seignur;
Ensemble od la dame l'ad mise
32 Pur li tenir meuz en justise.
Autres femmes i ot, ceo crei,
En un' autre chambre par sei;
Mes ja la dame n'i parlast,
36 Si la vielle ne comandast.

One is struck by the gap between the Prelude and the opening of the story; we had just been told about Yonec and Muldumarec, and now the reader is expecting to hear about Muldumarec and how he came to Yonec's mother — or, at least, to hear about the mother and how Muldumarec came to her. But instead, we hear about an old man who married a pretty girl. And we are told about him in a most leisurely fashion.

When the wife is mentioned (and it is she who will be Yonec's mother), it is only as part of a plan that is carried out by the old man. In fact, "femme prist" probably means only "he took a wife" — "he got married"; she is not yet an individual in any sense. Nor does the wife become an individual during the description: in the first three lines of her portrait she is presented as a person-given, in the last lines, as a person-guarded. In both cases the wife is completely controlled by others: first by her family,

---

only to avenge his parents. One further point: in *Yonec* no love-intrigue is allowed to the hero, the son of *la dame* and *li chevaler,* whereas in *Cligés* and in *L'Escoufle* the son himself has a love-story.

then by her husband. Even the description of her beauty is offered as a two-fold source of motivation for her husband: it is the reason for his "loving" her, and also the reason for his locking her up.

It is fitting to comment briefly upon the manner of presentation of *li sires'* family: this is in the form of a triptych, of parts approximately equal in length. In the triptych, *la dame* occupies, so to speak, the central panel, balanced by the figures of *li sires* and *la vielle*. Analogous to the encompassment of the lady by the wall of her husband's tower is the lady's position here, surrounded by the two custodians of her person. The slow emergence of the lady as an individual (for here she is treated as a possession) [3] is an important part of the first section of the lay: she will grow a little more in the summary of seven years (37-50), and still more in the next section (51-66).

Marie's presentation of the old husband is also noteworthy, for she refrains from directly portraying his character. She mentions only two things about his feelings: that he wanted an heir, and that he loved the lady for her beauty. Nothing whatever is said about his character. Marie does not call him cruel, does not even call him suspicious and jealous; she only suggests this by telling us what he does to the lady. This oblique presentation of his character is even more effective than would be an outright description. What is more, Marie reports on his cruel program very calmly. For one thing, the auctorial expression of pity for the lady's imprisonment that we might expect is lacking; for another, the comment of lines 25-26: "because she was so lovely" makes one expect something like "he treated her tenderly and wanted to make her happy." Instead, Marie uses the lady's loveliness to lead up to the description of the husband's cruelty; quite calmly, as if Marie were describing something normal: "she was so lovely — that of course he imprisoned her!"

Seven years go by: (37-50)

> Issi la tient plus de set anz—
> Unques entre eus n'eurent enfanz—

---

[3] We should note that the wife will never become individualized to the point of having her own name: she will always be called *la dame* throughout the entire lay.

>   Ne fors de cele tur ne eissi
> 40   Ne pur parent ne pur ami.
>   Quant li sires se ala cuchier,
>   N'i ot chamberlenc ne huisser
>   Ki en la chambre osast entrer
> 44   Ne devant lui cirge alumer. [4]
>   Mut ert la dame en grant tristur;
>   Od lermes, od suspir e plur
>   Sa beuté pert en teu mesure
> 48   Cume cele que n'en ad cure.
>   De sei meïsme meuz vousist
>   Que mort hastive la preisist.

In this section dealing with the seven years' duration of the lady's situation, we learn still more about this situation. The husband's insane jealousy is described in more detail (41-44), and we learn of two ironical developments: the marriage undertaken for the sole purpose of procreation is childless, and the lady's beauty, the reason for her husband's cruel program, is lost as a result of that program.

Two other things must also be stressed. First, the lady comes somewhat more into the foreground (one notes here that this is not a triptych, for the sister is missing; here we have a married pair). And for the first time, we have access to the lady's feelings. The first four lines of this section show her still only as a person-guarded, but in the last six she becomes a being who reacts (and of course it is this reaction on her part that precipitates the series of events of the narrative: if she hadn't been so sad, she would not have made her wish (103-4); if she had not made her wish, the knight would not have come).

In this section we also notice the change made in the reference to time. Up to line 36, the time had only been *jadis:* now (v. 37) we are made aware of the passage of time: seven long years (every night for seven years the husband goes to bed in the dark; day after day, for seven years, the lady mourns). We do not actually feel the movement of time yet: this is only a summary, an announcement of duration. Still, the statement *"Thus* he kept

---

[4] One notes the presence of seven negatives in the opening lines (37-44) of this summary of the lady's imprisonment.

her seven years" suggests that a change will come; we feel that we are on a threshold of the period when the time of the action must begin, when time will start moving ahead.[5] And this is what happens in 51.

One April morning the lady is left alone in her bed-chamber: (51-66)

>   Ceo fu al meis de avril entrant,
> 52   Quant cil oisel meinent lur chant.
>   Li sires fu matin levez;
>   De aler en bois s'est aturnez.
>   La viellë ad fet lever sus
> 56   E aprés lui fermer les hus.
>   Cele ad fet sun comandement.
>   Li sires s'en vet od sa gent.
>   La vielle portot sun psauter,
> 60   U ele voleit verseiller.
>   La dame en plur e en esveil
>   Choisi la clarté del soleil.
>   De la vielle est aparceüe
> 64   Que de la chambre esteit eissue.
>   Mut se pleineit e suspirot
>   E en plurant se dementot.

Although the preceding section (37-50) has hinted at a change to come (once the seven years are over), and though the opening line 51 sets the moment for things to start happening, nevertheless the present section begins with a description of a routine pattern: the husband, when he leaves in the morning, has his sister lock the door after him. Throughout the first part of the lay (11-464) how often is the locking of the door a constant reminder (as if the reader could not, and must not, forget) of the lady's imprisonment.

---

[5] An analogy to this summarization of the passage of time is found in the lay of *Guigemar*, in the presentation of the lady's suffering and "martyrdom" in her tower-prison: Marie states that the lady's imprisonment is said to have lasted "two years and more" (*Guigemar*, 665). In that lay, too, the lady mourns, and often, with the difference that her "frequent" lament is shown occurring on one occasion which, curiously enough, is not even particularized. Yet in both lays, *Yonec* and *Guigemar*, some extraordinary event takes place upon the completion of the lament.

This section also brings us closer to the lady. The old husband departs, the old woman goes into another room, and for the first time we are alone with the lady. Once again we are afforded knowledge of her feelings (by way of her perceptions: *choisi, est aparceüe*) and, this time, at a given moment.

And now we hear her speak: (67-104)

       'Lasse,' fait ele, 'mar fui nee!
68 Mut est dure ma destinee!
    En ceste tur sui en prisun,
    Ja n'en istrai si par mort nun.
    Cist viel gelus, de quei se crient,
72 Quë en si grant prisun me tient?
    Mut par est fous e esbaïz,
    Il crient tuz jurs estre trahiz.
    Jeo ne puis al muster venir
76 Ne le servise Deu oïr.
    Si jo puïsse od gent parler
    E en deduit od eus aler,
    Jo li mustrasse beu semblant,
80 Tut n'en eüsse jeo talant.
    Malëeit seient mi parent
    E li autre communalment
    Ki a cest gelus me donerent
84 E a sun cors me marïerent!
    A forte corde trai e tir!
    Il ne purrat jamés murir.
    Quant il dut estre baptiziez,
88 Si fu al flum d'enfern plungiez:
    Dur sunt li nerf, dures les veines,
    Que de vif sanc sunt tutes pleines.
    Mut ai sovent oï cunter
92 Que l'em suleit jadis trover
    Aventures en cest païs,
    Ki rechatouent les pensis:
    Chevalers trovoënt puceles
96 A lur talent gentes e beles,
    E dames truvoënt amanz
    Beaus e curteis, [pruz] e vaillanz,
    Si que blamees n'en esteient,
100 Ne nul fors eles nes veeient.
    Si ceo peot estrë e ceo fu,
    Si unc a nul est avenu,
    Deu, ki de tut ad poësté,
104 Il en face ma volenté!'

In this passage, we note the extremely careful development of the lady's feelings: this lament (the first instance of direct speech in the *Yonec,* and the longest address ever uttered by the lady) will end with a wish that precipitates everything. But just how does the lady reach that point? This development could be outlined as follows:

67-70: General lament in which her whole future life is anticipated.

Note that at the very moment before everything is about to change for her, the lady anticipates her whole future in terms of the past. In our lay, we shall see that the materialization of predictions plays a very important part. But here, the lady makes the first ("Ja n'en istrai si par mort nun": 70) of two predictions that will fail to materialize.

71-4: The needlessness of her husband's cruelty

It is most important that the lady stresses the needlessness of her husband's cruelty: it shows that at the moment she begins her lament, she is not thinking, even wistfully, of having a love affair. She is clearly saying: 'there was no need to lock me up, I would never have betrayed my husband.' As regards 73-4 ("Mut par est fous e esbaïz, / Il crient tuz jurs estre trahiz"), how doubly ironical it is that, despite his many and elaborate precautions, later the husband will be *trahiz* (i.e., cuckolded). For it is precisely because of his efforts that the husband precipitates the cuckoldry.[6] Moreover, that his wife should comment on his stupidity implies a sort of mechanical inevitability about the cuckoldry.

75-80: Her innocent desires

Then follows the most innocent of desires on the part of the lady: if only she would be able to go to church. And if only he would let her talk to people! And if he would take her out with him to have a good time, she would be so nice to him!

81-4: Her curse on her parents

Then as the lady thinks that these simple, innocent pleasures are denied her, she curses the parents who allowed this to happen

---

[6] The very same situation is also true in the *Roman de Flamenca,* where the husband Archimbaut, in spite of many efforts, is betrayed by his wife Flamenca with Guillem. Cf. the article by Kurt Lewent, "Zum Inhalt und Aufbau der Flamenca," *ZRPh,* LIII (1933), 1-86.

(as well as *li autre*, 82, who, along with her parents, are the objects of her curse).

85-90: Her despair over her husband's longevity

In her remarks about her husband's strong constitution that will not allow him to die, the lady is indirectly cursing him: she is wishing him dead with all her soul.

91-100: Her recollection of stories she has heard

It is probably the hideous idea of her husband living eternally that turns her mind toward the stories of loving couples that she has heard. This is an escape from reality for her, just to think about others who had a happier fate than she. And as she reminds herself of these happy, idyllic stories, the desire arises in her to re-live, to re-enact such a story.

101-4: Her wish

And so the lady makes her wish, still without revealing her explicit desire (note the curious phrase 'may my will be done' said to God!).

From a rational point of view, it might be objected that if, for seven years, it had never occurred to the wife to betray her husband if she ever had the opportunity, and if at the beginning of her lament it still had not occurred to her, why should she change so quickly? It would seem that this is an artistic foreshortening, presenting in the course of a few lines what must have been in reality a long, slow development toward the breaking-point.

Immediately a bird appears at the window who, once in the room, turns into a handsome knight: (105-18)

```
      Quant ele ot faite pleinte issi,
      L'umbre d'un grant oisel choisi
      Par mi une estreite fenestre.
108   Ele ne seit quei ceo pout estre.
      En la chambre volant entra;
      Gez ot as piez, ostur sembla,
      De cinc mues fu u de sis.
112   Il s'est devant la dame asis.
      Quant il i ot un poi esté
      E ele l'ot bien esgardé,
      Chevaler bel e gent devint.
```

> 116 La dame a merveille le tint;
> Li sans li remut e fremi,
> Grant poür ot, sun chief covri.

In this lay there is a dream-like, almost surrealistic atmosphere,[7] evident in this passage wherein the lady's desire becomes reality. We notice the very delicate detail of the shadow ("L'umbre d'un grant oisel choisi / Par mi une estreite fenestre": 106-7. First the lady perceives the shadow of a giant bird at the narrow window, then the bird, and then the handsome knight. The gradation in the realization of her desire into flesh is very beautifully done. Another delicate touch is that moment (or did several moments pass?) of silence in which the two being look at one another.

As for the lady's frightened reaction (118: "sun chief covri") to what will be the first metamorphosis on the part of the knight, it is obviously with the bedclothes[8] that she covers her head: the sheet that has not been mentioned of the bed that has not been mentioned. The bed will not be mentioned until the knight first lies beside her (166), and the sheets will not be mentioned until they are reddened with his blood (316).

We are struck by the lack of concrete details (and not only in this section) regarding the lady's physical background: her life has been, and up to a certain point it will continue to be, limited to her bed-chamber; yet this is never described, and only five objects in it are even mentioned: the bed, the sheets, a window (probably two windows), a curtain, the door: all of them the most inconspicuous, the most inevitable objects of the interior of a bedroom, yet all of them basically necessary to the plot.

The knight addresses her, asking her for her love: (119-44)[9]

---

[7] Indeed, *Yonec* is the lay with the most details that go a gainst common sense.

[8] It is somewhat humorous that for eighteen lines (from 118-136) the lady's head is covered with the sheets while the bird-knight is talking to her.
During her lament, the lady is evidently in bed; in fact, whenever we see her during the first part of the lay, she will always be in bed (until she leaves the tower).

[9] One remark must be made here which will hold true for all of the specified visits of the knight to the lady: the knight does most of the talking.

Mut fu curteis li chevalers:
120　Il l'en areisunat primers.
'Dame,' fet il, 'n'eiez poür!
Gentil oisel ad en ostur; [10]
Si li segrei [vus] sunt oscur, [11]
124　Gardez ke seiez a seür,
Si fetes de mei vostre ami!
Pur ceo,' fet il, 'vienc jeo [i]ci.
Jeo vus ai lungement amé
128　E en mun quor mut desiré;
Unques femme fors vus n'amai
Ne jamés autre ne amerai.
Mes ne poeie a vus venir
132　Ne fors de mun païs eissir,
Si vus ne me eüssez requis.
Or puis bien estre vostre amis!'
La dame se raseüra,
136　Sun chief descovri, si parla;
Le chevaler ad respundu
E dit qu'ele en ferat sun dru,
S'en Deu creïst e issi fust
140　Que lur amur estre peüst.
Kar mut esteit de grant beauté:
Unkes nul jur de sun eé
Si beals chevaler ne esgarda
144　Ne jamés si bel ne verra.

In this passage there are, in addition to the knight's transformation from a hawk, several other mysteries. The first involves a practical consideration: we wonder how the knight even knew

---

During this visit to the lady, she says only three brief things: (1) "I'll make you my lover if you believe in God, so that our love will be possible" (137-40); (2) "You have said something good" (165); and (3) "Please come back to see me often" (197-8). And these few remarks appear in indirect discourse, whereas the knight's words are (always) presented in direct address.

[10] Note the humor of line 122: "Don't be afraid: a hawk is a very nice bird" — as if the lady's horrified reaction to his transformation from a hawk were due only to her fear of hawks.

[11] The expression *li segrei* (123) poses a problem: we might think that the phrase refers to the secret of his transformation (yet he never explains that!), as well as to the secret of his coming, for that he will soon explain. Yet his explanation of his coming to the lady leaves so many things unexplained; perhaps that is the reference of the *segrei*. But this passage (123-4) is not too clear.

of the lady's existence. Often in medieval literature, it is true that one falls in love with an unknown persön through his reputation; this could hardly be the case in our lay, given the lady's isolation from society. The other two mysteries pertain to the knight's magical powers: how could he know the lady's wish; and why was he unable to come to her (or even leave his own land!) until she had wished for him?[12] Actually, the lady did not wish for *him,* only for a lover, whereas he, apparently, loved her personally. She was as necessary for his liberation, as he for hers!

The simplicity and quickness of the lady's answer to the knight's request for her love are remarkable. She might have hesitated, she might have offered objections, or she might have continued to feel afraid. The knight is not only a stranger, he is a most mysterious stranger. Yet the lady immediately answers yes. And her one condition is simply that he be a human being, that he have a soul: a bird can not believe in God.

And why does the lady answer 'yes' so quickly? Simply because he was so handsome: "E dit qu'ele en ferat sun dru, / ... Kar mut esteit de grant beauté": (138, 141). Surely these lines, and 142-144 as well, do not belong to the indirect discourse. When the knight replies, 'Vus dites bien' (145), he is agreeing to her conditions, not to her words about his beauty. It is Marie, then, who analyzes for us the lady's motives.

The knight assures her of his orthodoxy and asks to be put to the test: (145-68)

<pre>
       'Dame,' dit il, 'vus dites bien.
       Ne vodreie pur nule rien
       Que de mei i ait acheisun,
148   Mescreauncë u suspesçun.
       Jeo crei mut bien al Creatur,
       Que nus geta de la tristur,
       Ú Adam nus mist, nostre pere,
152   Par le mors de la pumme amere;
       Il est e ert e fu tuz jurs
       Vie e lumere as pecheürs .
       Si vus de ceo ne me creez,
</pre>

---

[12] *Yonec* is the second of Marie's lays (cf. *Guigemar*) in which the two lovers are destined for each other.

```
156  Vostre chapelain demandez;
     Dites ke mal vus ad susprise,
     Si volez aver le servise
     Que Deus ad el mund establi,
160  Dunt li pecheür sunt gari;
     La semblance de vus prendrai,
     Le cors [Damne]deu recevrai,
     Ma creance vus dirai tute;
164  Ja de ceo ne seez en dute!'
     El li respunt que bien ad dit.
     Delez li s'est cuché al lit;
     Mes il ne vout a li tucher
168  [Ne] de acoler ne de baiser.
```

In the knight's request, we learn about a second metamorphosis: he will assume the guise of the lady in order to take Holy Communion and to recite the Credo.[18] The lady, apparently, is *not* afraid of this particular transformation, for she agrees at once to his suggestion.

A striking feature of this section is the theological flavor of the knight's words. If he had said, simply: "Oh yes, I do believe in God," the lady probably would have been satisfied. But he must mention the Redemption and the Fall of Man (150-1); he must also characterize God in relation to sinners; he must point out the divine origin of communion and its efficacy for sinners. One may doubt whether the lady cares at all for all this theology; the only time (that we know about) that she has prayed to God, it was to ask to send her a lover. May there not be humor in this section — since all the lady really wanted to know was "are you human?"

The old woman is sent to fetch the priest: (169-90)

```
     Atant la veille est repeirie;
     La dame trovat esveillie,
     Dist li que tens est de lever;
172  Ses dras li voleit aporter.
     La dame dist que ele est malade.
```

---

[18] This second metamorphosis of the knight would indeed involve a problem: there would be two of the lady in her bed! But *la vielle* will apparently not notice that.

>   Del chapelain [se] prenge garde,
>   Sil face tost a li venir,
> 176 Kar grant poür ad de murir.
>   La veille dist: 'Or vus suffrez!
>   Mis sires est al bois alez;
>   Nul n'enterra ça enz fors mei.'
> 180 Mut fu la dame en grant esfrei;
>   Semblant fist que ele se pasma.
>   Cele le vit, mut s'esmaia.
>   L'us de la chambre ad defermé,
> 184 Si ad le prestre demandé;
>   E cil i vint cum plus tost pot,
>   Corpus domini aportot.
>   Li chevaler l'ad receü,
> 188 Le vin del chalice beü.
>   Li chapeleins s'en est alez,
>   E la vielle ad les us fermez.

In this passage we feel a swiftness of action (particularly in 180-90) which affords a strong contrast to the slowness of the preceding scene (in which the knight has made a long speech). Again, some humor is evident: the chaplain (probably an elder man, given the husband's jealousy) comes quickly with the *corpus domini* (why should Latin be used at that moment?) And do we not have to do with a third metamorphosis, since Christ is present in the Host?

Now the lovers are alone: (191-6)

>   La dame gist lez sun ami:
> 192 Unke si bel cuple ne vi.
>   Quant unt asez ris e jüé
>   E de lur priveté parlé,
>   Li chevaler ad cungé pris;
> 196 Raler s'en volt en sun païs.

This passage, in which the knight's desire in coming to the lady is now fulfilled, is notable for its elegance and delicacy. One could almost say that the love-making takes place in one line, the opening line: "La dame gist lez sun ami." And Marie, drawing near to the lovers, looks upon them and finds them beautiful;[14] that is all.

For in the next sentence it is all over, the knight is ready to depart; and the only details of their love-making that Marie reports *(rire, juer, parler)* are summarized in a dependent clause, a clause looking forward to the lover's departure. Yet in this section there is no feeling of swift action, simply calm: "La dame gist lez sun ami," and a summary of something that is already over.

Before leaving, the knight expresses a premonition: (197-210)

> Ele le prie ducement
> Quë il la reveie sovent.
> 'Dame,' fet il, 'quant vus plerra,
> 200 Ja l'ure ne trespassera.
> Mes tele mesure esgardez
> Que nus ne seium encumbrez:
> Ceste vielle nus traïra,
> 204 [E] nuit e jur nus gaitera.
> Ele parcevra nostre amur,
> Sil cuntera sun seignur.
> Si ceo avi[e]nt cum jeo vus di,
> 208 [E] nus serum issi trahi,
> Ne m'en puis mie departir,
> Que mei nen estuce murir.'

The knight's warning to the lady [15] (which will be the first of his many predictions to her) reveals a curious threefold development. First, whatever danger there may be is presented as something that can be avoided, if only the lady will be sufficiently careful; nor does the knight specify the danger ("... ne seium encumbrez"). Quite different in tone are the next four

---

[14] It may be noted that Marie's assertion in 192 ("Unke si bel cuple ne vi") is the last in a series of statements concerning physical appearance: first Marie mentions the lady's beauty (22 and 24); then the knight's beauty (115); next, the lady's appraisal of the knight's beauty (141-4); finally, there is Marie's own estimation of the couple's beauty.

[15] It should be noted that *Yonec* and *Guigemar* (the two lays where there is a surrealistic atmosphere) are also the two lays where prophecy and prediction are the most important.

lines (203-6) [16] where the danger is specified in detail; after the general reference to betrayal (203) come the three stages this betrayal will take. The betrayal is presented as if it were a fact, a fact of the future, as something inevitable.

Then again there is a shift: with "if" (207) we have passed from apparent certainty, to mere possibility. However, of one thing the knight is absolutely sure: he is sure of the result of the betrayal. He is sure that it would mean death to him if the events he predicated in the future tense were to be realized. And with this note of finality, with this emphasis on death, the account of his first visit closes.

So happy is the lady in the days that follow that she regains her beauty: (211-24)

```
        Li chevalers atant s'en veit,
212  A grant joie s'amie leit.
     Al demain lieve tute seine; [17]
     Mut fu haitie la semeine.
     Sun cors teneit a grant chierté,
216  Tute recovre sa beauté.
     Or li plest plus a surjurner
     Que en nul autre deduit aler.
     Sun ami volt suvent veer
220  E de lui sun delit aveir
     Desque sis sires [s'en] depart,
     E nuit e jur e tost e tart,
     Ele l'ad tut a sun pleisir.
224  Or li duinst Deus lunges joïr!
```

From these lines we learn of the radical transformation that has taken place in the lady, a transformation both mental and physical. Her deep grief has been turned to joy; as a result, her beauty that has been destroyed by her grief is now restored. And whereas she had once longed to *aler en deduit* ("Si jo puïsse od

---

[16] It is not too clear why in 203-6 the knight seems so sure: does he suddenly have a prophetic vision? Then why does he say *if*; does he not trust his prophetic powers? And if he doesn't trust them, why is he so sure of his own death (if . . .)?

[17] This line ("Al demain lieve tute seine") reminds us of her earlier feigned illness ("La dame dist que ele est malade": 173).

gent parler / E en deduit od eus aler...": 77-8), now she enjoys her confinement.

In this passage the emphasis on joy and the lady's complete happiness are conspicuous. The word *joie* with which the section opens is echoed in *mult fu haitie* (214), *li plest plus* (217), *de lui sun delit* (220), *a sun pleisir* (223). Furthermore, the absence of limits to this joy is described in *e nuit e jur e tost e tart* (222). This section is concluded by Marie's fervent wish that the joy may last long (224). Yet does not the wish itself suggest that the lady's happiness will inevitably end?

Her shrewd husband, noticing the change in her, questions his sister: (225-41)

   Pur la grant joie u ele fu,
   Que ot suvent pur veer sun dru,
   Esteit tut sis semblanz changez.
228 Sis sire esteit mut veiz[ï]ez:
   En sun curage se aparceit
   Que autrement est k'i[l] ne suleit;
   Mescreance ad vers sa serur.
232 Il la met a reisun un jur
   E dit que mut [a] grant merveille
   Que la dame si se appareille;
   Demande li que ceo deveit.
236 La vielle dit que el ne saveit—
   Kar nul ne pot parler od li,
   Në ele n'ot dru në ami—
   Fors tant que sule remaneit
240 Plus volenters que el ne suleit;
   De ceo s'esteit aparceüe.

The *joïr* of 224 is echoed in the *joie* of the next sentence in which Marie insists again on the complete transformation of the lady — this climax being followed immediately by the first suggestion of the falling movement of the lay: the lady's husband, Marie tells us, was very shrewd and noticed that a change had taken place in his wife. Although he does not voice his suspicions to his sister, her insistence that the lady has no lover ("në... dru në ami") makes it clear that she has guessed them. Apparently she, less sensitive to feminine beauty than her brother, had noticed not so much the change in the lady's appearance as her new contentment in captivity.

The husband sets his sister the task of spying upon his young wife: (242-56)

>   Dunc l'ad li sires respundue:
>   'Par fei,' fet il, 'ceo qui jeo bien!
> 244 Or vus estuet fere une rien:
>   Al matin, quant jeo erc levez
>   E vus avrez les hus fermez,
>   Fetes semblant de fors eissir,
> 248 Si la lessez sule gisir;
>   En un segrei liu vus estez,
>   E si veez e esgardez
>   Quei ceo peot estre e dunt ço vient
> 252 Ki en si grant joie [la] tient.'
>   De cel cunseil sunt departi.
>   Allas! cum ierent malbailli
>   Cil ki l'un veut si agaitier
> 256 Pur eus traïr e enginner!

About this rather brief section there is little to say except for the abstract, intellectual nature of the task imposed by the husband upon his sister in 249-52: from the vantage-point of a hiding-place she should seek to discover the nature and the origin ("Quei ceo peot estre e dunt ço vient...") of what it is that brings such joy to his wife. The husband, who soon will plan cold-bloodedly the knight's death, appears here as one interested only in ascertaining the truth about a psychological development his wife has experienced; he seems to have a clinical interest. And the word *joie* in his mouth has a sinister ring. (Note too, that the husband's reply (243-52) is the only instance when his words are given in direct address.)

Marie, who so recently had wished the lovers lasting enjoyment, must now lament their fate,[18] in words recalling the premonition of the knight: *agaitier* and *traïr*. Both these passages serve as a kind of foil to the *trahiz* used by the lady in her lament about her husband, whom she derided for his foolish fear of being betrayed.

Three days later the trap is set: (257-66)

---

[18] Does Marie pity the lovers because she, as the author, will do away with them?

> Tiers jur aprés, ceo oi cunter,
> Fet li sires semblant de errer.
> A sa femme ad dit e cunté
> 260 Que li reis [l]'ad par briefs mandé;
> Mes hastivement revendra.
> De la chambre ist e l'us ferma.
> Dunc s'esteit la vielle levee,
> 264 Triers une cortine est alee;
> Bien purrat oïr e veer
> Ceo que ele cuveite a saver.

These ten lines are reminiscent of the ten lines that open the first section of the lay:

> Ceo fu al meis de avril entrant,
> Quant cil oisel meinent lur chant.
> Li sires fu matin levez;
> De aler en bois s'est aturnez.
> La viellë ad fet lever sus
> E aprés lui fermer les hus.
> Cele ad fet sun comandement.
> Li sires s'en vet od sa gent.
> La vielle portot sun psauter,
> U ele voleit verseiller.   (51-60)

Again the husband leaves the bed-chamber (and the house), giving a reason for his departure. Again the old woman locks the door after him; and again she retires from the room. But this time it is not to another room that she goes, to read her psalter, but behind a curtain where, Marie assures us, she will be well able to learn what it is she is so eager to know.

The knight comes to the lady, and the old woman watches: (267-78)

> La dame jut; pas ne dormi,
> 268 Kar mut desire sun ami.
> Venuz i est, pas ne demure,
> Ne trespasse terme në hure.
> Ensemble funt joie mut grant,
> 272 E par parole e par semblant,
> De si ke tens fu de lever;
> Kar dunc li estuveit aler.
> Cele le vit, si l'esgarda,
> 276 Coment il vient e il ala;

> De ceo ot ele grant poür
> Que hume le vit e pus ostur.

In this section where great emphasis is placed upon the visual, the first two lines are given over to the lady and her desire for her lover; the next two lines to the lover, who arrives immediately (twice the quickness of his coming is stressed); four lines to their union (so briefly and delicately described), followed by his departure ("because the time had come").

But what we have just seen, someone else has seen; and the last four lines (275-8) concern this witness and her reactions. She has seen the love and the happiness of the couple, she has taken in the obvious fact that her brother has been cuckolded; but none of this, evidently, has impressed her. The old woman reacts (and reacts with fear, as the lady herself had done) to only one detail of the scene, the metamorphosis of the lover. In fact, this detail is twice mentioned: not only in 278 ("... Que hume le vit e pus ostur") [19] but also in 276: the couplet (275-6) "Cele le vit, si l'esgarda, / Coment il vient e il ala" (which, incidentally, sums up the whole visit) refers, of course, to seeing him come and leave in the form of a bird. This double insistence upon the metamorphosis seems to reflect the old woman's amazement and fear. [20]

The absence of truly audible speech between the lovers heightens the dramatic effect of this scene where they unknowingly become a spectacle to be watched. It is as if the old woman were all eyes, interested in only what she saw. Although there is a vague murmur in the background ("Ensemble funt joie mut

---

[19] Of the two metamorphoses the old woman must have seen (ostur > hume; hume > ostur) Marie chooses to mention only the second one.

[20] This insistence upon the old woman's fears also serves to remind the reader of something he may have temporarily forgotten. For Marie, after the description of the lover's first appearance, omits reference to the metamorphoses undergone by him: nothing is said of this when he leaves the first time ("Li chevaler ad cungé pris": 195; and also, "Li chevalers atant s'en veit": 211). There is no indication of it in the reference to his numerous, unspecified visits or in the description of his arrival and departure in the present scene (note that his nature is unspecified: "Venuz i est...", without subject (269). Thus, the one detail that Marie omits from her description is the only one that impressed the witness to this scene.

grant, / E par parole e par semblant": 271-2), yet it is mostly the visual senses, not the auditory, that are stimulated in this scene.

The husband, when informed, plans to murder the lover: (279-96)

>   Quant li sires fu repeirez,
> 280 Que gueres n'esteit esluignez,
>   Cele li ad dit e mustré
>   Del chevalier la verité;
>   E il en est forment pensifs.
> 284 Des engins faire fu hastifs
>   A ocire le chevalier.
>   Broches de fer fist [granz] forgier
>   E acerer le chief devant:
> 288 Suz ciel n'ad rasur plus trenchant.
>   Quant il les ot apparailliees
>   E de tutes parz enfurchiees,
>   Sur la fenestre les ad mises,
> 292 Bien serreies e bien asises,
>   Par unt le chevaler passot,
>   Quant a la dame repeirot.
>   Deus! qu'il ne sout la traïsun
> 296 Quë aparaillot le felun.

This interview, like the first one between the husband and his sister, is unstaged. It has been said that the bed-chamber, the scene of the main action (of the narrative), is never described. It is also true that when something takes place off-stage, as in the two interviews of the sire and his sister, we are never allowed to know where the characters are. This impossibility not only of visualizing the two schemers but also of locating them in space, is most effective: we simply hear voices in the air surmising and plotting. It is notable, too, that these two interviews form a sinister frame; the lover's second specified visit is both preceded and followed by plans for his betrayal.

We must also point out the brevity of this interview, the brevity of the old woman's words, and their abstract, intellectual nature, which reflect the tone of her brother's earlier command: she tells him "the truth" about the knight.

In her brother's reaction to her words, the word *pensifs* must be noted. Although this word in Old French usually suggests grief (or love-longing), it could be used of simple mental concentration; I prefer to interpret it in this same sense here. We should now remind ourselves that the first reference to his cruel jealousy is presented in terms of mental concentration ("De ceo kë ele ert bele e gente, / En li garder mist mut s'entente": 25-6). In our passage the "thoughtfulness" will lead to the invention of the instruments of death. As for the husband's mental activity, we must also point out the quality attributed to him in 228 ("mut veiz[ï]ez"), which signals the beginning of the falling action in our lay.

The eleven lines given to the description of the "engines" (one couplet of summary, 284-5, followed by nine lines of gruesome detail) lead immediately to Marie's sorrowful lament. It may be noted that the passages dealing with the activity of the brother and sister (her espionage and his fabrication of the "engines") are preceded and followed by auctorial interjections of pity ("Allas!...": 254; "Deus!...": 295), the first of which concerns both lovers, the second (naturally enough) the knight alone. [21]

The next day the lady again desires her lover, who comes immediately: (297-308)

>   Al demain en la matinee
>   Li sires lieve ainz l'ajurnee
>   E dit qu'il vot aler chacier. [22]
> 300 La vielle le vait cunveer,
>   Puis se recuche pur dormir, [23]

---

[21] Before leaving this particular section, one further comment is in order. Why does the lady not see the fastening of the "engines" to the window of her room? Is it perhaps that she is not there when they are being affixed? But we know that she is not allowed to leave her room; even if she were absent when they were being attached, she would have to see them at the window when she came back. If they had been placed below the window, then they could have been attached from the outside without her knowing it and she need not have noticed them. But then the "engines" would not have killed the knight!

[22] As for *li sires'* third departure, we must point out its connection with his first departure from his home: in both instances the woods are his destination. Yet "hunting" is mentioned only in the description in our passage, after the husband has set the traps for the bird!

[23] One would think that the old woman would want to see the unusual thing once again, as if to verify her own vision. But no, she goes back to

>   Kar ne poeit le jur choisir.
>   La dame veille, si atent
> 304 Celui que ele eime lëalment,
>   E dit que or purreit bien venir
>   E estre od li tut a leisir.
>   Si tost cum el l'ad demandé,
> 308 N'i ad puis gueres demuré:

Here we have the third and last (i.e., at a specified time) visit of the lover. Again the husband will arise early,[24] again the sister will accompany him to the door;[25] again the lady will desire her lover, who again, will come to her immediately. It is interesting that for this final, fatal visit, Marie elaborates more than ever on the lady's desire, stressing particularly her confidence in freedom from disturbance (*tut a leisir*: 306)!

Bleeding from his fatal wounds, her lover joins her on the bed: (309-18)

>   En la fenestre vient volant,
>   Mes les broches furent devant;
>   L'une le fiert par mi le cors,[26]
> 312 Li sanc vermeil en eissi fors.
>   Quant il se sot de mort nafré,
>   Desferré tut enz est entré;
>   Devant la dame al lit descent,
> 316 Que tut li drap furent sanglent.
>   Ele veit le sanc e la plaie,
>   Mut anguissusement s'esmaie.

---

bed to sleep, knowing that everything will be taken care of. And, as far as the reader is concerned, she will continue to sleep — for we never hear of her again.

[24] The husband arises before dawn — perhaps because he wishes his absence to bring the lover while it is still dark and the bristling prongs will not be perceived?

[25] The sister does this, evidently to lock the door behind him, but for some reason this reminder of imprisonment is lacking here. Or does this omission serve to anticipate the scene of the lady's escape from the tower? Perhaps one could even say that the very failure (yet serving no practical purpose) to mention the locking of the door faintly suggests the possibility of the lady's escape.

[26] Was his, like Guigemar's, a sexual wound? We can only wonder where he was wounded (and we must remember that he was in the form of a bird); for we are told only "... par mi le cors."

For this last visit, the lover is shown us in the same form [27] as when he first came to his love; but the line (*En la fenestre vient volant:* 309) reminding us of his first visit (and seeming thereby to guarantee continuity) is immediately followed by "But...": "Mes les broches furent devant." [28]

The crimson blood gushed forth, Marie tells us; the sheets on the lady's bed are made bloody. [29] For the first time a pictorial detail is offered us, for the first time we see a color. From this point on in the lay, descriptive details will abound.

He prophesies the birth of their son, and then departs: (319-35)

```
        Il li ad dit: 'Ma duce amie,
320     Pur vostre amur perc jeo la vie;
        Bien le vus dis qu'en avendreit:
        Vostre semblant nus ocireit.' 30
        Quant el l'oï, dunc chiet pasmee;
324     Tute fu morte une loëe. 31
        Il la cunforte ducement
        E dit que dols n'i vaut nïent;
        De lui est enceinte d'enfant,
328     Un fiz avra pruz e vaillant:
        Icil [la] recunforterat;
        Yonec numer le f[e]rat,
        Il vengerat [e] lui e li,
332     Il oscirat sun enemi.
        Il ne peot dunc demurer mes,
        Kar sa plaie seignot adés.
        A grant dolur s'en est partiz.
```

---

[27] Although the metamorphosis is not described, it must have taken place on this as on all other visits; and we may perhaps assume that it takes place immediately after his "descent" onto her bed: that is, in the space of the two lines describing the lady's anguish: 317-18.

[28] Why did the lover not notice the *broches*?

[29] The bloody bed of the lady is an analogy with that of Iseut, made bloody by Tristan's visit to her.

[30] *Yonec* is the second of Marie's lays where lack of *mesure* (here, on the part of the lady; in *Les Deus Amanz,* on the part of the youth) will lead to death.

[31] Although fainting was a stock gesture in medieval literature, such a phrase as *tute fu une loëe morte* is no cliché. The lady is probably sitting up in bed (that is where we have always seen her), and then falls backward; her backwards fall makes 324 ("Tute fu morte une loëe) all the more significant. Following upon the knight's words "...vostre semblant nus ocireit," it is surely intended to suggest an "as-if" realization of his prophecy:

The first and most important thing to be mentioned about this passage is the reproachful speech of the knight to the lady: he claims to have warned her that her appearance would destroy them, whereas, actually, he said nothing of the kind. He had not mentioned her "semblant." The only thing he had said to her was that she should *esgarder mesure,* without further explanation. Should we perhaps assume that in this general phrase he was warning her not to appear too happy?

There may, however, be another explanation: he had promised her in the first visit that he would come whenever she wished; immediately afterwards, however, he urges her to *esgarder mesure:* i.e., not to insist on too frequent visits. Now, the more often he comes, the more marked should be her transformation (and is this what the knight had in mind?). At any rate, she seems to have used no restraint in sending for him ("E nuit e jur e tost e tart"); and his last visit comes only one day after the preceding one. [32]

In addition to his words of reproach, the knight also speaks words of comfort to his love. After reminding her of his first prophecy, the knight prophesies (in a somewhat Biblical tone) a second time: he speaks of the son who will be born to her, whom she should name Yonec, and who will comfort and avenge her. [33] One question might be raised. In *De lui est enceinte d'enfant* is he reminding her, by way of comfort, of the child that she knows she will bear? Or is she still unaware of her pregnancy, so that this statement, too, is a prophecy? I would rather judge that to be the case.

---

an anticipation of its ultimate realization (when she will die, incidentally, in a faint). (Moreover, the lady, who now is lying — as if dead — in her bed, will find her lover, dying, in his bed.)

[32] One further remark about "... Vostre semblant nus ocireit": in his opening words of warning to the lady, the knight had not mentioned the possibility of their death, only of their being "encumbrez" (in the last line of his first prediction, he refers to his own death). It may be that the knight, who is ready to begin his second prophecy, has already foreseen her death — and it is true that her death will be a (belated) result of the tragedy of their betrayal (which, in turn, was a result of the lady's changed "semblant").

[33] For the expression *sun enemi* (332), there are three possible meanings: 'her enemi, his enemy, Yonec's enemy.' The most probable is that the knight means her enemy, i. e., *li sires.*

The lady leaps through a window and follows his course: (336-44)

> 336 Ele le siut a mut grant criz. [34]
> Par une fenestre s'en ist;
> C'est merveille k'el ne s'ocist,
> Kar bien aveit vint piez de haut
> 340 Iloec u ele prist le saut.
> Ele esteit nue en sa chemise.
> A la trace del sanc s'est mise,
> Que del chevaler [de]curot
> 344 Sur le chemin u ele alot.

This sudden move on the lady's part is breath-taking. For seven years she has been confined in the tower (and apparently, in the bedchamber; in fact, we have always seen her in bed). We have accepted the fact that, because of the carefully-guarded doors, all possibility of escape is precluded. The lady herself had proclaimed (line 70) that only after death would she leave her prison. [35] We knew there was a window, through which her lover could come and go [36] — but only by assuming the form of a bird. No reader could possibly have anticipated that, suddenly, the lady would rise from her bed and, rushing to the window, leap out. [37] And her jump is all the more remarkable in view of her pregnancy!

Not only had we accepted her perpetual confinement: we had accepted her character as one of utter passivity. The boldest thing the lady had ever done was to make a wish; before then she had

---

[34] This is the second time in Marie's lays that we have heard a character scream: the girl in *Les Deus Amanz* who laments her dead lover with screams, here, the lady, screaming, who follows her wounded lover. And these two are the only lays where the lover dies.

[35] As it turns out, it is not her own death but the imminent death of her lover that is the reason for her leaving the tower.

[36] *Yonec* is the second (cf. *Equitan*) of three lays in which there are three specified meetings of the protagonists.

[37] This window could not have been the one that has figured so far in the story, for it would have been called "la fenestre," not "une fenestre." One may compare here the description of the lover's arrival for his second specified visit, "En *la* fenestre vient volant" (309). Then, too, it is most obvious that if the lady leapt through the window to which the "engines" had been attached, she too would have been wounded.

languished in her prison for seven years, with apparently no idea of rebelling or even protesting (and surely not of attempting to escape). Afterwards, her happiness had also been of a primarily passive nature: her life consisted in lying in bed, desiring and receiving her lover. Now she springs into action, risking her life to follow him. And with this act, we have the climax of her slow emergence as a personality.

The drops of blood lead her to a beautiful city: (345-78) [38]

>   Icel senti[e]r errat e tient,
>   De s[i] que a une hoge vient.
>   En cele hoge ot une entree,
> 348 De cel sanc fu tute arusee;
>   Ne pot nïent avant veer.
>   Dunc quidot ele bien saver
>   Que sis amis entré i seit;
> 352 Dedenz se met en grant espleit.
>   El n'i trovat nule clarté.
>   Tant ad le dreit chemin erré
>   Que fors de la hoge [est] issue
> 356 E en un mut bel pre venue;
>   [Del sanc trova l'erbe muilliee,
>   Dunc s'est ele mut esmaiee;]
>   La trace en siut par mi le pre.
> 360 Asez pres ot une cité;
>   De mur fu close tut entur;
>   N'i ot mesun, sale ne tur,
>   Que ne parust tute d'argent;
> 364 Mut sunt riche li mandement.
>   Devers le burc sunt li mareis
>   E les forez e les difeis.
>   De l'autre part vers le dunjun
> 368 Curt une ewe tut envirun;
>   Ileoc arivoënt les nefs,

---

[38] In this section describing the lady's journey, we note for the second time Marie's concern with bodies of water and navigation. In other *lais* we find similar references, but in ours it serves no practical purpose: why this purely gratuitous reference? The first allusion immediately following the presentation of the old sire ("La cité siet sur Düelas; / Jadis i ot de nes trespas": 15-16) might indicate decay, as well as slow up the narrative; then the second surely should indicate a thriving condition: but the knight is dying! And more than 300 ships is a fantastic number of ships at one time! It should be pointed out that the town mentioned earlier (i. e. that of the sire) faintly anticipates the sea-girt city of the knight.

"YONEC" 195

>   Plus i aveit de treis cent tres.
>   La porte aval fu desfermee;
> 372 La dame est en la vile entree
>   Tuz jurs aprés le sanc novel
>   Par mi le burc deske al chastel.
>   Unkes nul a li ne parla;
> 376 Humme ne femme n'i trova.
>   Al paleis vient al paviment,
>   Del sanc [le] treve tut sanglent.

After having restricted the on-stage activity to the narrow area of a bedroom, suddenly, after the lady's leap, Marie sets the stage in space unconfined. After having offered nothing upon which the eye could dwell (until the moment when the life-blood of the knight gushes forth), now pictorial details abound, the one constant, colorful element being the drops of blood. And not content to describe the city, Marie must offer the topography of the surrounding country-side. Perhaps the river is there to give variety to the landscape, and the many, many ships are there to fill out the panorama.

At last she comes to her lover: (379-96)

>   En une bele chambre entra;
> 380 Un chevaler dormant trova,
>   Nel cunut pas, si vet avant
>   En un' autre chambre plus grant;
>   Un lit trevë e nïent plus,
> 384 Un chevaler dormant desus.
>   Ele s'en est utre passee;
>   En la tierce chambre est entree,
>   Le lit sun ami ad trové.
> 388 Li pecul sunt de or esmeré;
>   Ne sai mie les dras preisier;
>   Li cirgë e li chandelier,
>   Que nuit e jur sunt alumé,
> 392 Valent tut l'or d'une cité.
>   Si tost cum ele l'ad veü,
>   Le chevaler ad cuneü.
>   Avant alat tut esfrëe[e],
> 396 Par desus lui cheï pasmee.

The lady, after passing through two bed-chambers, in each of which she finds a sleeping knight, enters a third in which she finds her (mortally) wounded lover.[39] But why does Marie triple the beds and the knights? Probably because she could not have the lady come upon her lover immediately [40] (most fairy-tales attempts go through three stages).[41] As to why she chose precisely this mode of suspense, it could be not only that she wishes to multiply the reflections of the bed-image, but also because the sleep of the first two knights could be a prefiguration of death.

The elaborate description of the knight's bed [42] is doubly effective. Not only does it create suspense (for it is only after the bed has been described that the lady is shown going toward her

---

[39] When the lady finally sees her lover (in 394), note that he, too is called a *chevaler*. He must have been lying upon his bed as he would probably lie in state upon his bier, with his sword — although his sword is not mentioned until line 421.

The visit of the lady to her wounded lover is paralleled in the visit of Blancheflor to Rivalen, in the *Tristan* story.

[40] A parallel between *Yonec* and *Lanval* may be noted, for in both the device of 'double anticipation' is used. Toward the end of *Lanval*, two groups of two maidens (in contrast to just one knight in each of the two successive rooms in *Yonec*) precede the arrival of the fairy mistress. The maidens serve no purpose at all, although they pretend they do, by giving instructions about the rooms for their mistress.

As for *Yonec*, a close examination of Marie's presentation of the three knights and the three beds is very interesting. In the first room, the lady finds (380) a sleeping knight (which implies a bed); in the second, it is the bed (383) that is first predicated (it is as if the bed were gaining in prominence), then a knight (384); in the third, first the bed (387), on a large scale indeed, is seen (and it is very nice that the 'nothing more' of 383 anticipates what the lady will find in the third room, where there are so many furnishings), and finally, her lover (394).

Bédier, speaking of the final episode in *Lanval*, mentions the *émerveillement croissant* produced by the successive appearance of the two groups of two maidens, climaxed by the arrival of the fairy mistress. The purpose of the narrative method in the final episode in *Lanval* as well as in the scene in *Yonec* where the lady passes through a series of rooms to find her lover is one of postponement of the climax (Joseph Bédier, ed. *Roman de Tristan* par Thomas d'Angleterre (Paris, 1902, 1905), I, 335).

Because of Marie's manner of narration, in *Lanval* there is an increase in the climax. In *Yonec*, we can not really speak of an increase in the climax of this particular scene, although the lady surely must have wondered (because of the *cunut* in 381) each time she saw a knight 'Is that my lover?'; then, when she does find him, note the form *ad cuneü* (394).

[41] Note the rather frequent use of the number 3 in our lay: the three specified visits of the lover, the three gifts he gives to the lady.

[42] The knight's bed, unlike that of the lady, is not presented as bloody.

wounded lover),[43] but it offers a striking contrast to the lady's bed. Though that was the scene of their love-making, and the fixed spot to which the lady always seemed to be limited, it was never described in any way.[44]

Then, too, we note the symbolic differences or likenesses between the two beds: his bed, unlike hers, is for himself alone, to die upon, not a bed of union for the two lovers. Still the lady does share his bed, briefly (when she faints), as if sharing in his death. Furthermore, the knight's bed is a prefiguration of his second bed, the tomb in the abbey.[45]

The action related by the words "Par desus lui cheï pasmee" (396) is paralleled by the lady's later fainting spell when she hears the bells tolling her lover's death. But more significant, because fainting is such a stock device in medieval literature, is the parallel with 315, when the knight "descends" to her. Her movement toward him on the bed *(par desus lui)* parallels his toward her, just as her journey through space to him is a reciprocation of his journeys to her.

The whole progression of this section, as well as the preceding one (347-58), once the darkness of the narrow passage of the hill is left behind, is toward spaciousness and light. When the lady comes out from that dark passage, she first sees a beautiful meadow, then a city glittering bright, then a rather vast expanse of landscape — and finally, she will see a blaze of light concentrated on a small space (the knight's bed).

Her lover comforts her, gives her gifts, and sends her away: (397-440)

---

[43] The reader may note a parallel between *Yonec* and *Guigemar;* these are the only two lays in which the lady finds a wounded knight upon a bed.

[44] The failure to describe the lady's bed belongs to the over-all pattern of the lay: in the first part no object is described; in the second, pictorial descriptions appear, and not only of the bed and tomb. Perhaps the lack of description in the first part is in accord with the secrecy of the lovers' situation, with its gradual, final revelation (in the second part of the lay) occurring after the very elaborate description of the tomb (in which the lady will be placed, to lie eternally beside her dead lover).

[45] In this lay, there are three stages in the development of the *Symbolding*, the bed: A (the lady's bed) and C (the tomb) frame stage B which is three-fold (the three knights and the three beds).

Cil la receit que forment l'aime,
Maleürus sovent se claime.
Quant de pasmer fu trespassee,
400 Il l'ad ducement cunfortee: [46]
'Bele amie, pur Deu, merci! [47]
Alez vus en! Fuiez d'ici!
Sempres murai devant le jur;
404 Ci einz avrat si grant dolur,
Si vus [i] esteiez trovee,
Mut en serïez turmentee:
Bien iert entre ma gent seü
408 Que me unt par vostre amur perdu.
Pur vus sui dolent e pensis.'
La dame li ad dit: 'Amis,
Meuz voil ensemble od vus murir
412 Que od mun seignur peine suffrir.
S'a lui revois, il me ocira.'
Li chevalier l'aseüra.
Un anelet li ad baillé,
416 Si li ad dit e enseigné:
Ja, tant cum el le gardera,
A sun seignur n'en membera
De nule rien que fete seit,
420 Ne ne l'en tendrat en destreit.
S'espee li cumande e rent,
Puis la cunjurë e defent
Que ja nul hum n'en seit saisiz,
424 Mes bien la gart a oés sun fiz.
Quant il serat creüz e grant
E chevalier pruz e vaillant,
A une feste u ele irra,
428 Sun seignur e lui amerra.
En une abbeïe vendrunt;
Par une tumbe k'il verrunt
Orrunt renoveler sa mort
432 E cum il fu ocis a tort.
Ileoc li baillerat s'espeie.
L'aventure li seit cuntee

---

[46] One might wonder why Marie uses the word *cunforter*, since the words that follow are a warning! But we feel most strongly that the entire expression *cunforter ducement* (after the lady has fainted) is an echo of 325 (yet in the reverse order of events), when the knight, after having first spoken words of reproach to the lady, then "gently comforts" her.

[47] With the knight's words of "bele amie," the shift (begun when he first addressed his comfort to the lady, "Ma duce amie": 319) from his previous formal address ("Dame") is most striking.

>   Cum il fu nez, ki le engendra;
> 436 Asez verrunt k'il en fera.
>   Quant tut li ad did e mustré,
>   Un chier bliant li ad doné,
>   Si li cumandë a vestir;
> 440 Puis l'ad fete de lui partir.

The knight's final words to the lady fall into two parts. In the first (401-9) he urges her (twice in the very same line, 402) to leave before his people learn of her presence and do her harm; though, in a sense, she has caused his death, his only concern is for her welfare.[48] In the second section (416-36) he makes his third prophecy which is, indeed, mainly an amplification of his prophetic words uttered on his last visit to her, concerned with the avenging role of Yonec. Interestingly enough, instead of predicting outright this vengeance (as the knight had done earlier: 331-2), this time he leaves the outcome in suspense: "assez verrunt k'il en fera." There can surely be little doubt what Yonec, with the sword in his hand, will do with it, when he hears his mother relate the fateful "aventure"!

And one should (especially) note that the single line (435) in which this "aventure" is summed up, repeats the two details that Marie, in lines 6-8 of the Prologue had promised to clarify: "cum il fu nez" = "... e de sun pere / cum il vint primes a sa mere"; "ki l'engendra = "... d'Iwenec ... dunt il fu nez." Thus Marie's words in the Prologue to the story are repeated in the story itself by the knight to the mother who should repeat them to her (why not *their*) son! This last point is very important: in several other lays, it has already been pointed out that one of the most characteristic traits of Marie's narrative technique is that the events in a story become themselves a story to be told within a story.

In conjunction with Marie's narrative technique, we must also point out that the *Yonec* is the only lay where the point of view is that of the protagonist from beginning to end. The story is

---

[48] And this is the lady's sole concern, too! Indeed, in her only words of direct discourse to her lover (410-13) she shows no concern for him whatsoever: the lady prefers to die with him not because she cannot bear to live without him, but because if she goes home, her husband will kill her!

told entirely from the lady's point of view; we *never* see the lover alone.

Soon after leaving the city gates the lady hears the bells toll for her lover: (441-8)

>   Ele s'en vet, l'anel en porte
>   E l'espee ki la cunforte.
>   A l'eissue de la cité
> 444   N'ot pas demie liwe erré,
>   Quant ele oï les seins suner
>   E le doel al chastel mener;
>   De la dolur què ele en ad
> 448   Quatre fïees se pasmad.

One notes the rather grim touch given by "L'espee ki la cunforte": the lady is evidently comforted at the thought of her husband's slaughter at the hands of her unborn child![49] And along with the tolling of the bells, the lady hears the mourning of the people for the dead lord (as her lover had predicted) — the only signs she has perceived that indicate the existence of the city's inhabitants.

The lady's visit to her lover was not one of the events prophesied by the knight; it was necessary, however, to the fulfillment of the knight's prediction about his death, in the sense that the fulfillment must be known to have taken place; if the lady had not gone to his land, she would not have heard the mourning. Her journey to him was also necessary to his prophecy about Yonec's act of vengeance: she had to go to her lover to receive the ring which would protect herself and her son from harm, and the sword by means of which the act of vengeance would be performed. The beauty of the parallel offered by her journey to him (as he came many times to her, so she must go once to him) is unmistakable.

She returns home, to live in peace with her husband: (449-56)

---

[49] This "comfort" afforded by the sword may remind us of the lines in her lament deploring her husband's longevity (i. e. her wish for his death). And is there not a contrast afforded by the grim tone of the verb *cunforter* in this passage, with the "gentle" or "sweet comfort" of lines 325 and 400? But are *those* words, too, of gentle comfort to the lady?

> E quant de paumesuns revient,
> Vers la hoge sa veie tient;
> Dedenz entra, si est passee,
> 452 Si s'en reveit en sa cuntree.
> Ensemblement od sun seignur
> Aprés [i] demurat meint jur,
> Que de cel fet ne la retta
> 456 Ne ne mesdist ne ne gaba.

The long return journey of the lady is described in three lines (450-2),[50] and her subsequent life with her husband which ensues peacefully, thanks to the magic ring given her by the knight,[51] is treated in two couplets.[52] Indeed, the long passage of time is summed up in two lines (453-4).[53] One feels here the rhythm of a final movement, as if the story had come to an end — and indeed one story has come to an end.

The son Yonec grows up and is dubbed a knight: (457-64)

> Lur fiz fu nez e bien nuriz
> E bien gardez e bien cheriz.
> Yonec le firent numer;
> 460 El regne ne pot hom trover
> Si bel, si pruz e si vaillant
> E larges e bien despendant.
> Quant il fu venuz en eez,
> 464 A chevaler l'unt [a]dubez.

---

[50] A clear parallel between *Yonec* and *Le Fresne* may be noted. In both lays, a woman makes a trip in which she is finding or searching her way; the *meschine* in *Le Fresne* responds to aural and visual stimuli to find her way; the lady in *Yonec*, to visual stimuli. In both cases, the trip to the destination is described in great detail, whereas the return journey is summed up very briefly.

[51] The lady's assertion to the knight that her husband would kill her on her return (413) is the second of her (two) predictions that fail to materialize. (Cf. "Ja n'en istrai si par mort nun": 70).

[52] In the summary of the lady's life after her return home, no mention whatever is made of the old woman; nor will we hear of her again in the narrative. What did she say to her brother? And we ask ourselves — What did the brother say to his sister?

[53] The use of the expression *meint jur* is indeed significant: not only is *Yonec* the only lay where it occurs, it will be used again in a very important scene (cf. 522) by "the people from the country." In its first appearance, it is the lady's confidence that is important, in the second, the impatience on the part of "the people from the country."

These eight lines cover the period of time from Yonec's birth to his growth to early manhood,[54] thus overlapping almost exactly the period of time summarized in the four lines (453-6) preceding this section, which describe the years that the lady lived with her husband after her return from her lover's deathbed.

The part of the mother in the rearing of her son is obliterated: in the first couplet this effect is achieved by the use of the passive ("fu ... nuriz ... gardez ... cheriz"). In the third line, we find the third person plural ("... le firent numer"), even though it is obvious that it was the mother who suggested the name, in accordance with the knight's request. And in the two sections that follow (465-506; 507-24), the figure of the lady is similarly obscured. One notes here, at the beginning of the second section of the lay, the obvious parallel with the lady's role in the first section: at the very beginning, she is left in the background, and then emerges (emotionally and even physically) with her lament, the regaining of her beauty, and her trip to her dying lover. During the second section of the narrative, the lady will remain obscured, only to come into prominence toward the end of the lay.

That same year they leave to attend the feast of St. Aaron: (465-506)

        A l'an meïsmes qeu ceo fu,
        Oëz cum[ent] est avenu!
        A la feste seint Aaron,
468 C'on selebrot a Karlïon
        E en plusurs autres citez,
        Li sire aveit esté mandez
        Qu'il i alast od ses amis
472 A la custume del païs;
        Sa femme e sun fiz i menast
        E richement s'aparaillast.
        Issi avint, alez i sunt;
476 Mes il ne seivent u il vunt.
        Ensemble od eus ot un meschin,
        Kis ad mené le dreit chemin,[55]

---

[54] Concerning the qualities of the grown Yonec, it is to be noted that the father (the knight) had twice prophesied that the son would be *pruz e vaillant* (328 and 426); in addition, Marie speaks of his beauty and his generosity (that quality so essential to the knightly ideal).

[55] One must point out the parallel of *le dreit chemin* in 478, with its previous use in 354, where, too, the path led to the (then wounded) knight.

Tant qu'il viendrent a un chastel;
480 En tut le siecle n'ot plus bel.
Une abbeïe i ot dedenz
De mut religïuses genz.
Li vallez les i herberga,
484 Quë a la feste les mena.
En la chambre que fu l'abbé
Bien sunt servi e honuré.
A demain vunt la messe oïr;
488 Puis s'en voleient departir.
Li abes vet od eus parler,
Mut les prie de surjurner;
Si lur must[er]rat sun dortur,
492 Sun chapitre, sun refeitur,
E cum il sunt [bien] herbergiez.
Li sires lur ad otrïez.
  Le jur quant il orent digné,
496 As officines sunt alé.
Al chapitre vindrent avant;
Une tumbe troverent grant
Covert[e] de un paile roé,
500 De un chier orfreis par mi bendé.
Al chief, as piez e as costez
Aveit vint cirges alumez.
De or fin erent li chandelier,
504 D'ametiste li encensier,
Dunt il encensouent le jur
Cele tumbe pur grant honur.

In 475-6 we have the most striking couplet in the section: no reader can fail to be struck by the suggestion of mystery in these lines (and of a fate not suspected by the characters). But the whole passage is imbued with mystery.[56] Who is it that summoned the husband to attend the religious celebration, with friends and family,[57] richly attired? Was it by order of the king referred to in 260? To what place did they go? They went to

---

The phrase *le dreit chemin* has a poetic quality which is, however, difficult to analyze.

[56] One may compare, too, the air of mystery surrounding the stranger, Muldumarec, on his first visit to the lady.

[57] One notes the effectiveness of the simple, and on the surface, commonplace phrase "sa femme e sun fiz" (473), given the real facts that the reader knows and the speaker did not.

attend a celebration in honor of St. Aaron which was performed at Caerleon and "several other cities"; we are not told that they went to Caerleon.

Why should they need a boy to guide them? One thinks of a religious celebration as being performed in a place easily accessible. And did the boy belong to the same locality as the husband, or was he sent to guide the group by the unidentified person who summoned the husband? And finally, did they follow the same route taken by the lady years ago (for the castle must be the castle of her lover, since the tomb — as we soon learn — is his)? There is no mention of the hill with the passage cut through, just as there is no reference to the walled city where the knight's castle was located. When the lady saw the castle (which has been converted into an abbey?), must she not have recognized it? But in this section, and the one that follows, we are not allowed to penetrate into her feelings.

The description of the tomb [58] serves to remind the reader of the similar, if less elaborate, description of the knight's bed; thus it is clear that his bed was intended as a prefiguration of his tomb. When the knight's bed was described, we were told that the candles were lit night and day. This reference to a habitual, or rather, continuous (day and night = 'forever') illumination of a bed is most strange; this must be a feature of his tomb which was lent to his bed by way of prefiguration. The illumination of the tomb is described with specific details (the exact number of the candles and their exact position): we are forced to visualize this tomb surrounded on all four sides by lights. This was not so of the lights burning near the knight's bed. This difference in description would be due not only to the desire to present the tomb climatically, but also because it would not have been fitting to give a precise description in the earlier section: the lights that burned eternally were merely an *anticipation* of the lights of the tomb.

---

[58] In both *Le Fresne* and *Yonec*, a *paile roé* is meant to serve as a covering for some object. In *Le Fresne*, the *paile roé* has a double function: first, as covering for the baby (an object found), then later, as covering for the nuptial bed. And in *Yonec*, the *paile roé* covering the knight's tomb is the (more sumptuous) counterpart to the sheets which covered the lady's bed.

They are told that the tomb is that of the lord of the land: (507-24)

          Il unt demandé e enquis
508   Icels ki erent del païs
          De la tumbe ki ele esteit,
          E queil hum fu ki la giseit.
          Cil comencerent a plurer
512   E en plurant a recunter
          Que c'iert le meudre chevalier
          E le plus fort e le plus fier,
          Le plus beaus [e] le plus amez
516   Que jamés seit el secle nez.
          De ceste tere ot esté reis;
          Unques ne fu nul si curteis.
          A Carwent fu entrepris,
520   Pur l'amur de une dame ocis.
          'Unques puis n'eümes seignur;
          Ainz avum atendu meint jur
          Un fiz que en la dame engendra,
524   Si cum il dist e cumanda.'

The atmosphere of mystery, noted in the preceding section, still lingers on in this one. Why do the visitors to the abbey not ask the abbot himself about the tomb, since he is their guide within the abbey? And what are "Icels ki erent del païs" doing with them at the tomb (unless they were performing an act of reverence and homage)? Supposedly, the abbot was conducting a tour for the benefit of *li sires*, his family and friends!

The question-and-answer contained in this section presents a problem: "Those of the land" are asked whose tomb it was, but his name is never told. In fact, before telling the visitors of the dead man's royal station and his fate, they answer the request for information by a description of his personality! We may wonder whether the request was, after all, only for factual information. Two questions were asked: 'whose tomb was it?' and 'queil hum fu ki la giseit?' Do we have here the same information twice requested, or does the second question mean 'What kind of man?' In the latter case, the people's answer would follow much more naturally: they would simply begin with the second question. In any case, it is interesting that the name Muldumarec, which Marie de France gave us in the introduction, is not mentioned.

In the *Yonec,* the old husband has never seen Muldumarec alive; only *li sires'* agent, his old sister, saw the lover alive as he came and went on his second specified visit to the lady. But the old man does see the lover's tomb (in the lay's final episode), and hears his rival (whom he never saw) so highly praised by his rival's subjects.

The lady tells her son that this lord was his father; then she dies: (525-40)

           Quant la dame oï la novele,
           A haute voiz sun fiz apele.
           'Beaus fiz,' fet ele, 'avez oï
528   Cum Deus nus ad mené ici! [59]
           C'est vostre pere que ici gist,
           Que cist villarz a tort ocist.
           Or vus comant e rent s'espee:
532   Jeo l'ai asez lung tens gardee.'
           Oianz tuz, li ad coneü
           Que l'engendrat e sis fiz fu,
           Cum il suleit venir a li
536   E cum si sires le trahi; [60]
           La verité li ad cuntee.
           Sur la tumbe cheï pasmee,
           En la paumeisun devia;
540   Unc puis a humme ne parla. [61]

It might seem from the wording of 525-6 that the lady realizes for the first time the identity of the person buried in the tomb. But had she not recognized the castle? Had she not remembered the prophetic words of the knight (427-32): "A une feste u ele

---

[50] But in line 473 the husband had been told to bring his wife and son with him; and in line 428 (the knight's final prophecy and his instructions to the lady) it was the lady who was to bring her husband and son *(Sun seignur e lui amerra).* And now the lady declares it was God who brought them to this place. The allusion to God affords a sort of closure to the events, for it was the lady's prayer to God (toward the beginning of the lay) that precipitated the entire sequence of events!

[60] Once again, the motif of betrayal.

[61] The old husband (unlike the one in *Guigemar*) has been completely successful in separating the lovers during their lifetime.

irra..."? Most probably, the lady knew already when the summons came what the outcome would be. Furthermore, the lines "Quant la dame oï la novele, / A haute voiz sun fiz apele" indicate not that she had to wait for this information before she could know that it was her lover who lay in the tomb; rather, she was simply waiting for the moment to come, which the knight had predicted, when she should speak out:

> Par une tumbe k'il verrunt
> Orrunt renoveler sa mort
> E cum il fu ocis a tort.
> Ileoc li baillerat s'espeie.
> L'aventure li seit cuntee. (430-4)

Surely the lady remembered the knight's words; it was for this reason that she brought the sword with her! How effective the obliteration of her figure from the time she returns to her husband up to this moment when we hear her call out in a clear voice to her son, whom she tells "the truth" about his father.[62] The lady emerges from nothingness (bearing a sword!) to carry out the instructions of her lover.

For the second time in the narrative, we are reminded of the two facts which Marie de France promised to tell us in the Prologue: who Yonec's father was, and how he came to the mother. (To these the lady adds a third: "... e cum si sires le trahi": 536). This has been her only reason for living on after her lover's death; and having told her son the truth, she dies. Having spoken these words dictated by her lover, she never spoke again to any man ("Unc puis a humme ne parla": 540).[63]

---

[62] This is the second use of the term "la verité" applied to the knight (cf. its first instance, where *la vielle* tells her brother "del chevaler la verité").

[63] Concerning the entire episode at the abbey and near the tomb, there are several problems.

First, was the abbey merely a stopping-place on their way to the *feste*, or was it their destination? Was the celebration supposed to take place there?

Two facts speak against the latter interpretation: first, there is nothing to indicate that the mass they attended was a special religious celebration; and there is no other detail of the narrative which suggests that a feast-day was being celebrated there. Secondly, if the abbey had been their destination

Yonec kills the husband, and is accepted as lord by his father's people: (541-50)

> Quant sis fiz veit que el morte fu,
> Sun parastre ad le chief tolu;

one would expect that their proposed departure (488) would be presented as a return (home): "Puis s'en voleient retorner" rather than "departir."

But two facts speak in favor of this interpretation (that the *feste* was really celebrated at Karlïon): first, in his prophecy the knight speaks of "une feste u ele irra..." (427), and in 475 we find: "Issi avint, alez i sunt...." This parallel should mean that the travellers arrive at the place where the feast-day is being celebrated. Secondly, we must consider line 484: their young guide is described as the one "Quë a la feste les mena" — not the imperfect *menot* (it is true that the preterite was often used of imperfect aspect, but mainly with verbs of state: *fut* instead of *esteit*, *tint* instead of *teneit*).

Now Ewert and Wilhelm Hertz (*Spielmannsbuch*, Stuttgart-Berlin, 1886, 2nd. edn. 1900) take it for granted that the *feste* to which the group was summoned was held at Karlïon, but Marie does not say this: in fact, she might have mentioned Karlïon only because it was the chief place for this celebration. They also reason that, since the castle in which the abbey was housed must be that of the lover, Marie locates this castle at two different places: "The description of Muldumarec as a ruler of some supernatural realm which is reached through a hill not from Caerwent is in contradiction with the latter part of the story... where his domain is situated on the road from Caerwent to Caerlion" (Ewert, p. 179).

That is, Ewert and Hertz do not believe that the travellers followed the same route as the lady had, probably because there is no mention of the *hoge*, no mention of the beautiful walled city — and probably also because a "supernatural realm" (Hertz even believes it was in the underworld: the passage in the hill would have led her underground) can't be found on the road from one real city to another. As for the latter point, I am not sure that we must reason that way (even if it is true that the travellers were on their way to Caerleon, and we do not know that that is true). As for the first two points, just because Marie decides to summarize the journey in the briefest of formulas ("... tant qu'il viendrent a un chastel"), without describing anything on the way, or the environs of the castle — this does not mean that there was nothing to be seen on the way, or in the vicinity: and there very well might have been the *hoge* and the meadow and the walled-city — which Marie refuses to describe again. The lady's return from her lover had been described very briefly; this time, there would be no description whatsoever. Certainly the absence of detail in regard to the *feste* is in accordance with the over-all lack of detail in the beginning of this entire episode.

I believe that the group covered the same route the lady had (maybe the parallelism offered by the phrase *le dreit chemin* in both accounts of the journey is significant in this regard), and that the lady was recognizing all the landmarks, mention of which is suppressed in this account. It is obvious

>   De l'espeie que fu sun pere
> 544 Ad dunc vengié le doel sa mere.
>   Puis ke si fu dunc avenu [64]
>   E par la cité fu sceü,
>   A grant honour la dame unt prise
> 548 E al sarcu posee e mise.
>   Lur seignur firent de Yonec,
>   Ainz quë il partissent d'ilec.

In the first two couplets of this section, the last detail of the knight's prediction to the lady is fulfilled: first the brute fact is presented, then its significance. In the last couplet of this section is fulfilled the prophecy that the dying knight had made to his people ("Ainz avum atendu meint jur / Un fiz que en la dame engendra, / Si cum il dist e cumanda": 522-4).

If the first event in our lay (after the action has begun) represents the fulfillment of a wish (almost), everything that follows the first visit of the knight (211-540) represents fulfillments of prophecies (or of instructions about the future). Now perhaps we understand why Marie in her Prologue mentions only one event: how the knight came to Yonec's mother. This we have learned by line 210; but in the meantime we have learned something else: the betrayal of the lovers that must come, according to the knight's prophecy. Thus the events leading up to

---

that she knew before they set out that they would come to the knight's castle, or otherwise she would not have brought the sword along.

The lack of specific detail in the passage concerning the trip (465-506), as well as the temporary blotting-out of the lady, is most effective; she alone knows where their journey will take them, and what they will see on the way; she alone knows that a prophecy is about to be fulfilled — and Marie deliberately hides from us the details of this journey, as well as the lady's state of mind. We should not need to be told, for we know as much as the lady and should be able to imagine the state of her feelings.

As for the mysterious presence of "those of the land" at the knight's tomb — does that not somehow accord with the mysterious absence from the city (or seclusion) of these same people at the time of the lady's visit to her wounded lover? And the fact that their first reaction when questioned at the tomb is that of mourning, surely must remind us of the sounds of mourning the lady heard coming from the city she had left behind.

[64] Notice the parallel here with line 466 ("Oëz cum[ent] est avenu!"), where the verb *avenir* is used in the very same form of the verb; we observe, too, how these two lines serve to set off the "happening" of the scene at the tomb, and the vengeance.

this betrayal may be seen simply as a demonstration of the correctness of the lover's premonition. And by the time the betrayal (and the subsequent death of the knight) has taken place, we have learned, through his divinatory words, of the act of vengeance that must come about. Again, what follows is simply a demonstration of accuracy. Thus the rhythm of the lay is a movement of self-propulsion.

Yet there is one event in this section that was not predicted or prescribed earlier: that the lady should be buried in her lover's tomb was the spontaneous decision of the knight's people.[65] And with her burial there the significance of the tomb grows. It is not merely a more splendid version of the death-bed of the knight: it is also an analogue of the lady's bed. If this bed was the place of the lovers' union, the tomb becomes that of their reunion; a permanent reunion, openly manifested in death, of the lady and the knight who, in life, could not remain united in secret. In fact, the sharing of a common tomb is the sanction, even the legitimation of their love, by society. Moreover, just as the bed of the lady had served as the fixed point in space from which all incidents proceed and to which all events have some relation, so does the tomb become that fixed point in space toward which all the actions lead, becoming in a permanent, eternal form the culmination and symbolization of the action of the total narrative.

Years later a lay was made of the lovers' *aventure* (551-4):

>   Cil que ceste aventure oïrent
> 552 Lunc tens aprés un lai en firent,
>   De la pité, de la dolur
>   Que cil suffrirent pur amur.

The summary of this lay differs from the more factual one offered in the Prologue. Now that we know "how Yonec's father came to his mother," Marie stresses only the tenderness and grief that these suffered through their love.

---

[65] An analogy between *Yonec* and *Les Deus Amanz* comes to mind: the action at the end of each lay is in the hands of a crowd. In both lays, moreover, after the burial takes place, the people depart. The solitude thus created is oppressive, and weighs down upon the reader.

MILUN

The lay of *Milun*,[1] 536 verses in length, with an introduction of eight lines and a conclusion of four verses, discloses the tripartite structure so often noted in Marie's lays. The first two narrative sections are of approximately the same length (144 and 138 lines, respectively), whereas the final portion (283-524) is almost one hundred lines longer than the first.

In the first part Milun, a valiant and much honored knight, courteously accepts the love of a damsel who has fallen in love with him (sight unseen) because of his reputation. Discovering she is pregnant, she sends for her lover who promises to follow her instructions for the child, once it is born. After sending the infant to the damsel's married sister to be raised, Milun goes off to distinguish himself further, and the girl is married to another man.

In the second division of the narrative, Milun, upon returning to his country, devises a means of communicating secretly with his sweetheart. His squire manages to present to the lady Milun's pet swan, with a hidden letter containing instructions for their communication by means of the bird. For the next twenty years they thus communicate, also meeting several times.

In the final section, the exploits and fame of an unknown young knight reach Milun, who takes leave of his sweetheart to find the knight, and also to look for his son. In a joust, he is unhorsed by the young knight whom he discovers to be his son.

---

[1] *Milun* is the third of three lays in which a bird plays a rôle. Here the bird, in addition to being a sexual symbol, serves the practical function of a messenger between the lovers.

After a dramatic scene of recognition, the son decides to bring together his parents in marriage. On their way to the lady they are met by her messenger, bringing news of her lord's death. The parents are joined in marriage by their son, and live happily ever after.

In the Prologue Marie speaks of the duties of an author: (1-8)

>   Ki divers cunte veut traitier,
>   Diversement deit comencier
>   E parler si rainablement
> 4 K'il seit pleisibles a la gent.
>   Ici comencerai Milun
>   E musterai par brief sermun
>   Pur quei e coment fu trovez
> 8 Li lais kë issi est numez.

This is a most baffling Prologue. Lines 3 and 4 seem empty; the same is true of 1 and 2, and, in addition, it is not too easy to see how the opening of this lay differs appreciably from those of the others (unless it is the absence in the Prologue of a reference to the "matière de Bretagne"). As for the last four lines I have searched in vain for any allusion to the reason and the manner of the lay's composition.

Milun was a knight of widespread reputation: (9-20)

>   Milun fu de Suhtwales nez.
>   Puis le jur k'il fu adubez
>   Ne trova un sul chevalier
> 12 Ki l'abatist de sun destrier. [2]
>   Mut par esteit bons chevaliers
>   Francs [e] hardiz, curteis e fiers, [3]
>   Mut fu coneüz en Irlande,
> 16 En Norweië e en Guhtlande;
>   En Loengrë e en Albanie
>   Eurent plusurs de lui envie: [4]

---

[2] It is indeed appropriate that the knight who will be knocked off his horse (years later) has such a reputation. There will be four more explicit references (356-7; 419; 421; 443-5), and one indirect allusion (427-30) to being unhorsed.

[3] In Milun's description it may be noted that, just as was true of the portrait of the lover in Laüstic, we are not told that Milun was beautiful.

[4] This reference to envy reminds us of Lanval and his situation (Lanval, 21-6), but in that lay the situation is not only more developed, it is

>   Pur sa prüesce iert mut amez
> 20 E de muz princes honurez.

In the very first line of the narrative one of the lovers is mentioned. In this respect *Milun* parallels *Equitan:* in both lays the name of the hero is given in the Prologue (although here as title of the lay itself) and in both he is mentioned in the opening line of the story.[5]

In 9-20 there is surely a suggestion, although not a predication, of movement. Milun is a knight who is evidently constantly on the go, since he is known in many countries. That there is this suggestion so early in the narrative is very significant, for movement (particularly that of departure) will be the most salient feature of this lay.

A damsel, in love with Milun sight unseen, sends word to him: (21-8)

>   En sa cuntree ot un barun,
>   Mes jeo ne sai numer sun nun;
>   Il aveit une fille bele,[6]
> 24 [E] mut curteise dameisele.
>   Ele ot oï Milun nomer;
>   Mut le cumençat a amer.
>   Par sun message li manda
> 28 Que, si li plest, el l'amera.

In the very first line of this rather brief section, a new character is presented: a baron, who exists only to have a daughter (and later on, to give her away in marriage), and who remains nameless, because Marie is ignorant of his name.

After the brief, conventional description of the daughter, the abruptness of her actions recounted in 25-8 is startling. In 25, she hears about Milun; in 26, she loves him; and in 27-8, she sends

---

essential to the plot-development. Here in *Milun* others' jealousy of the knight is mentioned only once, and nothing comes of it.

[5] Although both men demonstrate great fidelity in love, Marie probably uses the above-mentioned device to stress their great dissimilarity.

[6] Of the four unmarried girls in Marie's lays (*Le Fresne, Les Deus Amanz, Milun,* and *Eliduc*) the parents, with the exception of the father in *Milun,* play a more or less prominent rôle.

word for him to love her. The reader wonders whether Marie intended this account to appear humorous. Or did she choose this accelerated rhythm to emphasize the abrupt awakening of emotion in the young girl, the sudden passion, and also, the sudden willfulness? [7]

Milun replies to the message: (29-48)

>   Milun fu liez de la novele,
>   Si'n merciat la dameisele;
>   Volenters otriat l'amur, [8]
> 32 N'en partirat jamés nul jur. [9]
>   Asez li fait curteis respuns;
>   Al message dona granz duns
>   E grant amistié [li] premet.
> 36 'Amis,' fet il, 'ore entremet
>   Que a m'amie puisse parler [10]
>   E de nostre cunseil celer.
>   Mun anel de or li porterez [11]
> 40 E de meie part li direz:
>   Quant li plerra, si vien pur mei,
>   E jeo irai ensemble od tei.'
>   Cil prent cungé, atant le lait,
> 44 A sa dameisele revait.
>   L'anel li dune, si li dist
>   Que bien ad fet ceo kë il quist.
>   Mut fu la dameisele lie[e]
> 48 De l'amur issi otrïe[e].

Milun's reaction to the news of the damsel's offer of love strikes the reader as somewhat flat emotionally *(Milun fu liez de*

---

[7] It might be pointed out that *Milun* is the fourth (and final) lay (cf. *Le Fresne, Lanval, Les Deus Amanz*) where both lovers (when we first meet them) are unmarried.

[8] Upon several occasions the feudal verb *otrïer* is used to relate the granting of love by a woman in the normal situation of a man going after a woman, yet this is the only instance of its use in the four cases when a woman goes after (i. e., sends for) a man.

[9] The promise made by Milun here he is unable to keep. Not only does he leave her, but they will be separated for twenty years.

[10] Note that Milun calls the damsel (sight unseen!) *m'amie.* Could Marie be making sport of *curteisie*, of Milun's immediate use of this endearment?

[11] Milun's gold ring, mentioned here for the first time, will never be described; yet much later the sight of that ring will set the recognition-scene into motion.

la novele); one might expect more response than is described in this terse summary. This represents the first of very many references to happiness in this lay.[12] Yet with three exceptions, the reader does not feel the warmth and spontaneity of a character's happiness.

Lines 29-32 of Milun's reply (whose gist is 'all right') are rather amusing to the reader. For just as the girl had offered her love to him, sight unseen, he pledges eternal fidelity to her,[13] also sight unseen. His thanking the girl for her love reminds us of two other instances when the lover thanked the lady: the lover in *Bisclavret* (whose reaction, too, was emotionally flat, given his assiduous — and unsuccessful — courting of the lady), and the youth in *Les Deus Amanz.*

In 27-35 one message and one movement may be noted.[14] In 36-42 there is another message (Milun's speech to the messenger) and another movement (back to the place where the messenger started from). These two stages of a round-trip, as well as Milun's explicit mention of future movement ('Quant li plerra, si vien pur mei, / E jeo irai ensemble od tei': 41-2) anticipate the extraordinary amount of coming and going to be noted in the story.

This section ends with a fitting circularity: the emotional flatness ("Mut fu la dameisele lie[e] / De l'amur issi otrïe[e]": 47-8) of the damsel's reactions to the knight's message echoes his reported reaction to her offer of love ("Milun fu liez de la novele").

We learn of their frequent meetings: 49-54

---

[12] Indeed, the reaction of 'happiness' is mentioned so often in this lay that it almost seems to be (but it is not) a stock response. Since *Milun* will be the only one of Marie's lays with a truly happy ending, could all the references to happiness serve to anticipate that conclusion?

[13] Thus Milun is the second man (cf. *Lanval*) to immediately pledge his fidelity to the woman. But of course Lanval had seen the *pucele*'s body, whereas Milun had not! And Milun's immediate acceptance of the girl's offer of love makes us wonder if he had been waiting for someone to ask him!

[14] It is interesting that as early as 27-35 the two central themes of the narrative are introduced: communication (which is the framework of the lay) and movement. The rhythm of movement (particularly that of going away from where one is, and then coming back to where one was) will be in evidence throughout the entire lay.

> Delez la chambre en un vergier,
> U ele alout esbanïer,
> La justouent lur parlement [15]
> 52 Milun e ele bien suvent.
> Tant i vint Milun, tant l'ama [16]
> Que la dameisele enceinta. [17]

For a second time Marie's brevity of narration is notable: in this short passage there is both a telescoping of time and a condensation of activity. Note that Milun is already there, with the girl; the first four lines (49-52 are a summary of their love-affair in a *vergier*. It is remarkable that this lay, purportedly the story of a man in love with a woman, rarely mentions their feelings toward each other. The reader feels no vibration of emotion on their part toward each other.

In 53-4, Marie treats of pregnancy in a brutal manner. [18] With the *tant ... tant* we feel the force of the almost sexual rhythm;

---

[15] The reader's attention may well be struck by the expression *jouster parlement,* an "official" phrase used here in an erotic context.

[16] The couplet ("Tant i vint Milun, tant l'ama / Que la dameisele enceinta": 53-4) is the second instance of a summary of frequent meetings between a knight and a maiden in which the quantitative *tant ... tant* construction is employed (cf. *Le Fresne,* 273-4: "Tant li pria, tant li premist, / Que ele otria ceo kë il quist"). In the passage from *Milun,* the abruptness of the report is even more notable.

That these two passages are found in the lay *(Le Fresne)* where there is great emphasis upon, and much talk by the man of, pregnancy (and where no pregnancy results from the lovers' union), and in the lay *(Milun)* where there is no talk between the lovers that the reader is allowed to hear before the pregnancy resulting from the lovers' union, is another instance of Marie's subtle artistry.

[17] That the only two lays where a woman is made pregnant by her lover are the 'bird-lays' *Yonec* and *Milun* surely can not be mere coincidence, for there are far too many parallels (and contrasts) to have been accidental.

Although *enceintier* can be either intransitive or transitive, here in 54 I prefer to read it as transitive, with *he* (i. e., Milun) as subject. It can thus be said that in both *Yonec* and *Milun* Marie presents the moment of conception from the point of view of the man. In *Yonec,* there are three references to this: in the Prologue *(Cil ki engendra Yuuenec:* 9), in the lover's announcement to the lady *(De lui est enceinte d'enfant:* 327), and the lady's revelation at the tomb *(Oianz tuz, li a coneü / Que l'engendrat e sis fiz fu:* 533-4). In *Milun,* line 54 is the first of several references to conception.

[18] It may be interesting to compare the manner in which Marie treats of pregnancy in *Milun* and *Yonec.* In *Yonec,* pregnancy is mentioned in a

half of the reason given for the girl's becoming pregnant is Milun's movement *(Tant i vint;)* the prase *tant l'ama* (which recalls the girl's statement that 'she will love him' when she sends her messenger to Milun) obviously refers to physical love-making.

Realizing her plight, the girl sends for Milun: (55-66)

>   Quant aparceit que ele est enceinte, [19]
> 56 Milun manda, si fist sa pleinte.
>   Dit li cum[ent] est avenu:
>   S'onur e sun bien ad perdu,
>   Quant de tel fet s'est entremise;
> 60 De li ert fait[e] grant justise:
>   A gleive serat turmentee,
>   [U] vendue en autre cuntree;
>   Ceo fu custume as anciens,
> 64 Issi teneient en cel tens.
>   Milun respunt që il fera
>   Ceo që ele cunseillera.

The opening portion of the girl's words to Milun is her lament over the situation; these words are given, as is her lover's reply, in indirect discourse. The damsel's fear of punishment strikes the reader as quite exaggerated; she is so certain that she will suffer.[20]

(Indeed, a few lines later she will mention her suffering as a *fait accompli:* 'Si'n ad suffert meinte dolur': 74.)

What Milun's feelings must have been as he hears the news, we do not know. In his reply, there must be some irony; we might expect this famous warrior to spring into action, but instead, he simply agrees to do whatever she advises (65-6).

---

more tender manner than in *Milun:* the mortally wounded lover is comforting the lady; the news that she is pregnant is brought in parenthetically (327-9). Muldumarec's revelation of her pregnancy is done delicately, in the act of comforting, and, in this scene, there is no love-making. Moreover, in *Yonec,* it is the man, in *Milun,* the girl, who speaks of pregnancy.

[19] Note how pregnancy is mentioned in two consecutive lines.

The girl's pregnancy, which occurs toward the beginning of the lay, is the first of only two unplanned events concerning the lovers.

[20] Ernest Hoepffner, "La geographie et l'histoire dans les Lais de Marie de France," *Romania,* LVI (1930), cites vv. 63-4 as an instance of Marie's care to emphasize the antiquity of the story of *Milun* (p. 8).

The damsel gives him instructions concerning the unborn child: [21] (67-86)

>   'Quant l'enfant,' fait elë, 'ert nez, [22]
> 68   A ma serur le porterez, [23]
>   Quë en Norhumbre est marïee,
>   Riche dame, pruz e senee;
>   Si li manderez par escrit
> 72   E par paroles e par dit [24]
>   Que c'est l'enfant [a] sa serur,
>   Si'n ad suffert meinte dolur;
>   Ore gart k'il seit bien nuriz,
> 76   Queil ke ço seit, u fille u fiz.
>   Vostre anel al col li pendrai,
>   E un brief li enveierai:
>   Escrit i ert le nun sun pere
> 80   E l'aventure de sa mere.
>   Quant il serat grant e creüz
>   E en tel eage venuz
>   Quë il sache reisun entendre,
> 84   Le brief e l'anel li deit rendre;
>   Si li cumant tant a garder
>   Que sun pere puisse trover.'

For the first time we hear the maiden speak, as she plans in detail the child's life for the next twenty years or so. [25] Note that whereas in 76 (*Queil ke ço seit, u fille u fiz*) the mother-to-be is uncertain of the baby's sex, only a few lines later she shifts to absolute certainty: the child can not be anything but a son (*Quant il serat grant e creüz:* 81). The last of her instructions concerning the son (when he is grown up he is to look for his

---

[21] The prolixity of the girl's instructions to her lover are in amusing contrast to the brevity of her first message to him.

[22] In this lay where written communication will be so important, the reader will also be struck by the inordinate amount of talking.

[23] This is the fourth time (cf. *Le Fresne, Les Deus Amanz, Yonec*) in Marie's lays that there is an aunt, and the second time (cf. *Yonec*) that there is a sister who plays a significant rôle. Here in *Milun* the aunt will be specifically helpful to the child of the protagonists.

[24] Note how communication *(manderez)* is stressed by the phrase *par escrit / E par paroles e par dit.*

[25] In *Yonec*, Muldumarec's words to the lady concerning their unborn son are somewhat similar; yet they are also different, for Muldumarec is a magical being who is able to prophesy.

father: 85-6) will prove to be very important in the development of the story.

The baby is born: (87-95)

>   A sun cunseil se sunt tenu,
> 88 Tant que li termes est venu
>   Que la dameisele enfanta.
>   Une vielle, ki la garda, [26]
>   A ki tut sun estre geï,
> 92 Tant la cela, tant la covri, [27]
>   Unques n'en fu aparcevance
>   En parole në en semblance.
>   La meschine ot un fiz mut bel.

Once again succinctness of narration is noted; this is evident not only in the first three lines (87-9) where there is telescoping of time (by the use of the *tant que* construction), but also in 92: *Tant la cela, tant la covri* (where the use of *tant ... tant* is a parallel to its first appearance in 53: *(tant i vint Milun, tant l'ama)*. Although the baby's birth is reported in the third line of this passage, it is a nice detail that Marie suspensefully withholds from us, until the very last line, the sex of the infant: the mother-to-be's certainty is made flesh!

The maiden and her guardian prepare the infant for travel: (96-106)

> 96 Al col li pendirent l'anel
>   E une aumoniere de seie,
>   E pus le brief, que nul nel veie. [28]
>   Puis le cuchent en un bercel,

---

[26] In both *Yonec* and *Milun* (and in no other of Marie's lays) there is a character named *la vielle*. Yet there is a notable difference in her function and relationship to the other characters: in *Yonec la vielle* not only is the guardian whose actions will be injurious to the lady's interests, she is also the sister of one of the married couples; in *Milun la vielle* who is the helpful guardian of the maiden is no relation of any character.

[27] For a second time (cf. the concealment of the lovers' intention, 38) there is reference to secrecy.

[28] The letter from the maiden to her married sister represents the first of five sealed letters (or written messages) which will be mentioned specifically in the course of the story. Yet the *seel* will not be predicated until the sister receives the letter in 118.

>   100 Envolupé d'un blanc lincel; [29]
>   Desuz al testë a l'enfant
>   Mistrent un oreiller vaillant
>   E desus lui un covertur
>   104 Urlé de martre tut entur.
>   La vielle l'ad Milun baillié;
>   Cil [l]'at [a]tendu al vergier.

The reader can not fail to be struck by the many details of the loving and tender preparations of the baby for its journey. Just as the damsel had said she would do, the ring is hung around the infant's neck. Does Marie offer the detail of the *aumoniere* (97) which the girl herself had not mentioned because in it the letter will be concealed from sight? The delicate touch of the pillow [30] placed under the baby's head effectively epitomizes the women's concern for his comfort.

Note that the *vergier*, the place where the maiden became pregnant, is also the place where the infant son is handed over to his father (106).

Milun carries out his sweetheart's instructions: (107-22)

>   Il le cumaunda a teu gent
>   108 Ki l'i porterent lëaument.
>   Par les viles u il errouent
>   Set feiz le jur [se] resposoënt;
>   L'enfant feseient aleitier, [31]
>   112 Cucher de nuvel e baignier:
>   Nurice menoënt od eus,
>   Itant furent [ic]il lëaus.

---

[29] This is the third (and I believe, the last) time that the verb *enveluper* is found in Marie's lays; in all three instances, it is used in the account of the preparation of someone (or something) precious for travel. In both *Le Fresne* (cf. 122) and the present lay, it is an infant that is tenderly prepared for a journey; in *Laüstic* (cf. 137) it is the body of a dead bird which is given such care.

[30] With the reference to the pillow we are reminded of the one other pillow in Marie's lays. What a difference there is between this pillow for the infant in *Milun*, and the magic pillow (cf. *Guigemar*, 178-80: *Mes tant vos di de l'oreillier: / Ki sus eüst sun chief tenu / Jamais le peil n'avreit chanu*) of the magnificent bed upon which the wounded Guigemar rests to ease his pain.

[31] Could the nursing of the baby seven times a day be over-solicitude on the part of the new father?

> Tant unt le dreit chemin erré
> 116 Que a la dame l'unt comandé.
> El le receut, si l'en fu bel.
> Le brief receut e le seel.
> Quant ele sot ki il esteit,
> 120 A merveille le cheriseit.
> Cil ki l'enfant eurent porté
> En lur païs sunt returné.

Milun, who had entered the story as a virile and faithful lover, is now seen in a new rôle: that of a concerned and loving father. And just as he had obeyed the maiden completely, so do the loyal *gent* to whom Milun entrusts his *enfant* son obey him, Milun, completely.

Although this passage represents another instance when the narration is expanded, note that the movement of the journey (the two stages of going forth and coming back) is briefly summarized (in 115-16 and 212-22). Had the girl given instructions about the seven rest-stops to Milun? It seems far more likely that it was Milun himself who, in his tenderness for the infant (he is already showing the great love and tenderness for the child which he will manifest later) planned the details of the trip to Northumberland. [32]

It may be pointed out that in the first few dozen lines of the lay, the love-story of the two young lovers has been told, then rounded off by the maiden's pregnancy, the birth of the son and his protection. [33] And this story (or phase of the story) which closes at the end of 122 is brief, quick, and uncomplicated in movement.

Just as Milun, and then the people loyal to him, had acted in an almost mechanical fashion after the birth of the infant, so does the sister. But whereas we were left to imagine Milun's feelings as he held his infant son in his arms for the first time,

---

[32] There are only five lays in which a journey is described in any detail. *Milun* is the second of two lays (cf. *Le Fresne*) where details are given of a journey with an infant.

[33] We may note here the first of several parallels between *Milun* amd the Tristran story: the story of the parents is given before that of the son (the same narrative device is used also in *Yonec*). Another analogy is the secret birth of the son, and his upbringing away from his country.

Marie explicitly reports the sister's emotion [34] ("Elle receut, si l'en fu bel": 117) upon receiving the baby.

Milun leaves his country, and his sweetheart is married: (123-52)

```
         Milun eissi fors de sa tere
124  En sude[e]s pur sun pris quere. [35]
     S'amie remist a meisun;
     Sis peres li duna barun, [36]
     Un mut riche humme del païs,
128  Mut esforcible e de grant pris.
     Quant ele sot cele aventure,
     Mut est dolente a demesure
     E suvent regrette Milun.
132  [Kar] mut dute la mesprisun
     De ceo que ele ot [eü] enfant;
     Il le savra demeintenant.
     'Lasse,' fet ele, 'quei ferai?
136  Avrai seignur? Cum le prendrai?
     Ja ne sui jeo mie pucele;
     A tuz jurs mes serai ancele.
     Jeo ne soi pas que fust issi,
140  Ainz quidoue aveir mun ami;
     Entre nus celisum l'afaire, [37]
     Ja ne l'oïsse aillurs retraire.
     Meuz me vendreit murir que vivre;
144  Mes jeo ne sui mie delivre,
     Ainz ai asez sur mei gardeins
     Veuz e jeofnes, mes chamberleins,
     Que tuz jurz heent bone amur
148  E se delitent en tristur.
     Or m'estuvrat issi suffrir,
     Lasse, quant jeo ne puis murir.'
```

---

[34] We can only wonder what the reaction of the sister's husband (who is never mentioned) may have been. He is an even more shadowy figure than the girl's father.

[35] Is being a *soudeür* an act of desperation for Milun, as well as a way of embellishing his reputation?

Milun is the first of two lays (the other is *Eliduc*) where the hero becomes a hired soldier, but the emphasis placed upon that position differs greatly in the two lays.

[36] *Milun* is the only one of Marie's lays where, in the course of the narrative, the lady is married to someone she does not love.

[37] In this line, note the third instance of the verb *celer*.

Al terme ke ele fu donee,
152 Sis sires l'en ad amenee.

In the opening couplet of this new section, Milun is dismissed, as it were, from the narrative for a brief time; the rest of the passage is devoted to his sweetheart who is left behind.

In the line immediately following *S'amie remist a meisun*, we learn that her father marries her off. The substantive *barun* is used in 126 in the sense of 'husband,' not as a designation of rank. If *riche* does here signify 'powerful' (in a social sense), why does Marie tell us again, in the very next line, that the husband is *mut esforcible*?[38] It is noteworthy that the husband, like Milun the lover, is also of good reputation.

The gist of the maiden's continuous laments (*E suvent regrette Milun:* 131) is summed up in 135-50: it is as if we hear her speak on a single occasion. This monologue[39] may remind us of her first lament (presented as indirect discourse), except that here she reveals less fear of punishment.

It is remarkable that the girl (who is so full of self-pity: 'Lasse' and who thinks that she will be treated as a servant), does not voice her fear that her loss of virginity will be recognized and punished. Rather, she seems to say (in 137) that she has no right to take a husband because she is not a virgin. And surely she has a very naïve reaction to have thought (140-42) that she and her lover would be able to continue their relationship forever, concealing it. It is odd that even before she is married she talks about the guardians[40] whose presence will prevent her from committing suicide. Yet they had not kept her from meeting Milun before the marriage!

In the final line of this section ("Sis sires l'en ad amenee") we learn of what is to be her only movement throughout the entire

---

[38] Could the adjective *esforcibles* have here a suggestion of physical strength (which is a possible reference of this word)?

[39] Note the circularity created by the use of the same exclamation ('Lasse') at the beginning of the opening and closing lines of her lament.

[40] The expression *bone amur* is found in only two of Marie's lays, here and in *Eliduc*, with a significant difference in its use. Here in *Milun*, where the love between the protagonists is not chaste (in contrast to the situation in *Eliduc*), the girl is attempting to justify herself (147).

lay: she is taken from the home of her father to that of her husband.[41]

It is a deliberate omission on Marie's part, after she has built up to the wedding-night, not to tell us of it (and this is a notable contrast to *Le Fresne* where we see the preparations for the wedding-night take place). Moreover, it is also a deliberate omission not to tell us of the husband's discovery that the girl is no longer a virgin — and Marie has had her talk at length about her loss of virginity! Did the girl perhaps try to do what Iseut did? If she did not do so, would her husband not then have found out the truth? And did he then treat her cruelly? (For we recall that he was described as "mut esforcible.")

With the information 'her husband took her away' (152), the first narrative division comes to a close.

Milun returns to his country: (153-74)

> Milun revient en sun païs.[42]
> Mut fu dolent e mut pensis,
> Grant doel fist, grant doel demena;
> 156 Mes de ceo se recunforta
> Que pres esteit de sa cuntree
> Cele k'il tant aveit amee.[43]
> Milun se prist a purpenser
> 160 Coment il li purrat mander,[44]
> Si qu'il ne seit aparceüz,[45]
> Qu'il est al païs [re]venuz.

---

[41] The manner in which the maiden is presented in this line reminds us of La Codre in *Le Fresne*: they are both passive figures (although not to the same degree) in that things are done to them. In this passage, the father marries off his daughter (126); then, at the proper moment, she is taken away by her husband (152).

[42] Although we had been told (124) that Milun became a hired soldier to enhance his reputation, yet when Marie re-introduces him into the story at 153, nothing whatever is said about his reputation. It is as if being back in his country, and near his sweetheart obliterates any other preoccupation; he will leave off being the knight, and become the faithful lover once again.

[43] It is an effective detail that his sweetheart is now characterized as "Cele k'il aveit tant amee" — for the reader knows with what result!

[44] Milun is surely a tender-hearted man.

[45] The second letter, as was the first (cf. 96-8), is tied around the neck of something living. Indeed, the swan is a parallel to the baby: both are messengers, and both have letters around their neck.

>   Ses lettres fist, sis seela.
> 164 Un cisne aveit k'il˘ mut ama,
>   Le brief li ad al col lïé
>   E dedenz la plume muscié.
>   Un suen esquïer apela,
> 168 Sun message li encharga.
>   'Va tost,' fet il, 'change tes dras!
>   Al chastel m'amie en irras,
>   Mun cisne porteras od tei;
> 172 Garde quë en prengez cunrei,
>   U par servant u par meschine,
>   Que presenté li seit le cisne.' [46]

There is an abrupt shift of scene and of characters in the very first line of the second narrative division. Although the reason for Milun's great grief (predicated four times in two lines!) is not made explicit, it must be because of his sweetheart's marriage.

Milun's solution to his problem [47] is to make use of a pet swan which he entrusts to his squire (in the first speech we hear him utter) [48] to be delivered to his sweetheart. [49] (It is notable that the swan, destined to play so important a rôle in the story, is never described in a visualizable manner; in a later passage (216), we learn only that the bird is *bons e beaus*.) And thus Milun initiates the action that will lead to a renewal of the love-affair. This situation is one which we do not find in any other of Marie's

---

[46] In both *Laüstic* and *Milun*, a servant is charged with a message by one member of the love-pair, and carries a bird to the other. Yet there are differences to be pointed out between the lays: first, not only in the size of the bird, but in one lay *(Laüstic)*, it is the man, in the other *(Milun)*, it is the woman to whom the bird is carried; thirdly, the bird signifies the possibility or impossibility of communication: in *Laüstic* the bird is an indication that at least overt love has ended, whereas in *Milun*, it signifies that a new stage in their love will begin for the lovers.

[47] The same situation (how can a lover, without being discovered, send word to his *amie* that he has returned) which has a parallel in the Tristram story will be repeated later in *Chevrefoil*.

[48] From the phrase 'Al chastel m'amie...' addressed to the squire, it would seem as though he knows exactly where the castle is, and who the *amie* is. Indeed, we are told as much in 177: "Tut le dreit chemin quë il sot".

[49] The device of the swan as the carrier of his letter seems absolutely gratuitous; it would seem that Milun could have sent his message some other way. It will not be until almost the end of the narrative that Milun will disclose his reason for his choice.

lays; the renewal of their love forms a second story which, in contrast to the first story, is not brief and not brusque.

As for Milun's letter to his sweetheart, this, the second of the five sealed written communications mentioned specifically in the lay, is also the first of two (specifically mentioned) letters which Milun writes to his sweetheart. Although in this passage the plural noun *ses lettres* ("Ses lettres fist, sis seela": 163) has a clear singular meaning, Marie employs the plural *lettres* (rather than a singular noun, e.g., *sa lettre* or *sun brief*) also to suggest writing which could be extended indefinitely and which could repeat itself. Since Milun's letter is the first of countless written communications which will be exchanged between the lovers, the choice of *ses lettres* is a very artistic detail. (Moreover, the very first of the letters to be written by the lady is also indicated (241) by the same plural noun, *ses lettres*, in Milun's instructions to her; it will be used for the last time in 497, when Milun tells of the many years of communication between the lady and himself.)

The lady receives the swan: (175-208)

```
       Cil ad fet sun comandement.
176    Atant s'en vet, le cigne prent;
       Tut le dreit chemin quë il sot ⁵⁰
       Al chastel vient, si cum il pot;
       Par mi la vile est trespassez,
180    A la mestre porte est alez;
       Le portier apelat a sei.
       'Amis,' fet il, 'entent a mei!
       Jeo sui un hum de tel mester,
184    De oiseus prendre me sai aider.
       En un pre desuz Karlïun ⁵¹
       Pris un cisnë od mun laçun;
```

---

[50] In this line, note the second instance in our lay of the phrase *le dreit chemin*. In both cases (cf. 115) the trip to one's destination seems to take place without delay or misfortune.

[51] This is the second time (the first was in *Yonec*) that in a 'bird-lay' there is reference to *Karlïun*.

Of the use of the name *Karlïun* in this passage, Hoepffner, "La géographie et l'histoire," questions: "N'est-ce pas encore pour retremper le récit dans l'atmosphère arthurienne? ... Il suffisait d'évoquer ce nom pour donner aussitôt au récit une couleur archaïque et bretonne." (p. 11).

Pur force e pur meintenement
188 La dame en voil fere present,
Que jeo ne seie desturbez,
E[n] cest païs achaisunez.'
Li bachelers li respundi:
192 'Amis, nul ne parole od li;
Mes nepurec j'irai saveir:
Si jeo poeie liu veeir
Que jeo te puïsse mener,
196 Jeo te fereie a li parler.'
A la sale vient li portiers,
N'i trova fors deus chevalers;
Sur une grant table seiëent,
200 Ad uns eschiés se deduiëent. ⁵²
Hastivement returne arere.
Celui ameine en teu manere
Que de nului ne fu sceüz,
204 Desturbez në aparceüz.
A la chambre vient, si apele;
L'us lur ovri une pucele.
Cil sunt devant la dame alé,
208 Si unt le cigne presenté.

The squire's words to the door-keeper (in 182-90) merit our attention in several respects. Had Milun told him to give the pretext of poaching to explain his possession of the swan? Or is this the servant's own idea? In saying that he had been poaching he may be following Milun's advice to him in 172 ('... prengez cunrei': i.e., 'use your brains,' 'take measures'). And why does the squire tell the door-keeper where ('En un pre desuz Karlïun': 185) he caught the bird?

We may wonder about the servant's brief reply (192-6) expressing his willingness to help. Do his words mean that the lady is closely guarded (in which case, access to her would be most difficult)? Or is he exaggerating the difficulty in order to make himself important?

In 197-204 the gratuitousness of the two knights playing chess is arresting. For Marie creates, *ex vacuo*, ⁵³ two nameless figures

---

⁵² In only one other lay *(Eliduc)* do we see people playing the game of chess.
⁵³ This is the second time in Marie's lays that there is creation *ex vacuo*. In *Laüstic* and *Milun* the creation has something in common. In *Laüstic*,

which could be an impediment to the passage of the servant and Milun's esquire; but then she makes them oblivious, thus quickly cancelling out, as it were, yet not completely, the impediment. The result of this is a picture of two men, absorbedly playing chess. We are briefly made spectators of their game; the two knights who could have been spectators (as we are) of the two men passing by with the swan, are not.[54] What Marie has invented here (I can name neither the procedure nor its effect) is unique.

Three connotations of the game of chess are possible, all of which are significant in the present, as well as future, context of our lay: face-to-face communication; military encounter (and for the twenty years of the lovers' communication nothing will be said of Milun's military exploits); and movement, back and forth on the chess-board. (Except for a (later) brief reference in passing to a few meetings of the lovers, the only movement, the only activity, will be that of the swan.)

The lady finds the letter: (209-32)

>   Ele apelat un suen vallet;
>   Puis si li dit: 'Or t'entremet
>   Que mis cignes seit bien gardez
> 212 E kë il eit viande asez!'
>   'Dame,' fet il ki l'aporta,
>   'Ja nul fors vus nel recevra;
>   E ja est ceo present rëaus:
> 216 Veez cum il est bons e beaus!'
>   Entre ses mains li baille e rent.
>   El le receit mut bonement;
>   Le col li manie e le chief,
> 220 Desuz la plume sent le brief.[55]

---

we suspect that there was no nightingale until the wife mentioned it; the husband's hatred made the bird exist, only to be killed. As for *Milun*, it is one of the two lays (*Guigemar* is the other) where Marie arbitrarily brings in extra characters. The two knights playing chess in the hall have no function (for they are not the obstacle they could have been). Marie may well have created them for reasons of a symmetrical composition: as two static figures in the background they complement the two moving figures in the foreground.

[54] Note how the fact that the two men are not seen is underlined by the three past participles of (almost) synonymous verbs of perception.

[55] This is the third (and final) instance of the verb *sentir* in the lays. Whereas in *Lanval* and *Les Deus Amanz* it appears in a context of sensuality (yet with a difference between the two examples, cf. *Lanval* 254-6, and

> Le sanc li remut e fremi:
> Bien sot qu'il vient de sun ami. [56]
> Celui ad fet del suen doner,
> 224 Si l'en cumandë a aler.
> Quant la chambre fu delivree, [57]
> Une meschine ad apelee.
> Le brief aveient deslïé;
> 228 Ele en ad le seel brusé.
> Al primer chief trovat 'Milun'.
> De sun ami cunut le nun;
> Cent feiz le baisë en plurant,
> 232 Ainz que ele puïst lire avant.

The squire makes certain the lady herself receives the swan, by placing it in her hands. Not only is the tenderness with which she treats the bird delicately mentioned, it also reminds us of the tenderness we had seen her show her infant son.

Although we are not allowed to see the lady react to her lover when he will visit her, we do see her, now responding to her tactile sense, [58] react to the swan ("Le sanc li remut e fremi": 221). [59] Her physiological reaction is the first immediate reaction that we have seen in the story.

Les Deus Amanz, 184), here it is used in a more delicate frame of reference, the lady's caressing of the swan.

[56] In this line Marie calls Milun the lady's sweetheart for the first time.

[57] It is significant that Marie does not specifically tell us of the esquire's return trip which is suggested in 224 ("Si l'en cumandë a aler"); moreover, his departure is indirectly mentioned in the following line ("Quant la chambre fu delivree": 225). This omission has some connection with setting the stage for the following scene: we are meant to stay with the lady.

The 'when' *(quant)* clause in OF usually recapitulates what the reader has already been told. Twice in Marie's lays a *quant* clause is not recapitulatory, first in *Le Fresne*, 409 ("Quant la chambre fu delivree"), and here again, in *Milun*, 225 ("Quant la chambre fu delivree"): in both instances, an event is telescoped or passed over.

[58] The reader may well think back to the use of the verb *tater* in *Le Fresne* (v. 189): the porter's fingers tell him that this mass of cloths is a human being: here, the lady's fingers tell her that this animal is a messenger from her lover.

[59] Her physiological reaction is the third (and final) instance (cf. *Le Fresne* and *Yonec*) when a lady experiences a *frémissement;* it is also the second case (cf. *Yonec*, 117: "Li sans li remut e fremi") where a lady experiences a *frémissement du sang* that has some connection with a bird. In contrast to the lady in *Milun*, the lady in *Le Fresne* and the lady in *Yonec* react to what they have seen.

In 231 we are offered a second immediate reaction on the lady's part. Although she knows who sent the letter (cf. 222), at the moment of reading the name Milun at the heading of the letter she is overwhelmed by emotion ("Cent feiz le baisë en plurant"). The manifestation of her feelings reminds us (although the basic situation is quite different) of the release of the king's emotions upon finding the lost knight in *Bisclavret* ("Li reis le curut enbracier, / Plus de cent feiz l'acole e baise": 300-01). In all the lays, the lady and the king are the only characters whose effusive emotions are mentioned in a similar manner.

Now the lady reads the contents of the letter: (233-48)

>   Al chief de piece veit l'escrit,
>   Ceo k'il ot cumandé e dit,
>   Les granz peines e la dolur
> 236 Que Milun seofre nuit e jur.
>   Ore est del tut en sun pleisir
>   De lui ocire u de garir.
>   S'ele seüst engin trover
> 240 Cum il peüst a li parler,
>   Par ses lettres li remandast
>   E le cisne li renveast.
>   Primes le face bien garder,
> 244 Puis si l[e] laist tant jeüner
>   Treis jurs, quë il ne seit peüz;
>   Le brief li seit al col penduz;
>   Laist l'en aler: il volera
> 248 La u il primes conversa.

After a one-line summary ("Ceo k'il ot cumandé e dit") of the contents of the letter, we are given its details. The brief reference to Milun's grief (235-8) is followed by lengthy instructions (239-48) concerning the care of the bird, and how the lady is to send a return letter. This pedantic set of instructions [60] reminds us of the prolixity of the girl's speech to Milun when she instructed him in the care of the infant (cf. 67-86).

The lady carries out her lover's instructions: (249-78)

---

[60] Milun's somewhat mechanical list of instructions about the swan represent another example of the expansion of the narration through use of details.

Quant ele ot tut l'escrit veü
E ceo que ele i ot entendu,
Le cigne fet bien surjurner
252 E forment pestre e abevrer;⁶¹
Dedenz sa chambre un meis le tint.
Mes ore oëz cum l'en avint!
Tant quist par art e par engin
256 Kë ele ot enke e parchemin;
Un brief escrit tel cum li plot,
Od un anel l'enseelot.
Le cigne ot laissié jeüner;
260 Al col li pent, sil laist aler.
Li oiseus esteit fameillus
E de viande coveitus:
Hastivement est revenuz
264 La dunt il primes fu venuz;
A la vile e en la meisun
Descent devant les piez Milun.
Quant il le vit, mut en fu liez;
268 Par les eles le prent haitiez.
Il apela un despensier,
Si li fet doner a mangier.
Del col li ad le brief osté;
272 De chief en chief l'ad esgardé,
Les enseignes qu'il i trova,
E des saluz se reheita:
'Ne pot sanz lui nul bien aveir;
276 Or li remant tut sun voleir
Par le cigne sifaitement!'
Si ferat il hastivement.

Would the reader wonder that the lady would keep the swan for a month? Might we not think that she was just petting the bird and keeping it there with her? And would not her husband notice the bird? But perhaps it did take her one month to obtain the writing-materials mentioned in 256; Marie's address to the reader in 254 *(Mes ore oëz cum l'en avint!)* is immediately followed by a line in which is suggested the difficulty of obtaining the ink and the parchment *(Tant quist par art e par engin*: 255).

---

[61] This is the fourth (and last) case where food and drink are important in Marie's lays *(Guigemar, Bisclavret, Les Deus Amanz)*. In lines 244-86, the reader will not fail to be struck by the many references to starving and feeding.

Instead of giving the details of the contents of the lady's letter (as in the case of Milun's), Marie delicately and succinctly describes the lady's reply as 'one that pleased her.' As Milun's sweetheart puts his instructions into practice, for a third time (260) a letter is hung upon the neck of something living (cf. the infant, in 98; the swan, in 165).

Particularly notable in the brief account of the bird's return [62] is the feeling of gradual movement through space, ending with precise finality (*A la vile e en la meisun / Descent devant les piez Milun*: 265-6). The swan's arrival before its master somewhat parallels the account of the arrival of the mortally-wounded bird-lover before the lady in *Yonec*, 315-16: *Devant la dame al lit descent, / Que tut li drap furent sanglant*. For the lover in *Yonec*, his "descent" opens the scene of his last trip to the lady; for the swan, this "descent" marks only the end of the first of its countless trips between the lovers.

Twice we are told of Milun's happiness [63] upon seeing the swan (267-8). [64] At first it does seem odd that Milun (who has waited for what must have seemed an interminable time) would wait even longer, until the bird is fed, before taking the letter. Yet his delay represents another example of his gentle nature of his consideration.

When Milun sees the letter attached to the swan's neck, he does not seem to manifest as much emotion as did the lady; no reaction except that of happiness (*se reheita*, 274) is predicated. At the moment when he is reading the letter, Marie summarizes its contents (275-7).

Milun and his sweetheart communicate for twenty years: (279-90)

---

[62] Toward the beginning (263) and in the final line of the account (in 261-78) of the swan's flight home to Milun, and his reactions to its arrival, the reader will notice the repetitive use of *hastivement*.

[63] The phrase *mut en fu liez* in 267 recalls Milun's reaction to the damsel's offer of love (*Milun fu liez de la novele*: 29).

[64] This is the second time is Marie's lays that the rhyme-scheme *liez / haitiez* is used to report and emphasize the deep joy of a character who finds something (or someone) he had believed lost forever.

>   Vint anz menerent cele vie
> 280 Milun entre lui e s'amie.
>   Del cigne firent messager,
>   N'i aveient autre enparler,
>   E sil feseient jeüner
> 284 Ainz qu'il le lessassent aler;
>   Cil a ki li oiseus veneit,
>   Ceo sachez, quë il le peisseit. [65]
>   Ensemble viendrent plusurs feiz.
> 288 Nul ne pot estre si destreiz
>   Ne si tenuz estreitement
>   Quë il ne truisse liu sovent.

The opening couplet summarizes the life of Milun and the lady. Does Marie include the six apparently superfluous following lines (281-6) in order to inform the reader that the lovers carried out their plan perfectly, [66] and perhaps also to give us the sense of time going on? [67]

After a brief reference (287) to the lovers' meetings (about which nothing is specified), [68] Marie vaguely suggests (in 287-8) that the lady was guarded. And with the author's affirmation that such difficulties can be overcome, the second large narrative division comes to a close.

Now we learn of their son: (291-318)

>   La dame que sun fiz nurri—
> 292 Tant ot esté ensemble od li

---

[65] Is it possible that the starving and the feeding of the swan is a (grotesque) symbol of the starving and feeding of their love and their life?

[66] The back-and-forth movement of the countless trips of the swan is a movement of union, for both the end-points (the lady and the man) help to connect the movement.

[67] Here a forceful contrast is to be noted with *Yonec*. In *Milun*, the story is, at this point, concerned less with the son than with the parents. A period of twenty years (during which, almost quite incidentally, the son grows up) is filled with the communication of the lovers. But in *Yonec*, in order that the dying knight's prophecy be fulfilled, the son must come to manhood; the period in which he does so is rapidly summarized. And the story can once again move forward.

[68] In its brevity, this reference to their meetings is somewhat similar to the *Tant i vint, tant l'ama* of line 53.

It may be that the *enseignes* ('information') in the lady's first letter which made Milun so happy (273-4) included instructions about how they could meet.

Qu'il esteit venuz en eé—
A chevalier l'ad adubé.
Mut i aveit gent dameisel.
296 Le brief li rendi e l'anel;
Puis li ad dit ki est sa mere [69]
E l'aventure de sun pere,
E cum il est bon chevaliers,
300 Tant pruz, si hardi e si fiers,
N'ot en la tere nul meillur
De sun pris ne de sa valur.
Quant la dame li ot mustré
304 E il l'aveit bien escuté,
Del bien sun pere s'esjoï;
Liez fu de ceo k'il ot oï.
A sei meïsmes pense e dit:
308 'Mut se deit hum preiser petit,
Quant il issi fu engendrez
E sun pere est si alosez,
S'il ne se met en greinur pris
312 Fors de la tere e del païs.'
Asez aveit sun estuveir;
Il ne demure fors le seir,
Al demain ad pris [sun] cungié.
316 La dame l'ad mut chastïé
E de bien fere amonesté;
Asez li ad aveir doné.

The final division of the narrative opens with the re-appearance of two characters whom we had left very long ago. Of these, one, now grown to maturity (in a telescoping of time, 292-3) will rise to prominence, and will be present until the very end of the story; the other, once her rôle has been played, will cease to exist.

In the present passage (291-318) the lady finally carries out (in 296) instructions given her by her sister. Yet part of them she does not fulfill: we are not told precisely that the son was told to look for his father. It is significant that the aunt begins her characterization of the youth's father (which substantially reproduces that offered when Milun was introduced at the beginning of the lay) with the descriptive phrase *bon chevaliers:* this phrase

---

[69] For a second time (cf. 79-80), the name of one parent and the adventure of the other are mentioned. But in 297-8, there is a reversal of the names.

not only repeats Marie's initial words about Milun in 13, but also anticipates his later characterization in 392.

The first time that we really see the son close-up is in 305-6: he reacts with such joy to the news of his father's reputation! Note that once his decision to acquire an even greater reputation has been made, [70] how hastily he initiates his plan ("Il ne demure fors le seir, / Al demain ad pris [sun] cungié": 314-15). That we do not even know on what day he left heightens our impression of the youth's eagerness — he is so impatient to be on his way! It is a pleasing detail that the passage ends, as it began, with the aunt who, after bestowing both advice and money, then fades out of the story.

Through his exploits the son acquires fame: (319-42)

> A Suhthamptune vait passer;
> 320 Cum il ainz pot, se mist en mer.
> A Barbefluet est arivez;
> Dreit en Brutainë est alez.
> La despendi e turneia,
> 324 As riches hummes s'acuinta.
> Unques ne vint en nul estur
> Que l'en nel tenist a meillur.
> Les povres chevalers amot:
> 328 Ceo que des riches gaainot
> Lur donout e sis reteneit,
> E mut largement despendeit.
> Unques, sun voil, ne surjurna:
> 332 De tutes les teres de la
> Porta le pris e la valur;
> Mut fu curteis, mut sot honur.
> De sa bunté e de sun pris [71]
> 336 Veit la novele en sun païs
> Quë un damisels de la tere,
> Ki passa mer pur [sun] pris quere,
> Puis ad tant fet par sa prüesce,
> 340 Par sa bunté, par sa largesce,
> Que cil ki nel seivent numer
> L'apel[ou]ent par tut Sanz Per.

---

[70] It is as if the knight needed to hear of the reputation of his father to set himself into motion, to compete with his unknown father.

[71] It may be pertinent to recall that the substantive *bunté* signifies not only 'goodness,' but also 'knightly capability.'

In the first part (319-334) of this passage we learn how the young knight acquires the reputation he so desired; the rapidity (especially in the first four lines) and the purposefulness of his actions are arresting. As the son sets out to accomplish his intent, everything seems to be taking place mechanically, as it were, without any obstacle.

Three details are remarkable in the characterization of the young knight. As in the portrait of the knight Milun, so, in that of his son, Marie omits any reference to physical qualities; [72] it is the knightly and moral qualities of the son that are stressed. Yet the son displays the quality of *largesse* [73] (indeed, Marie refers to it several times, in 323, in 328-30, and again in 340) never mentioned in his father's portrait. From the information given in the narration of the son's activities, it would seem that he has indeed surpassed the reputation of his father ("De tutes les teres de la / Porta le pris e la valur; / Mut fu curteis, mut sot honur": 332-4). [74]

The young knight's reknown travels from where he is to his homeland over the sea. In Marie's explanation of his sobriquet *Sanz Per*, [75] she uses the occasion to name his virtues *(prüesce, bunté, largesce)*; it is almost as if she wishes to be absolutely certain that the reader has recognized them.

---

[72] The only description offered of the youth is that "Mut i aveit gent dameisel" (295).

[73] Note the opposition of the *riches hummes* (324) whom the young knight meets in combat, with the *povres chevalers* (327) to whom he shows such great liberality.

[74] In the report of the son's achievements, it is an artistic detail that Marie repeats words used earlier by the aunt of the youth's father: cf. 301-2, "N'ot en la tere nul meillur / De sun pris ne de sa valur."
Still another analogy between *Milun* and *Yonec* is that the son, toward the end of the narrative, achieves at least the same reputation or rank as that of his father: in *Yonec*, the son is raised to the kingship held by his late father; in the present lay, the son achieves even greater reknown as a knight than his father.

[75] In 341-3, there is another instance (cf. 22 and 25) of the preoccupation with names and naming evident in this lay. Yet the name of the young knight need not be known, for his deeds name him *Sanz Per*. The omission of his name is probably done in purposeful contrast to the naming of Yonec by his father in the lay of *Yonec*.
It should be pointed out that the son of Milun is the sole character in all of Marie's lays who has a sobriquet.

The news about Sanz Per reaches the ears of Milun: (343-50)

>   Milun oï celui loër [76]
> 344   E les biens de lui recunter.
>   Mut ert dolent, mut se pleigneit
>   Del chevaler que tant valeit,
>   Que, tant cum il peüst errer
> 348   Ne turneier ne armes porter,
>   Ne deüst nul del païs nez
>   Estre preisez në alosez.

Milun's extremely personal reaction to the hear-say about Sanz Per can not fail to impress the reader. That he takes this news so to heart (note the synonymic iteration, used in 345 to underscore Milun's anguish) and that he categorically refuses to be bested makes us suspect that he had indeed been devoting the aforementioned twenty years exclusively to his communication with the lady, not to increasing his knightly reputation.

Milun leaves to find the unknown knight: (351-80)

>   De une chose se purpensa:
> 352   Hastivement mer passera,
>   Si justera al chevalier
>   Pur lui leidier e empeirer;
>   Par ire se vodra cumbattre, [77]
> 356   S'il le pout del cheval abatre: [78]
>   Dunc serat il en fin honiz.
>   Aprés irra quere sun fiz
>   Que fors del païs est eissuz,
> 360   Mes ne saveit qu'ert devenuz.
>   A s'amie le fet saveir,
>   Cungé voleit de li aveir;

---

[76] In lines 342-3, note the juxtaposition of father and son before they meet in combat. Does Milun grieve because the name *Sanz Per* is the one that he has mentally given to himself, the renowned knight?

[77] The expression *par ire* recalls Milun's hostility (345-50) upon hearing of the young knight's reputation. Here, too, it is as though the youth's reknown were a personal affront to Milun's reputation.

It is notable that the mention of Milun's aggressive intentions concerning the young knight (in 354-7) is immediately followed by the expression of his desire to go to find his son. This opposition of the two extremes of his character is very effective.

[78] Once again (cf. 10-12) there is reference to unhorsing an opponent on the field of combat.

>   Tut sun curage li manda,
> 364   Brief e seel li envea
>   Par le cigne, mun escïent:
>   Or li remandast sun talent.
>   Quant ele oï sa volenté,
> 368   Mercie l'en, si li sot gre,
>   Quant pur lur fiz trover e quere
>   Voleit eissir fors de la tere
>   [E] pur le bien de lui mustrer;
> 372   Nel voleit mie desturber.
>   Milun oï le mandement;
>   Il s'aparaille richement.
>   En Normendië est passez,
> 376   Puis est desque Brutaine alez.
>   Mut s'aquointa a plusurs genz,
>   Mut cercha les turneiemenz;
>   Riches osteus teneit sovent
> 380   E si dunot curteisement.

At the beginning of this passage, Milun's decision to quickly cross the sea (note the repetition of *hastivement* in 352) is reminiscent of the son's eagerness to start out on his way to acquire a reputation (cf. 314-15): both father and son are impulsive!

It is noteworthy that the one who does the seeking is the father. In two ways Milun goes to find his son: to find the unknown knight, and then, to seek his son (and his two purposes become one). But why is Milun now so eager to see his son after twenty years? Does the fame of the young knight make Milun think of his young son? And how does he know that his son has left the country (359)? Could it be that he has been sending letters inquiring about his son to his sweetheart's sister all those twenty years?[79] Or did the lady write to him of the son's departure in one of her letters?

In 361-6, the letter written by Milun and sent to his lady is the fourth sealed letter to be particularized;[80] it is also the third letter mentioned specifically as being carried by the swan. To the reader, Marie's auctorial aside in 365 ("Par le cigne, mun escïent")

---

[79] If this is true, his behavior would harmonize thoroughly with his great tenderness and concern for his infant son at the beginning of the narrative.

[80] In 363 ("Tut sun curage li manda"), the phrase *tut sun curage* summarizes the content of Milun's letter which Marie has detailed for us earlier in 352-60.

is somewhat amusing: of course the letter was carried by the swan; how else? But Marie has to remind us that at this time, as during the period of twenty years, the bird is the trusted messenger of the lovers' communications. In her reply, the lady reverses the order of Milun's requests: she refers first (369) to the son (it is natural that, as a mother, she would be more interested in that part of Milun's message), then (in 371) to the opportunity for Milun to show off his reputation. Thus, the presentation of Milun's requests and of her replies to them offers a chiasmus.

In the closing lines (373-80) of this section, three details deserve comment. Milun's desire to cross the sea quickly seems to have been fulfilled: in a rapid summary we learn not only of his sea-voyage to Normandy but also of his arrival at his destination. Secondly, his knightly activities at this time (377-8) are a repetition of those suggested (cf. 10-13) at the very beginning of the narrative. Finally, we learn that Milun, like his son, shows great generosity.

Milun and the son find themselves on the same field of combat: (381-403)

>   Tut un yver, ceo m'est avis,
>   Conversa Milun al païs.
>   Plusurs bons chevalers retient, [81]
> 384 De s[i] que pres la paske vient,
>   K'il recumencent les turneiz
>   E les gueres e les dereiz.
>   Al Munt Seint Michel s'asemblerent,
> 388 Normein e Bretun i alerent
>   E li Flamenc e li Franceis;
>   Mes n'i ot gueres de[s] Engleis. [82]
>   Milun i est alé primers,
> 392 Que mut esteit bons chevalers.

---

[81] It is artistically meaningful that Milun, the "good knight" (although he is not now characterized as such) engages "good knights" in his service. But it may be even more meaningful in terms of the development of the story: his recognition of excellence which Marie mentions at this time seems to prefigure his recognition of the most outstanding excellencë at a later time.

[82] Of the onomastic list given in 388-90, Hoepffner, "La géographie....," p. 13, singles out the term *Engleis* as an "anachronisme," which, however, he thinks, scarcely weakened for Marie's readers the archaic effect she wished to give to this tale.

>   Le bon chevaler demanda;
>   Asez i ot ki li cunta
>   De queil part il esteit venuz.
> 396 A ses armes, a ses escuz
>   Tut l'eurent a Milun mustré;
>   E il l'aveit bien esgardé.
>   Li turnei[e]menz s'asembla.
> 400 Ki juste quist, tost la trova;
>   Ki aukes volt les rens cerchier,
>   Tost pout perdrë u gaaignier
>   E encuntrer un cumpainun.

In the opening line of this new passage, Marie's own voice is heard once again, telling us of the length of Milun's stay in Brittany. There is a suspension of knightly endeavors during the winter's lull, but in 384 ("De s[i] que pres la paske vient") we are given to understand that time will again move forward, that activity will be resumed.

Thus, only a few lines later (387) we learn of a tournament to be held at Mont-Saint-Michel [83] where Milun is the first to arrive. [84] For a second time there is a juxtaposition of the father and son before their encounter in the joust. This juxtaposition (392-3) is all the more remarkable, for both father and son are described as "good knights": they are now on equal footing.

As for 393-5, is Milun (knowing to what region the infant son had been taken so long ago) beginning to wonder about the identity of the knight? His careful look at the young knight pointed out to him (398) may be one of mere curiosity. Yet his look is nevertheless reminiscent of that of the mother in *Le Fresne* (cf. 383) who, although wanting to hate the maiden, is forced to admire her and love her.

Now we learn of the father's and son's encounter: (404-21)

---

[83] Hoepffner's thesis that Marie's intention to "... situer son récit à l'époque des grandes conquêtes du roi Artus" is confirmed, so he feels, by the localization of the combat between father and son at Mont-Saint-Michel. With the choice of this site, "elle évoque de nouveau chez ses lecteurs la grande époque légendaire de l'histoire bretonne." (Hoepffner, "La géographie...,"), pp. 10-11.

[84] Milun's eagerness ("Milun i est alé primers": 391) reminds the reader of the eagerness of the youth in *Les Deus Amanz* (line 168) who was the first to arrive in the meadow on the day of the test.

"MILUN" 241

> 404 Tant vus voil dire de Milun:
> Mut le fist bien en cel estur
> E mut i fu preisez le jur.
> Mes li vallez dunt jeo vus di
> 408 Sur tuz les autres ot le cri;
> Ne s'i pot nul acumparer
> De turneer ne de juster.
> Milun le vit si cuntenir,
> 412 Si bien puindrë e si ferir;
> Par mi tut ceo k'il l'enviot,
> Mut li fu bel e mut li plot.
> Al renc se met encuntre lui,
> 416 Ensemble justerent amdui.
> Milun le fiert si durement,
> L'anste depiece vereiment;
> Mes ne l'aveit mie abatu.
> 420 Cil raveit si Milun feru
> Que jus del cheval l'abati.

In this section, Marie twice intervenes in her auctorial competence: in the first line she turns to Milun whose performance at the tourney is indeed that of a "good knight"; then, three lines later, she speaks of the youth whose jousting is beyond equal. And Milun, who sees the young knight perform, appreciates (somewhat grudgingly?) the youth's excellence (414).[85] Is he, when he responds to the youth's behavior on the field of combat, already beginning to think 'that is my son'?

Immediately after Milun's appreciation of the youth's excellence, he seeks him out as a jousting-companion. And now the father and son, whom Marie has twice juxtaposed, meet each other in combat. In their encounter, the rapidity with which events succeed each other is impressive. Is Milun's stroke (418) just a clumsy move resulting from twenty years of non-combat? Or is it that his blow (note that he still has the strength to strike "durement," breaking the shaft of his opponent's lance) is simply

---

[85] If it is true that Milun recognizes the beauty of the young knight's prowess, then *Milun* is the third of four lays in which a character appreciates beauty. In *Le Fresne*, there are two instances of such appreciation: that of the mother for the (unknown) daugther, and that of the daughter for the *paile roé*. In *Laüstic*, it is the wife who is fully conscious of the beauty of the nightingale's song. The final example of such a response is, as we shall see, in *Eliduc*.

not perfect? The young knight (whose lance is obviously still in a condition to be used advantageously) returns the blow, immediately succeeding where Milun had failed.

Sanz Per reacts to what he sees: (422-31)

>   Desuz la ventaille choisi
>   La barbe e les chevoz chanuz;
> 424 Mut li pesa k'il fu cheüz.
>   Par la reisne le cheval prent,
>   Devant lui le tient en present;
>   Puis li ad dit: 'Sire, muntez!
> 428 Mut sui dolent e trespensez
>   Que nul humme de vostre eage
>   Deüsse faire tel utrage.'
>   Milun saut sus, mut li fu bel:

Upon seeing the gray hair of his opponent (who must be lying on the field), the young knight grieves for what he has done to an older knight. His immediate reaction is compassionate and tender: he returns his fallen opponent's horse and apologizes for his outrageous act. In the final line of this brief passage, we see Milun, delighted with the young knight's behavior, spring into action.[86] If the reader had any doubts about the knightly capability of the grey-haired Milun, his leap from the ground surely cancels them completely.

Milun recognizes his son: (432-68)

> 432 Al dei celui cunuit l'anel,
>   Quant il li rendi sun cheval.
>   Il areisune le vassal.
>   'Amis,' fet il, 'a mei entent!
> 436 Pur amur Deu omnipotent,[87]
>   Di mei cument ad nun tun pere!
>   Cum as tu nun? Ki est ta mere?
>   Saveir en voil la verité.

---

[86] This is the second and final time when we see a man leap onto the back of a horse. The contrast between the movement of Milun and Lanval (cf. *Lanval*, 637-40) is remarkable, given the fact that Milun, still dressed in his armor, unlike Lanval, has no *perrun* from which to spring.

[87] The adjective *omnipotent* in Milun's oath "Par amur Deu omnipotent" is very strong, and appears only one other time in Marie's lays (in Guigemar's prayer: "E prie Deu omnipotent": 624).

440 Mut ai veü, mut ai erré,
     Mut ai cerchiees autres teres
     Par turneiemenz e par gueres:
     Unques pur coup de chevalier
444 Ne chaï mes de mun destrier.
     Tu m'as abatu al juster:
     A merveille te puis amer.'
     Cil li respunt: 'Jol vus dirai
448 De mun pere, tant cum jeo'n sai.
     Jeo quid k'il est de Gales nez
     E si est Milun apelez.
     Fillë a un riche humme ama,
452 Celeement m'i engendra. [88]
     En Norhumbre fu[i] enveez,
     La fu[i] nurri e enseignez;
     Une meie aunte me nurri.
456 Tant me garda ensemble od li,
     Chevals e armes me dona,
     En ceste tere m'envea.
     Ci ai lungement conversé.
460 En talent ai e en pensé:
     Hastivement mer passerai,
     En ma cuntreie m'en irrai;
     Saver voil l'estre [de] mun pere,
464 Cum il se cuntient vers ma mere.
     Tel anel d'or li musterai
     E teus enseignes li dirai:
     Ja ne me vodra reneer,
468 Ainz m'amerat e tendrat chier.'

Up to this moment, Milun has thought of Sanz Per only as a knight. But now, he looks upon him as a young man who reminds him of his own son. The use of *le vassal* (434) immediately preceding Milun's speech is very meaningful. [89]

---

[88] As in *Yonec* (cf. line 9 of the Prologue, and also 523), here too conception is presented from the point of view of the man.

[89] The substantive *vassal*, appearing in a context of service (*Guigemar*, 107; *Lanval*, 3, and *passim*) is used here to stress the idea of youth. Indeed, the only times when terms denoting the son's youth (e. g., *dameisel*, 295; *vallez*, 407; and now, *vassal* in 434) are not used is when son is presented from the point of view of Milun who thinks not of the youth of Sanz Per, but of the fact that he is a knight (cf. 346, *chevaler;* 353, *chevalier;* 393, *le bon chevaler*).

In this scene, Milun recognizes his son in two ways: first by the ring on his finger (432), then later by the words his son will speak. We can not fail to note the comic effect resulting from the 'staging' of this scene: during this portentious occasion the two knights are seated upon their chargers!

Milun's speech to the youth opens with three questions (437-8), all of which have to do with names.[90] When he asks his first question ('Di mei cument ad nun tun pere!'), does he suspect that he is the knight's father? At the end of 439, Milun could have stopped, but his words flow on; he gives Sanz Per seven lines of praise (440-6) at his own expense, but he also indirectly praises himself: this is the first time that he has even been knocked off a horse. In the two final lines there is a notable opposition: he can love the youth (and we recall his earlier intention to joust with him *par ire,* 355) simply because the young knight has unhorsed him!

The young knight begins his reply with the disclosure of his father's name, and even place of birth (449-50); note that he does not give the name of his mother or of himself. He then goes on to speak for eighteen more lines (451-66), first telling the story of his own life after his birth (which the father had not asked for). We are left to imagine what Milun's feelings must have been as the youth continues to speak. Between the first part of the son's speech and the words of the father in which both tell of their life as a knight there is a very fine balance.

---

[90] Since we do not know that Milun and the damsel discussed the name of the child before its birth, nor are we told that they did so at a later date, it is conceivable that the youth's name would not mean much to Milun — unless, of course, it was something mentioned during the lovers' communication.

Note that Marie does not have father first ask about the ring (although she could have done so) becaues she had already chosen a similar question ('Where did you get the silken cloth?') for the mother's opening words to the maiden in *Le Fresne.* It is very elegant that Marie never repeats exactly the same situation.

There is another reason why Marie does not let the father ask about the golden ring, and this reason may have come to her first. For Milun, after his three questions, does not stop (although he does say in 439 ('Saveir en voil la verité'): he is really not so impatient at that point for an answer that he can stop before he indirectly compliments himself.

Could the youth's decision to go to seek his father have been motivated by the sight of the older knight? Note that he too, like the father earlier (cf. 352), intends to "cross the sea quickly" (461). We, the reader, who can not fail to respond to his youthful eagerness and naïveté as we hear him (in 460-8) tell of his plan [91] (he is so confident that his own father will not reject him!) marvel that his father can continue to sit there, just listening!

Milun identifies the knight as his son: (469-82)

> Quant Milun l'ot issi parler,
> Il ne poeit plus escuter;
> Avant sailli hastivement,
> 472 Par le pan del hauberc le prent.
> 'E Deul' fait il, 'cum sui gariz!
> Par fei, amis, tu es mi fiz.
> Pur tei trover e pur tei quere [92]
> 476 Eissi uan fors de ma tere.' [93]
> Quant cil l'oï, a pié descent,
> Sun peire baisa ducement.
> Bel semblant entrë eus feseient
> 480 E iteus paroles diseient
> Que li autres kis esgardouent
> De joie e de pité plurouent.

Milun, unable to contain his emotions any longer, springs "hastily" into action for a second time: he is as eager and spontaneous as his son! This time his speech, in contrast to his opening words, is very short. Now we may note the third and final stage in Milun's feelings toward the young knight: [94] when he first hears of Sanz Per, he is full of hostility; then when he sees him in action, he prizes him for his prowess; and finally, the outburst

---

[91] Note that the father and mother are coupled together in the end-rhyme of 463-4, which may be an anticipation of the same device in the son's plan enunciated later in 500-502.

[92] Not only is the use of hysteron proteron very effective in this line (because he has found the son *before* he has even sought him), it is an echo of the mother's words summarizing the contents of Milun's request ("... lur fiz trover e quere": 369).

[93] This line, too, echoes the words of the lady's message (cf. 370, "Voleit eissir fors de la tere").

[94] We may recall that the mother in Le Fresne also passes through three very similar stages in the development of her feelings toward the maiden.

of his joy when he realizes the knight is his son ('E Deu!'...
'cum sui gariz!').

The youth's acknowledgement of his father is also emotional
("Sun peire baisa ducement": 478). His sweetness is so natural
an accompaniment to his eagerness and confidence.[95] In 481-2,
we see the two knights (still upon the field of combat!), expressing
their emotion and they, in turn, are seen by those around them
who experience a perfect empathy.[96] It is as if the joy of the
father and son had such breadth that it could spread to those
near by; never again will we see a similar situation in any of
Marie's lays. Moreover, the fact that the only expansion of emotion in the entire lay is that which Marie allows to the father
and son (469-80) heightens the impact of this recognition scene.

The father and son spend the night in talk together: (483-502)

```
       Quant li turnei[e]menz depart,
484    Milun s'en vet, mut li est tart
       Que a sun fiz parot a leisir
       E qu'il li die sun pleisir.
       En un ostel furent la nuit;
488    Asez eurent joie e deduit,
       De chevalers eurent plenté.
       Milun ad a sun fiz cunté
       De sa mere cum il l'ama
492    E cum sis peres la duna
       A un barun de sa cuntre[e],
       E cument il l'ad puis amee,
       E ele lui de bon curage,
496    E cum del cigne fist message,
       Ses lettres lui feseit porter,
       Ne se osot en nului fier.
       Le fiz respunt: 'Par fei, bel pere,
```

---

[95] Of the two sons who are born to the lovers in Marie's lays, it is pleasing to the reader that Marie has let one son have the youthful and eager reactions that we have just witnessed, and that she has also allowed one of the two sons to meet his father.

[96] In the mention of the emotional reaction of the crowd of knights, the use of the noun *joie* in 482 is very significant. This the second (and final) instance when this substantive, normally used to refer to an erotic ex-perience, appears here, just as in *Le Fresne* (cf. 488, 'Grant joie nus ad Deu donee'), in a context of family relationship.

500 Assemblerai vus e ma mere;
Sun seignur que ele ad ocirai
E espuser la vus ferai.'

For a second time, there is an audience (489) to witness (and share) the happiness of the father and son. The warmth of their emotion is doubly stressed by the nouns *joie* and *deduit*, usually reserved for an erotic context.

And now Milun tells *his* story to his son, filling in details. As he speaks of his love for the youth's mother, he mentions the two phases of their love: before (491-3), and after (494-8) her marriage. That Marie allows Milun, after twice telling of his love for the lady, to speak of her love for him (how she loved him "de bon curage"), is an effective touch: this is the only explicit reference to the lady's feelings for her lover. With the detail of the swan, we learn Milun's reason for his choice of such a messenger: "Ne se osot en nului fïer" (498).

For a second time, we see the son react eagerly and confidently: after his opening words [97] he immediately announces his intention to bring together his two parents [98] (after first beheading the husband!). In his rashfulness, he is again certain that there would be no difficulties he could not overcome.

The father and son return to their country: (503-8)

Cele parole dunc lesserent
504 E al demain s'appareillerent.
Cungé pernent de lur amis,
Si s'en revunt en lur païs.
Mer passerent hastivement,
508 Bon oré eurent e fort vent. [99]

---

[97] Note the parallel in the use of the expression *par fei* in the son's words 'Par fei, bel pere' (499), and in the father's speech 'Par fei, amis, tu es mi fiz' (474).

[98] Thus the husband (of whom nothing has been said since he took away his bride) is brought back into the story, as the son anticipates his death.

[99] The tautology of this line (and because of the *fort vent* they did cross quickly) reminds us of the description of Guigemar's first, slower trip in the magic ship ("Bon oret out e suëf vent": 194).

The haste of their preparations for departure ("Al demain s'apareillerent") reminds us of the son's hasty departure from his aunt's home ("Al demain ad pris [sun] cungié": 315).

A striking detail in this passage is the reference in 505 to *lurs amis:* the knights who shared the joy of the father and son, and who spent the evening with them after the tournament, have become their friends from whom they now take leave. The final movement of the lay is that of Milun (now accompanied by their son) coming toward the lady.

For the third time in the narrative (cf. 352 and 461), the phrase *mer passer hastivement* appears. From 507 to the end of the narrative, there will be an impression of increasing rapidity in the unencumbered succession of events.

They meet a messenger from Milun's sweetheart: (509-18)

>
> Si cum il eirent le chemin,
> Si encuntrerent un meschin:
> De l'amie Milun veneit,
> 512   En Bretaigne passer voleit; [100]
> Ele l'i aveit enveié.
> Ore ad sun travail acurcié.
> Un brief li baille enseelé;
> 516   Par parole li ad cunté [101]
> Que s'en venist, ne demurast;
> Morz est sis sire, or s'en hastast!' [102]

Marie, who has been silent for some time, offers a brief practical comment upon the encounter of the two knights with the lady's messenger ("Ore ad sun travail acurcié"). As for the letter from Milun's sweetheart (the second letter brought by a

---

[100] Here again, the intention of crossing over the sea. In this lay the reader feels that Marie has done so much with movement: the movement of Milun toward the damsel; the movement of sexual union; the movement of communication during the twenty years; the drama of the father and the son, which is also one of movement and meeting, and of course, the constant movement back and forth of various characters.

[101] The phrase *par parole* is reminiscent of the damsel's words to Milun about the letter he is to send (along with the infant) to her married sister: "Si li manderez par escrit / E par paroles e par dit" (71-2).

[102] For the final time the husband enters the story — as a dead person.

messenger from one lover to another), only two lines are devoted to its contents (517-18):[103] in its four-fold message, note that the lady's eagerness is shown three times! — and the death of her husband [104] is announced in a hemistich.

The father and son arrive at the lady's castle: (519-32)

```
        Quant Milun oï la novele,
520     A merveille li sembla bele;
        A sun fiz ad mustré e dit.
        N'i ot essuigne ne respit;
        Tant eirent quë il sunt venu
524     Al chastel u la dame fu.
        Mut par fu lie de sun fiz,
        Que tant esteit pruz e gentiz.
        Unc ne demanderent parent:
528     Sanz cunseil de tut' autre gent
        Lur fiz amdeus les assembla,
        La mere a sun pere dona.
        En grant bien e en [grant] duçur
532     Vesquirent puis e nuit e jur.
```

Could it be that the messenger gives the news only to Milun ("Par parole li ad cunté": 516 and "Quant Milun oï la novele": 519), who then transmits the same news to his son in 521? Or does Milun (in 521) simply point out the letter to his son, saying that "the lady says such-and-such"? We are not specifically told (after those twenty years spent in written communication with her!) that Milun read her last letter. Although it would be odd that he would not do so, yet it may well be that, in his eagerness to be on his way to her, he does not take the time. Milun's somewhat flat emotional reaction when he hears the news ("A merveille li sembla bele": 519) is reminiscent of that when he receives the message from the girl ("Milun fu liez de la novele": 29).

---

[103] We may wonder whether her message was actually so brief, or whether Marie has given us a summary of it (just as she had summarized the damsel's first message to Milun ("Par sun message li manda / Que, si plest, el l'amera": 27-8) at the opening of the story.

[104] The necessity for Sanz Per to kill his mother's husband (in contrast to the situation of Yonec) is thus removed.

The husband's death toward the end of the tale is the second of the two events not planned by the lovers.

The last time we saw the mother was when she gave permission (and thanks) to her lover to go to find their son. Now when she finally sees the son, only one line (525) is given to her reaction: "Mut par fu lie de sun fiz" (and none at all to that of the son).[105] The brief reference to her feelings purposely contrasts with the description of the expansive emotions of father and son in the recognition scene.

In the account of the marriage, the assertion *Unc ne demanderent parent* (527) is somewhat humorous: why should the couple do so, after all those years? In 529, the son carries out his intentions; note the repetition of the verb *assembler* used in his earlier statement of purpose (511).

In a repetitive mood, Marie twice tells us (just as the son had earlier twice stated his intention, 500 and 502) of the parents' marriage.[106] And what we learn of their life thereafter is something that Marie says of no other lovers: "En grant bien e en [grant] duçur / Vesquirent puis e nuit e jur."[107]

In the Epilogue we learn two things: (533-6)

>   De lur amur e de lur bien
>   Firent un lai li auncïen;
>   E jeo que le ai mis en escrit
> 536 Al recunter mut me delit.

Marie now tells us who (*li auncïen*,[108] not the Bretons) composed a lay about the love and goodness of the pair, and of her great joy in retelling it in written form. Thus the Epilogue, just as the story, ends on a note of deep happiness.

---

[105] That there is no reference to the lady's emotions upon seeing the son's father is perhaps not surprising: we do know that they did manage to see each other during the twenty years of their separation.

[106] The term *amdeus* is explained (as though it need be!) in the second line of the account of the marriage. Note the contrastive use of *la mere* with the emphatic *sun pere*.

[107] *Milun* is the only one of Marie's lays that has an obviously happy ending.

[108] The allusion to *li auncïen* harmonizes with Marie's intent of locating her tale in the far-off past.

BIBLIOGRAPHY

Baring-Gould, Sabine. *The Book of Were-wolves*. London, 1865.
Battaglia, Salvatore. "Lupus in Fabula," *Filologia Romanza*, III (1956), 292-5.
―――. "Il mito del licantropo nel "Bisclavret" di Maria di Francia," *Filologia Romanza*, III (1956), 229-53.
Bayrav, Sühela. *Symbolisme médiéval: Béroul, Marie, Chrétien*. Paris, 1957.
Bédier, Joseph. "Les Lais de Marie de France," *RDM*, CVII (1891), 835-63.
―――. (ed.) *Le Roman de Tristan* par Thomas. 2 vols. Paris, 1902-05.
The Bestiary: A Book of Beasts, being a translation from a Latin Bestiary of the twelfth century. Translated and edited by T. H. White. New York, 1960.
Bezzola, Reto Roberto. *Le sens de l'aventure et de l'amour: Chrétien de Troyes*. Paris, 1947.
Conigliani, Camilla. "L'Amore e l'avventura nei 'Lais' di Maria di Francia," *Arch Rom.*, II (1918), 281-95.
Crosland, Jessie. *Medieval French Literature*. Oxford, 1956.
Cross, Tom Peete. "Celtic Elements in the Lays of Lanval and Graelent," *Mod. Phil.*, XII (April 1915), No. 10, 1-60.
―――. "The Celtic Origin of the Lay of Yonec," *Revue Celtique* (1910), 413-71.
Damon, S. Foster. "Marie de France: Psychologist of Courtly Love," *PMLA*, 44 (1929), 968-96.
Delbouille, Maurice. "Le nom et le personnage d'Equitan," *le Moyen-Age*, LXIX (1963), 315-23.
Ewert, Alfred, ed. *Marie de France: Lais*. Oxford, 1947. (Reprinted in 1958.)
Faral, Edmond. *Les Arts poétiques du 12e et du 13e siècles, Recherches et Documents sur la Technique littéraire du Moyen-Age*, in *Bibliothèque de l'École des Hautes-Études*, CCXXXVIII. Paris, 1927.
Fauchet, Claude. *Recueil de l'origine de la langue et poésie françoise*. Paris, 1581.
Ferguson, Mary H. "Folklore in the *Lais* of Marie de France," *RR*, LVII (1966), (February), no. I, 3-24.
Flum, P. N. "Additional Thoughts on Marie de France," *Romance Notes*, III, i (1961), 53-6.
Foulet, Lucien. "Marie de France et la Légende de Tristan," *ZRPh*, XXXII (1908), 161-83 and 257-89.

Foulet, Lucien. "Marie de France et les lais bretons," *ZRPh*, XXIX (1905), 19-56 and 293-322.

———. "Thomas and Marie in their relation to the Conteors," *MLN*, XXIII (1908), 205-8.

Fox, J. C. "Marie de France," *Engl. Hist. Rev.*, XXV (1910), 303 ff., and XXV (1911), 317 ff.

Francis, E. A. "Marie de France et son temps," *Romania*, LXXII (1951), 78-99.

Frappier, J. "Remarques sur la structure du lai, Essai de définition et de classement," *La Littérature narrative d'imagination*, Colloques de Strasbourg, avril 1959, pp. 23-39.

Godefroy, Frédéric. *Dictionnaire de l'ancienne langue française, et de tous ses dialectes du IXe au XVe siècle, composé d'après le dépouillement de tous les plus importants documents, manuscrits ou imprimés, qui se trouvent dans les grandes bibliothèques de la France et de l'Europe, et dans les principales archives départementales, municipales, hospitalières ou privées.* 10 vols. Paris, 1880-1902.

Grandgent, C. H. (ed.). *La Divina Commedia di Dante Alighieri.* Revised ed. Boston, 1933.

Hatcher, Anna G. "Le lai du Chievrefueil," *Romania*, LXXI (1950), 330-44.

Hertz, Wilhelm. *Spielmannsbuch.* Stuttgart-Berlin, 1886, 2nd edn. 1900.

Hoepffner, Ernest. "The Breton Lais," in *Arthurian Literature in the Middle Ages,* ed. R. S. Loomis. Oxford, 1959.

———. "La géographie et l'histoire dans les Lais de Marie de France," *Romania*, LVI (1930), 1-32.

———. *Les Lais de Marie de France.* Paris, 1935.

———. "Marie de France et l'*Énéas*,'" *Studi Medievali*, V (1932), 272-308.

———. "Marie de France et les Lais anonymes," *Studi Medievali* (Nuova Serie), IV (1931), XXX, 1-31.

———. "Pour la Chronologie des Lais de Marie de France. 1. — Le Lai de Lanval," *Romania*, LIX (1933), 351-70.

———. "Thomas d'Angleterre et Marie de France," *Studi Medievali*, VII (1934), 8-23.

Hofer, Stefan. "Der Tristanroman und der Lai du Chievrefueil der Marie de France," *ZRPh*, LXIX (1953), 129-31.

Hollyman, K.-J. *Le Développement du vocabulaire féodal en France pendant le haut moyen âge.* Genève, 1957.

Holmes, U. T. *A History of Old French Literature.* New York, 1937.

Johnston, O. M. "Sources of the Lay of the *Two Lovers*," *MLN*, XXI (1906), 34-9.

Levi, Ezio. "I lai brettoni e la leggenda di Tristano" (reprinted from *Studj romanzi*, XIV). Perugia, 1918.

———. "Maria di Francia e le abbazie d'Inghilterra," *Arch. Rom.*, V (1921), 472-93.

———. "Il Re Giovane e Maria di Francia," *Arch. Rom.*, V (1921), 448-71.

Lewent, Kurt. "Zum Inhalt und Aufbau der Flamenca," *ZRPh*, LIII (1933), 1-86.

Mall, E. "Noch Einmal: Marie de Compiègne und das "Evangile aux femmes," *ZRPh*, I (1877), 337-56.

New Catholic Encyclopedia. 15 vols. New York, 1967.

Painter, Sidney. *Medieval Society.* Ithaca, 1951.

Painter, Sidney. "To Whom were dedicated the Fables of Marie de France?" *MLN*, XLVIII (1933), 367-9.
Politzer, Robert L. "Synonymic Repetition in Late Latin and Romance," *Language*, XXXVII (1961), 484-87.
Pollock, Frederick and Maitland, Frederic W. *The History of English Law before the time of Edward I.* 2nd. ed. Cambridge, England, 1898.
Réville, André. "L''Abjuratio Regni,' Histoire d'une institution anglaise," *Revue Historique*, 1892 (50), 1-42.
Rickard, Peter. "*Toute jour, tout le jour, et toute la journée* en français médiéval," *Romania*, LXXXV (1964), 145-80.
de Riquer, Martín. "La 'aventure,' el 'lai' y el 'conte' en Maria de Francia," *Fil. Rom.*, II (Fasc. I, num. 5), Gennaio-Marzo 1955, 1-19.
Roquefort, B. de. *Poésies de Marie de France*. 2 vol. Paris, 1819-25.
Salverda de Grave, J. J. "Marie de France et Énéas," *Neophil.*, X (1925), 56-8.
Schofield, W. H. "The Lays of Graelent and Lanval," *PMLA*, XV (1900), 121-80.
Schürr, F. "Komposition und Symbolik in den Lais der Marie de France," *ZRPh*, L (1930), 556-582.
Scott, Anne (trans.). *The Hans Christian Andersen Fairy Tale Book*. New York, 1959.
Smith, Kirby Flower. "An Historical Study of the Werwolf in Literature," *PMLA*, IX (New Series, vol. II) [1894], 1-42.
Spitzer, Leo. "Marie de France, Dichterin von Problem-Märchen," *ZRPh*, L (1930), 29-67.
Stephenson, Carl. *Medieval Feudalism*. Ithaca, 1956.
Thompson, Stith. *The Folktale*. New York, 1946.
——. *Motif-Index of Folk Literature*. 6 vols. Bloomington, 1955-58.
Tobler, Adolph. *Altfranzösisches wörterbuch*. Adolph Toblers nachgelassene materialen bearbeitet und mit unterstüzung der preussischen Akademie der wissenschaften, hrsg., von Erhard Lommatzsch. Berlin, 1925-1936; Wiesbaden, 1954—.
Warnke, Karl. *Die Lais der Marie de France*, 3rd ed. (Bibliotheca Normannica, III), with comparative notes by Reinhold Köhler. Halle, 1925.
von Wartburg, Walther. *Französisches etymologisches wörterbuch; eine darstellung des galloromanischen sprachschatzes*. Bonn, 1928—.
Wathelet-Willem, Jeanne. "Equitan dans l'œuvre de Marie de France," *le Moyen-Age*, LXIX (1963), 325-45.
Wilmotte, Maurice. "Marie de France et Chrétien de Troyes," *Romania*, LII (1926), 353-5.
Winkler, E. *Französische Dichter des Mittelalters: II. Marie de France*. Vienna, 1918.

www.ingramcontent.com/pod-product-compliance
Lightning Source LLC
Chambersburg PA
CBHW030618230426
43661CB00053B/2052